T0328558

MORAL DILEMMAS, IDENTITY, AND OUR MORAL CONDITION

MORAL DILEMMAS, IDENTITY, AND OUR MORAL CONDITION

A GUIDE FOR THE ETHICALLY PERPLEXED

MICHAEL S. PERRY

Algora Publishing
New York

Library of Congress Cataloging-in-Publication Data —

Perry, Michael S., 1980-
  Moral dilemmas, identity, and our moral condition / Michael S. Perry.
     pages cm
  Includes bibliographical references and index.
     ISBN 978-1-62894-075-6 (soft cover: alk. paper) — ISBN 978-1-62894-076-3 (hard
cover: alk. paper) — ISBN 978-1-62894-077-0 (ebook: alk. paper) 1. Ethics. 2. Identity
(Philosophical concept) I. Title.
     BJ1031.P47 2014
     170—dc23
                                    2014025796

Printed in the United States

For my parents, Geoff and Eileen.

ACKNOWLEDGEMENTS

This work is the result of many struggles, both personal and intellectual. I have benefited greatly from the education provided by Dartmouth College, the Philosophy Department at Johns Hopkins University, and the University of Michigan Law School. Though I have been interested in moral dilemmas since high school, this book began in the last year I was at Johns Hopkins and it was in this time that the central views and themes were forged. Parts were developed while at the University of Michigan. Any deficiencies, omissions, or plain confusions, however, are my own. I would like to thank the editors at Algora Publishing for their hard work and for reminding me that difficult thoughts need not be difficultly stated.

I have been very fortunate in life and am deeply thankful for the intellectual stimulation and support provided by teachers, colleagues, friends, and, most of all, my family.

Table of Contents

This is a book about moral dilemmas. Or more particularly, a book that uses moral dilemmas to approach ethics generally in attempting to develop a way to think about and understand our ethical condition as autonomous, self-conscious, rational beings thrown into a world and facing the question of who and what sort of person one ought to be. As such it touches on some very central questions in ethics, broadly conceived. What should I do with my life? How ought I live? How should I understand myself as an ethical being? How can ethics be objective and yet allow for reasonable variance? How can I find meaning and peace? This project proceeds on the idea that moral dilemmas are a tool, not problem, and can be used to fruitfully discuss and understand our perplexing moral condition.

I do not offer an ethical theory here. That is not my interest, and if it were I would have no book to write, as I have no ethical theory to defend. Neither do I have an ontology or metaphysics to offer or defend. These disclaimers may appear surprising for a book that purports to address central questions in ethics. Hasn't philosophy been concerned with offering theories of the good and the just from the beginning (whatever *that* is)? And isn't our ontology, whether "theistic" or "naturalistic," the place to begin in ethics? The obvious approach seems to be to lay out an ontology and then from that develop some theory that accounts for our ethical existence. Sometimes ethical experience is used as part of an argument for an ontology. So, crudely put, a "theist" might argue that without a god or gods there can be no moral truths and so there must be a god or gods, while a "naturalist" will begin with her ontology and theories and give a theory of ethics based on, say, evolutionary factors. Or perhaps a philosopher may begin with some basic moral truths and from these develop a complex, detailed moral theory that operates as a function of sorts to determine morally-correct actions. Such theories are then squared with an ontology, and moral puzzles, like moral dilemmas and unfriendly intuitions, are then dealt with.

When I began my intellectual and active life I often repeated a prayer, or goal, really, to guide me and express what I sought from the world and my life: "May I live a life of beauty, love, and peace, striving for justice and searching for truth." I still try to live by this prayer, and the values within it are important to me. Yet intellectual and personal struggles have convinced me to humbly take a step back, to temper my enthusiasm and confidence that I was to create justice and discover truth. This may be my aim, but what I must work towards is not the true theory of everything and the creation of a just society but an *understanding* of our human condition, epistemic and moral; freedom from consuming fear and ambition and blind, dogmatic certainty; and with understanding of my condition and my limits, a share of peace.

These are not un-ambitious goals, but they change the shape of the inquiry I engage in. Rather than offering a theory I offer an understanding of or approach to our moral condition. We are faced with the question of who and what sort of person one ought to be. I don't seek to answer this question. I am concerned instead with how we ought to *think about* and *understand* this question. Too often we presume we understand the question and how to approach it, only to become lost in dogmatism or intellectual chaos when we hubristically answer it. I want to step back, as it were, and query how we should think about ethics by coming to understand our condition as moral beings.

Moral dilemmas are the way I approach this task. They are situations of various sorts in which there are two incompatible ethical duties, and thus, either what one ought to do or who one ought to be is over-determined because there are too many right answers. Put another way, it is underdetermined since there are no right answers because any answer violates an ethical duty we think we have. When such dilemmas are addressed philosophers aim to solve them or dissolve them in some way, getting us out of dilemma through theory. I do not aim for such heights. I want to understand them and understand why we get into them. Rather than solving or dissolving them, I want to *accept* them as a feature of our moral life and use them as a way to better understand our moral condition. They lead us to a quest for grounding and this leads us to seek grounding in who we are, the sort of beings that we are. Eschewing ontology and theory, I seek to explicate identity as an ethical concept, proposing that we understand ourselves as ethical beings as a system of roles that form both facts about who we are and at the same time have normative import with rights and duties implicit in the role. Using this understanding of identity, I argue we can come to an enlightening understanding of our moral condition, how we ground norms, how to accept and make sense of an objective pluralism, and how to better think about the question of who and what sort of person one ought to be.

So this is a book about moral dilemmas, but much more as well. Moral dilemmas, for me, are not intellectual curiosities or irksome puzzles for theory but a tool to a better our moral understanding. The way to the larger picture takes time, and we must start somewhere. I ask the reader, then, to be patient and open to the challenge posed by moral dilemmas. Taking them seriously and trying to comprehend them at face value pays great dividends for moral understanding, and perhaps opens the path to a measure of peace.

A Moral Dilemma

Imagine that you are on vacation in a country that is politically unstable and lacks strong central authority. You venture, alone, into the beautiful countryside and happen upon a small village. Immediately you are held at gunpoint and brought to the local strongman. He has taken control of the village over some perceived slight to his authority and is holding the villagers captive. As you watch, he has his armed minions select three villagers from the group at random and lines them up to be executed as both a punishment of and a warning to the village. Your sense of right and justice is outraged and, perhaps unwisely, you protest to the strongman, pleading that what he is about to do is wrong as these are innocent men and women. He looks at you and laughs at your privileged naiveté about the ways of the world. Then he tells you that he won't hurt you because he doesn't want to create problems for himself by killing foreigners. He says he is amused by your scruples and wishes to offer you a choice. Either he will have his men execute all three or you can personally execute one and the others will live. What would you do? What should you do?

This is a slightly dramatized moral dilemma. Intuitions vary and arguments can get surprisingly heated. On the one hand, it seems morally correct to kill one person yourself because the end result is that two fewer people are killed. And surely we ought to minimize the loss of innocent life. But conversely it seems morally wrong for you to *personally* kill someone. As the situation stands, you are not responsible for the killing—the strongman is—but if you take the gun and kill an innocent person, you become very involved personally in a grievous wrong.

And it gets worse. We can change the details to play on intuitions. What if the choice is between 100 people being killed by the strongman and one being killed by you? Or what if three bad actors, though innocent in this case, can be killed by a strongman or you can personally strangle a baby to death? Intuitions shift, theories crumble, and all appears to be uncertain. Avoiding this ethical chaos is the challenge posed by moral dilemmas.

Moral Dilemmas and Ethical Inquiry

Ethics, broadly conceived, is the study of what one ought to do and, more importantly, who and how one ought to be. In contemporary thought we tend to think of ethics as concerning only actions, but in my usage (which is more accurate historically) it extends to who one is and how one structures one's life—so, for example, whether one ought to be a lawyer or doctor or father or volunteer, etc., are questions with an ethical dimension. Ethics is the study of how one ought to structure one's life and it is from this that ethically correct actions follow.

In his last philosophical work, a treatise on ethics ostensibly addressed to his son, Cicero wrote, "Above all we must decide who and what sort of people we want to be, and what kind of life we want to lead; and this is the most difficult question of all."[1] Ethics is hard and it is pressing. In moments of reflection we know that death awaits and we crave purpose for our lives—to somehow get it right, so to speak. We do not want the death of Tolstoy's brother from illness: "He suffered for over a year and died an agonizing death without ever understanding why he lived and understanding even less why he was dying."[2] We seek, ultimately, to arrive at some sort of peace with and understanding of our being. Ethical inquiry is an attempt to understand our lives and to be able to structure it, to the best of our ability, so as to find purpose and peace. To philosophize can be a way to learn how to die.[3] We also hope to avoid the death of Tolstoy's Ivan Ilyich—finding that our life and death are senseless and disgusting, terrorized by confusion, and realizing too late, all too late, that we have not lived as we ought to have, that our life was not the real thing.[4] Ethical inquiry is the exploration of where we are in life, how we got here, and where we ought to go to live a good life. By "doing" ethics we hope for understanding, and with it, peace.

In this endeavor moral dilemmas can play an important role. Moral dilemmas are situations in which there seems to be either no correct action or, from another perspective, too many correct but conflicting actions.

---

1 Cicero *On Duties* I.117.
2 Tolstoy, *Confession*, 23.
3 Montaigne *Essays* I: 19; Plato *Phaedo* 103.
4 Tolstoy, Leo. *The Death of Ivan Ilyich.*

Moral dilemmas can be used to test ethical theories and to develop ethical insights because of the acute challenges they pose. In this essay I aim to develop a deeper understanding of the human moral condition through the exploration of moral dilemmas. I differentiate and examine three types: pedestrian dilemmas, theoretical dilemmas, and critical dilemmas. Though each is different, I claim that they all lead us to seek the grounding of ethical theory and can only be correctly understood by adopting an identity-based approach to our moral condition, as one subject and sensitive to ethical norms.

My principal aim is to produce a better understanding of our moral condition. This is neither a moralistic exercise nor an attempt at pure, scholarly ethics. The former almost inevitably fails to engage the real ethical difficulties we face but rather papers over them with rhetoric. Moralistic exercises aim to excite our moral passions in such a way that what we ought to do and how we ought to be seems altogether clear and consequently we are driven enthusiastically to what appears to be right action, yet such clarity rarely survives rational scrutiny or even the vicissitudes of ordinary life. Scholarly ethics is pursued with such erudition and in such abstraction that it is often unclear how it relates to our lives at all. It is hard to see why such theories are worthwhile beyond intellectual amusement.

I hope to steer a middle course, one that is relevant to the ethical questions we struggle with in life and that approaches these issues with the rational scrutiny characteristic of academic inquiry rather than the rhetorical flourish of moralistic revival. This is a practical exercise aimed at a struggle with ethical problems that develops when a critical, philosophical approach is taken within one's life rather than in abstraction from it. I take the problems of theoretical ethics seriously but do not attempt to pursue inquiry in such abstraction that it becomes meaningless to life. Ethics is important because it affects all aspects of our lives, and hence it is best pursued at a colloquial level with the aim of seriously confronting the tensions and difficulties in our human ethical condition. Moral dilemmas are situations in which these tensions and difficulties are exacerbated and made explicit and hence are a valuable resource for ethical investigation.

This sort of inquiry aims at ethical self-understanding. I do not know what the "good life" is and I am uninterested in stirring others with inspired preaching. Neither do I have a theory to attack or defend. I find ethics to be difficult, perhaps the most difficult form of inquiry, because it has such import. If engaging in ethical inquiry requires one to have a clear idea of what the good life is, or a particular theory, then ethical inquiry is in serious trouble. Better we start by understanding the terrain before we run about imposing theories upon it.

This sort of ethical thought is particularly difficult in the present atmosphere. There is certainly no dearth of answers to how one ought to be but they tend to require acceptance of a grand theory of the nature of things. But what of the perplexed? What about critical inquiry? Discussion of ethics is often considered impolite in serious inquiry. It is common to believe that professionalized philosophy does not have any place answering the grand questions of life; instead it is best concerned with concrete, scholarly issues arising within a particular research program philosophers engage in. Maybe so, but that doesn't make those questions disappear. If we decline to engage in the big ethical questions in philosophy as a whole, we end up isolating ethical questions from critical discussion. I hope for more: a way to think critically and productively about ethics and who and how I ought to be.

Rather than arguing for a particular ethical theory, I will be motivating a particular perspective on ethics. And rather than offering solutions to moral dilemmas, I will be suggesting particular understandings of them. To borrow a phrase from Wittgenstein, I seek to be able to find my way about ethical issues and questions rather than lay down the law as to ethical truth.[1] Put another way, I aim to develop a better way to think about how one ought to be rather than providing robust answers to that question. Too often in philosophical inquiry we engage in theory building without adequate reflection on the nature of the inquiry engaged in and what it is we are after, what we can expect, and how we ought to conduct the inquiry in question. If the blind must lead the blind, it is best to begin by tracing the terrain and its features rather than assuming we magically know it all already. This is not to say that I am engaged in an intellectually un-ambitious project—I aim to do no less than shift the way we think about ourselves as ethical beings, the questions we engage with in ethical inquiry, and how we can understand what it means to lead a good life and find peace. Moral dilemmas are important because they are a good, concrete entry point into a better understanding of our ethical condition.

Moral dilemmas are rarely if ever given serious systematic treatment. Most often they are presented as intellectual amusements to be puzzled over. Indeed most peoples' exposure to them as a matter of inquiry is likely to have been polite conversation aimed at producing amusement and intellectual stimulation. Many ethicists and moralists will dismiss them as contrived intuition pumps that are only created to confuse the real issues and should be ignored.[2] Sometimes they are taken quite seriously and put to

---

1 Wittgenstein *Philosophical Investigations* 123: "A philosophical problem has the form: I don't know my way about."

2 Daniel Dennet coined the term in *Consciousness Explained*. His point was that we can construct hypotheticals and thought experiments that exploit intuitions to the detriment of good theory.

various ends in inquiry, but this almost always occurs to a very specific end the theorist finds for them alone. To do the needed work the theorist will offer one type of moral dilemma while ignoring the others. The needed work is almost invariably the refutation of a rival theory by casting the dilemma in such a way that the rival theory cannot deal with it. There seems to be little need or desire to come to a general understanding of moral dilemmas outside of a particular sort and a particular theory. This is a mistake. Moral dilemmas are important because they bring out difficulties within our ways of thinking about ethics. They make flaws in theories apparent and lead us to seek more from ethical theory. As such it would be beneficial to arrive at a general understanding of them.

I find moral dilemmas to be of the utmost importance and am troubled that they seem to be given little serious consideration. In popular ethics or moralistic treatises they are almost uniformly denied as real. Indeed it is sometimes the case that they are thought to be situations in which one shows true moral worth and fortitude in resisting temptation. Such treatment, however, fails to accurately account for the real crises moral dilemmas can engender. Instead the moralist uses them to ultimately laud one solution and expose the other as masked evil. True goodness is shown in the ability to resist and overcome the evil parading as the good. In scholarly academics they are more discussed as proper dilemmas, but here there is almost no effort to deal with them in any unifying way. The major debate on the issue seems to be as to whether or not there are any moral dilemmas, and if so, what this means for doctrines like moral realism. This rather abstract debate is important in reference to academic inquiry of some sort, no doubt, but it appears to me to be overly theoretical for the questions and issues that interest me.

In addition, scholarly discussion of moral dilemmas often suffers from the blunder of pretending to make an inquiry serious and scholarly by awkwardly transposing common problems into inscrutable formal logic and invented terminology that because new appears to be rigorous and/or insightful.[1] Formal logic has its place, yet as Aristotle tells us, we should not demand more precision than the subject permits.[2] This should be taken in the current context as an injunction, not a recommendation. Obsession with formality and specificity isn't just being more careful than necessary but can pervert the issues by giving them a foreign form that transforms nuance into contradiction and eliminates various ways of thinking not amenable to

---

1 Our sense of profundity and the obscurity of language are often linked. I doubt that this is because the language must be new and obscure in order to express what is already profound rather than something appearing profound because new and obscure language has been deployed to express it.
2 Aristotle *Nicomachean Ethics* I.3.

formal expression. We should give up the dogma that it is always possible to transform the nuanced and complex into the clear and systematic by applying a method foreign to the issues being considered. The result of the use of formal logic when discussing moral dilemmas is the loss of the salient issues in the need to transform genuine tensions into formal contradictions. It does strike me that moral dilemmas are instances of contradictions of a sort, but my work here does not hinge on the question of whether or not they are real in the sense that they present strict logical contradictions. Even if they do not there is still an important ethical issue to attend to in the clear tension that arises in moral dilemmas.[1]

Hence from the beginning I am bracketing one question that has been sometimes treated as of the utmost importance: whether or not there even are moral dilemmas. This question can seem important because exuberance for logical rigor turns tensions into dreaded logical contradictions that to some are simply intolerable. By thinking of moral dilemmas in a formal manner, the real issue of the tension they signal is lost and instead we debate whether or not they exist as transmuted into a particular logical program. Clearly there are moral dilemmas in the informal, colloquial sense of dilemma, and it is this sense I am concerned with regardless of how a particular philosopher seeks to analyze them formally. The problem with the logicians' approach is that by imposing a rigorous form foreign to the way moral dilemmas emerge in life, the dilemmas are fundamentally changed and the problem they really pose is lost. Rather than solving the problem moral dilemmas actually present, this approach changes that original problem so it can be solved.

I aim to understand our human ethical condition in a better way and hold that to do so we must confront moral dilemmas as challenges that push us towards a better understanding of our moral condition. In my view, the normative foundation of ethics lies in human identity, and that human identity is complex and pluralistic, constituted by a multitude of roles that are often in tension with one another. Moral dilemmas bring such tension to the fore and hence, if I am correct, are crucial to our understanding and coming to terms with our human moral condition. I do not seek to resolve

---

1 I do not mean, however, to deny the importance of analytical rigor and logic across the board. Formalized treatment can be quite enlightening and productive in ethics. For example, Wilfred Sellars' discussion and analysis of ethical norms as "We shall" intentions asserted on behalf of a community (real or imagined) is quite insightful and helpful for understanding moral judgments (and though I do not pursue the line of argument here, many of the points I make regarding roles below could be stated in terms of his framework, especially given his insistence that we must retain the concept of a person). See esp. Wilfred Sellars, *Science and Metaphysics* VII, "Objectivity, Intersubjectivity and The Moral Point of View." My objection is to a cruder approach that insists everything must fit into a certain "rigorous" framework and thereby bluntly transforms real questions into imaginary problems.

them but to understand them and, through them, our ethical condition. Ultimately, moral dilemmas are crises of who one is and resolving them in life means making choices about one's identity. Viewed as such, moral dilemmas are still pressing but hardly an embarrassment to ethics or the impetus for a radical ethical revolution. They are rather simply a fact about what it means to be a human being or an ethical being.

Since I aim to explicate our moral condition, this inquiry is different from most inquiries into the questions of morality. I am attempting to sketch our moral condition as autonomous self-conscious rational beings as we face it in our lives, in the world as we find it. I do not seek to go back to the beginning or to advance any complex final word as to moral truth and how that fits into the rest of our worldview.

In seeking a new approach to moral questions, I will consider traditional moral theories, but do so only to argue that they fail to really solve or confront the problem. Moral dilemmas lead us to seek a grounding for moral norms, and theories that purport to provide such a robust grounding fail to do so and do not really solve the problems they claim to address. But rather than offering a new theory to replace them, I want to articulate a new approach to moral problems based on identity and the myriad of roles that constitute it. This is not some sort of ultimate grounding, but a grounding that begins at where we are within a moral situation, as we find ourselves in daily life in the world. My hope is that by approaching the issue in a different way we can better understand the problems, tensions, and issues of our moral condition.

Instead of detailed interpretations of the various historical theories of the great ethicists, I offer thumbnail sketches of various ethical theories boiled down to their simplest form and core claims. Of course it is important and interesting to delve into the complexities of each theory and attempt to figure out what exactly the great philosophers of the past held, but this is not the place for such a project. I am attempting to figure out how we should think about moral problems, and a focus on the complexities of theories would obscure that background issue. Hence I use simple forms of positions that highlight what I believe to be the approach that defines, in large part, each sort of ethical theory. By looking at these and arguing that they are flawed, I aim to develop another sort of approach that is perhaps less ambitious but also more enlightening.

Neither am I going to play the moralist. A moralist is a sort of preacher who utilizes rhetoric to inspire what he or she believes to be moral action. The aim is to stir up the spirit by telling people exactly what they ought and ought not do in the most appealing way. I will make few prescriptions as to the content of the good, and those that I do make will be quite general and based on intuitions we generally share (e.g., killing for no reason is wrong).

Partly I avoid this because it tends to start with the answers and then go in search of questions, but mostly because I have no full account of the good action or the good life. My focus is the structure of moral inquiry, not its result.

This is ultimately a project of self-examination. For those who do not find themselves morally conflicted as to what they ought to do in various situations and who they ought to be in life, this essay will be perplexing. But I am conflicted and find it difficult to know how to think about ethics, and I believe many others are as well. The aim of this essay, in the end, is to figure out how to think about that conflict, understand that conflict, and live with that conflict.

Outline

In chapter two I make a number of points that serve to clarify what I am focusing on, what I mean by basic terms, and how I am approaching the inquiry. Some of these claims will be argued for as the project progresses, but it is important to be clear what I am up to at the beginning and to motivate, to some degree, my background views. Next I sketch each type of dilemma and explain the various examples and how exactly each sort of dilemma works. Chapter four turns to a consideration of the use each sort of dilemma is put to and then argues that what we seek in investigating moral dilemmas is a secure moral grounding.

Many ethical theories, whether or not they address moral dilemmas, are in search of moral grounding. In chapter five I lay out some criteria for a successful grounding and then argue that four predominant approaches from theory—theological, utilitarian, deontological, and virtue-based—fail to rise to the challenge. Essentially I argue that each fails because it tries to find an extrinsic grounding for moral space but, in so doing, fails either to provide something that can be understood for someone who is engaged in critical ethical inquiry or to provide something that could really ground the norms in question as genuine norms.

If an extrinsic approach will not work then an intrinsic approach is needed, even though this will not provide the sort of theory that many are looking for. But I gladly sacrifice the prospect of the great pay-off that would come with such a theory for a better understanding of our moral condition and the problems therein. Chapter six argues that, from the perspective of the moral agent, grounding is found in the identity of the moral agent. I follow norm x because I am y. We can search for more, but at some point asking for more justification of why one ought to be z fails to make sense because without z the particular moral agent is incomprehensible, i.e., taking away z would result in a different moral agent altogether (or no moral agent at all) rather than the same agent in a different shape, so to speak.

Pointing to identity alone shows little, and indeed it is compatible with all of the theories I found wanting earlier. Hence in chapter seven I explain what I mean by identity. Identity is a web of roles that we take on by nature, by the particular facts of our particular existence, or by implicit or explicit choice. The rest of the chapter explains the various sorts of roles that encompass who we are. Chapter eight fills in the approach by making a number of points about identity and the web of roles that constitute it. Chapter nine provides a detailed example of how this approach plays out by considering legal ethics and how we can better understand the ethical problems that lawyers face. It also addresses several other similar examples, examines the tension between solidarity and cosmopolitanism, and engages in an analysis of addiction and recovery from the perspective of identity and roles in order to offer a discussion of the ethical crisis of the addict in a way that well illustrates some aspects of how roles constitute identity.

The approach given, I return to moral dilemmas in order to provide a better understanding of why they arise and how in fact we deal with them. Though I do not attempt to solve them, I show how they work, why they can and must be accepted, and how their occurrence provides evidence that the approach I take is on the right track. Moral dilemmas are important because trying to understand them leads us away from absolute abstract theories to a better self-understanding of our moral condition. Ethical norms are grounded in identity, and identity is constituted by a myriad of various roles that encompass who we are by nature or by choice (and a good deal in between). These roles in turn give rise to a plurality of valid maxims that apply to various situations. We strive to live a unified life and hence avoid contradictions in roles we play. But since we are complex human beings, there is a constant tension that in some situations will lead to genuine moral dilemmas. The existence of moral dilemmas is hence good evidence that my approach is on the right track.

Chapter eleven turns to the crucial issue of avoiding both insulation and imperialism in ethics. On the one hand it seems that anything goes, while on the other we are forced to posit one strict way of being. Either we are left with a relativism that leads to nihilism or with an implausible and intolerant absolutism. Neither is palatable and thus the chapter argues that identity-based ethics offers a way between the two because it opens up the possibility of an objectively anchored ethical pluralism. Finally, chapter twelve concludes by taking a broad perspective on our moral condition and how to think about it following this approach.

CHAPTER TWO: PRELIMINARY QUESTIONS, DISTINCTIONS, AND DEFINITIONS

Before turning to moral dilemmas in more detail, I must address several background issues to clarify the nature of the project and the distinctions that are important in what follows. These points situate my project in relation to other questions, terms, and distinctions that are often discussed and thus provide a frame for the rest of the inquiry.

Why Be Good?

At the beginning of the *Republic*, Plato has Socrates frame the discussion around whether or not it is good to be just, or if it is better to be unjust.[1] The issue is presented in the memorable story of the Ring of Gyges. A shepherd, Gyges, finds a ring and discovers that if he turns it a certain way he becomes invisible. He uses this power to kill the king, marry the queen, take over the kingdom, and get anything he wants. He does so, of course, unjustly. Yet he appears quite happy. So the question is whether or not someone really ought to be just if one could get away with being unjust. Put otherwise, the question is what you ought to do if you had the ring. Note that this is not a question about personal psychology alone—we aren't concerned with what a particular individual would in fact do if he or she had possession of such a ring. Rather the question is normative—in possession of the ring, what should one do?

Socrates then begins a long journey to determine what justice is both for the city and the individual and ends up concluding that the just person is in fact happier than the unjust person. Throughout both ancient and modern philosophy there has been anxiety to show that it is in fact beneficial to be good or just.

---

1 Plato, *Republic* I.

The problem can be put starkly: is the just man being slowly tortured to death really happier than the unjust man enjoying a banquet? Clearly not, we want to say—but if this is so, isn't it only good to be just when there is some external benefit that one will achieve? The issue has been much discussed. Cicero, following the Stoic Panaetius, structures *On Duties* into one book devoted to determining what is honorable, a second book delineating what is advantageous, and a third combining the two to show that we ought to act honorably. In more recent times, contemporary ethicist Peter Singer frames his argument in *How Are We to Live?* on the problem.

The question is interesting but needs clarification. First, philosophers, like the Stoics, who claim that the just man is happier than the unjust man, mean a sort of happiness that is different in kind and more valuable than mere sensual pleasure. For such philosophers pleasure and happiness must be decoupled. Further, happiness of this sort is to be evaluated over a lifetime, not at an individual moment. The lesson is that the question of whether or not it is good to be just is very unclear. Indeed, the same question could be posed as to whether or not it is good to be good. But it is of course good to be good. Unless, that is, "good" refers to different things. And it seems to, when the question is posed. Our conception of justice or good is anchored to ordinary conventional senses of goodness and justice. When we ask whether acting that way is good we are getting at the different issue of whether or not that is advantageous in some undefined sense of maximal happiness.

But we are still dealing with "wiggle" words—words that seem simple but take on varying senses that are importantly different, though they are confounded when we use the same word to indicate them. Use of wiggle words without sufficient attention to their slippery usages and meanings is a bane of ethical thought (and indeed of philosophical thought generally). Advantageous in what sense? And doesn't this turn on what we want out of life? A question that originally seemed so clear becomes more difficult as we try to figure out what it means. The problem is simply that we attach quite colloquial senses to the terms in the original question, but any analysis of it requires that we fill in, upon reflection, what is advantageous and what is just or good.

And this is exactly what Plato has Socrates do in the *Republic*. I think this is right. We should not be overly anxious about whether it is good to be good. Instead we should ask how we ought to be and work from there to more understanding of what form of life that leads to, and what the state of that person is. Indeed the two inform each other: if we have an account of how one ought to be that leads to miserable forms of existence, that is a good sign that we are on the wrong track in our account. In the same way, if we think it expedient to have lots and lots of money but determine that, on balance, this creates bad character traits that decay a person's moral worth and character, then it isn't really good to have lots of money.

The question I ask is how one ought to be, and I pose this question without a set conception of what it means to be good or just, or what it means to be expedient, or what constitutes the most advantageous life, or what constitutes happiness. These are questions to consider, but if we want to figure out who and what we ought to be, we need to bracket these prior questions and conceptions. We cannot pretend we have clear ideas about what they are.

Ethics vs. Morals

It is currently fashionable in some circles to distinguish ethics and morals and to chide those who use the two interchangeably with falling into a silly and dangerous confusion. Colloquially, however, the two are often used interchangeably. I use both here and intend no deep difference. Depending on context, one word or the other is more natural, and I attempt to speak naturally. Nothing deep is to be found in the use of one word or the other here.

Though they are sometimes thought to be importantly different, I have seen several quite different ways of drawing those distinctions. For example, some say that morals refer to specific maxims while ethics refers to a broader system of those norms. Under this usage, morals are a part of an ethic. Others seem to think that morality refers to something absolute and objective while ethics, especially in the sense of an ethical code, refers to the norms in reference to a certain group or practice or role. Still others characterize morality as composed of various virtues while ethics consists of norms of action towards others or in various situations. And others view morals as picking out a narrower category of what duty requires, while ethics concerns larger issues or "all things considered" what one ought to do. A.C. Grayling finds an essential distinction for his project between morals, which are limited to constraints on how we relate to others, and the broader category of ethics that captures the sort of person one is overall.[1] These various distinctions may be compatible. But given that the "experts" seem unable to agree on what the important distinction is, I doubt there is really an important distinction captured in the words alone. Better to be clear

---

1 A.C. Grayling. *The God Argument: The Case Against Religion and for Humanism.* Esp. ch. 16. Though he draws on some historical usage for his distinction it is still an artificial imposition on *current* usage. The distinction is important for him and I'm not criticizing it—just flagging that I do not use it here.

about what we mean when we use either word than to rely on some implicit difference in sense between the two that isn't apparent to most people and is made explicit in different ways.

Now, of course it is important to distinguish individual norms and a system of norms. And virtues of character are different from virtuous actions, just as how one ought to be is different from what one ought to do. And we can explore how one ought to be, in reference to some code we hold fixed, or ask the same question more broadly, holding less fixed. But these are all related and differ more in the angle of inquiry into ethical or moral space than in the topic of inquiry. And while the distinctions are important, I doubt that merely using one word rather than another accomplishes the laudable goal of clarity, given ordinary usage and the lack of agreed technical meanings. Distinctions are good, but it is dangerous to overly rely on the bare sense of individual words like 'ethics' and 'morals', and claim to have thereby accomplished something important. When a distinction is necessary, it is better to make it explicitly. Here generally no deep distinction is meant to be conveyed merely by the use of 'morals' or 'ethics'.

Ethics vs. Meta-Ethics

Ethics is the study of various practical norms, tracing out what is morally required of someone. Meta-ethics is the study of questions about those norms. Do they have grounding? Are they an illusion? Are they expressions of emotion? Is there any reason we ought to follow them? The distinction is plain enough and the inquiries can be separated. Ethics, on this approach, would engage in the task of theorizing what we ordinarily take to be morally correct based on intuitions. Of course we could have surprising conclusions, or even come to see that there is no consistency, or too much variety, and hence there is no theory. But we would still operate within a framework that took ethical intuitions and maxims at face value. Meta-ethics would question the framework as a whole and offer some account of ethics itself. For emotivists, for example, ethical assertions are not true or false (and hence not assertions) but emotional responses of approval or disapproval.[1] Skeptics at this level might claim that ethics lacks any real normative force, which is to say that there is nothing deep to ethics at all.

The distinction can be important depending on the project at hand, but I will shift between the two throughout. I do so because I think that the idea of a totally abstracted, sideways-on investigation of ethical life, absent all

---

1 This sort of view was once held by A.J. Ayer. To understand it we must place it in its context: if, as many did, one holds a statement must be verifiable to be meaningful then either all moral language is meaningless or something like emotivism must be posited: by transforming moral language emotivists save it from becoming nonsense.

perspective on and participation in ethical life, is nonsense. This is not to say all of meta-ethics is nonsense, but rather that setting it as fundamentally different from, and over and above ethical inquiry from the perspective of a human being immersed in the world, is a dangerous mistake and fantasy. I will not argue for that claim now, but it is important to flag here as it explains why I shift between questions that are sometimes treated as importantly different.

Additionally, I do not see great value in a project that assumes a full meta-ethical theory and then attempts to engage in ethics. What we answer in response to questions normally treated within meta-ethics will have profound effects on our account of the norms that bind us. They may lead us to view them in a quite different way, solve some problems, and create others. I am interested in what one ought to be and do and how we are to understand moral dilemmas and our moral condition. I will focus on general moral intuitions and what we take to be ethical behavior but also query generally how these norms are grounded.

Reasonable and Rational

What it means to be reasonable and what it means to be rational are sometimes treated as crucially different, especially in moral and political philosophy. Generally, being rational is considered more basic, as following certain rules of reasoning that we generally attach to instrumental sorts of reasoning; that is, given various ends, making decisions about means that maximize those ends. Being reasonable is something more, adopting certain ends that are deemed intrinsically reasonable in and of themselves. Depending on what this entails, a great deal can be developed from what it means to be reasonable.[1]

Though the distinction can be important, it is not essential here. I don't want to adopt either conception. Rather when I speak of being reasonable I mean only that the person is engaged in the game of giving and asking for reasons. Otherwise put, the person follows certain sorts of inferences that are recognized as rational inferences and seeks to justify beliefs and actions to himself or others.

It may seem that in the last few sections I have been opening the road to sloppy thinking by rejecting various distinctions thought to be crucial. I am not, however, rejecting the distinctions wholesale insofar as they are important for a particular inquiry. Rather I am doing two things. First, I am rejecting the idea that the ordinary use of the words and our ordinary

---

1 This distinction can be drawn from Kant in his treatment of hypothetical and categorical imperatives as depending on different sorts of mental processes. As stated I am followed Rawls' usage.

way of talking in ethics automatically commits us to the various technical distinctions philosophers impose. We may, of course, employ such distinctions in ordinary practice, but they are not automatic functions of the words used. The upshot is that we should not think that there is anything magically picked out merely by using one word or another. If we intend to use them differently, we must be explicit and recognize a departure from ordinary, and perhaps sloppy, ways of talking. Second, I have merely been indicating that the various distinctions that are made with the words in question in different parts of the literature are generally unimportant here. I will not be using a complex technical apparatus to answer ethical questions and do not mean to implicitly pick one out in the use of words ordinarily employed in ethical discourse.

"Ought to Do" and "Ought to Be" Norms

Ethics can be talked about both in terms of what one ought to do in a particular situation and who and how one ought to be as a human being. Modern ethics focuses almost exclusively on the former, at least on the surface. It looks for principles that determine what the good acts are. Ancient ethics, by contrast, is generally more concerned with who and how one ought to be. We can see this strand in virtue ethics wherein the good is defined in terms of character traits. For the modern ethicist one is x because one takes action y. For the ancient ethicist one does y because one is x.

Both are important and they are deeply related. I stress ought to be norms because I think that this gets at the deeper parts of our moral condition. Investigation through reflection concerns inquiry into ourselves rather than concrete norms we apply in the course of actual situations. We are after the good life and it is helpful to think about horizons beyond the immediate action one will take. This need not be limited to virtues. We can look at what sorts of projects a person ought to undertake in life, and these projects will come to define her through time. The choice of whether to become a parent is another example. If we look at the issue through the ought to do lens, we look for duties to procreate, perhaps given our situation at the time. This is helpful, but a richer discussion can be had by looking at the question in terms of whether or not one ought to be a parent and undertake those responsibilities over a long stretch of time. This will depend on many other factors about who one is, and it is not easily reduced to abstract principles that give rules for conduct.

I do not, however, want to suggest that there is a stark difference in the end. Aspects of identity and character traits are reasons and causes for action, but at the same time if one acts in a certain way that is a reason for and cause of embodying various aspects of identity and character traits. The two are intimately related. We can imagine acting against character on occasion (and an examination of the way we punish reveals that we countenance this), but it is hard to think that a person would be *x* but never do actions *y* that follow from that trait. And if someone always takes *y*-type actions, it is rather absurd to say that he nonetheless does not embody trait *x* even though someone who is *x* usually does *y*. Hence though I think the question of who one ought to be is the essential question we face in our moral condition, focusing on it this way is done as a way of better framing the issues rather than moving away wholeheartedly from a focus on actions. What one does is a reflection of who one is, and vice-versa.

A related and more familiar point is captured in James 2:26, wherein the author points out that just as the body without the spirit is dead, so too faith without actions is dead. Christians may focus on their faith and know that they fail to live up to it. But if there are people who profess faith and yet it has no effect on their life and actions, then it is hard to think that the faith is alive and real. Coming to possess faith transforms a person in a way that will generally be reflected in action. In the same way there is a tight link between who one is and what one does. Though the two may diverge in particular instances, they are essentially connected.

Reduction vs. Explication

What follows may seem perplexing to many familiar with contemporary theory because I say nothing regarding the ontological constitution of identity or roles, or what it means to be a human being, beyond a colloquial explication of who we are when conducting ethical inquiry and acting in the world. Such a theory would be the ordinary way of pursuing a theory of human identity. So what of the ontological status of these roles and thus identity? In my explanation of identity that follows, I say nothing about the soul, mind, or brain.

This may seem puzzling. Usually when one discusses identity, the primary question is ontological—of what substance is one made? Spiritual? Mental? Physical? How does the mind relate to the brain? Where do these things come from and what is *really* real? I don't answer these questions and yet claim to give an explication of identity. I don't even address the question of the persistence of an integrated identity over time—an issue much discussed by philosophers. Nor do I engage in any thought experiments of the Star Trek variety about malfunctions in the "beaming up" process in which duplicates and the like are made. My account may thus seem a failure, or rather an embarrassing misunderstanding of the question being posed.

No doubt all of these questions are interesting, though in my view they are thought to be much more important than they really are. We have become obsessed with providing a reductive account of what we are that conforms to antecedent metaphysical prejudices and proclivities. The theories are often quite perplexing and questionable. We simply don't know how identity emerges biologically or spiritually. We quickly become lost and confused when we start postulating different sorts of substances. And once we begin with various thought experiments, our intuitions fail us—we don't understand what exactly identity is in an ontological sense and so are easily prey to thought experiments. In giving "accounts" of identity, we point to what must be the case, given what we already believe, and then claim to have an account of identity. I take the opposite approach.

I have no clue how we physically or spiritually come to have personal identity. I don't know whether to identify it with the brain, mind, soul, or something else. I'm not even sure there is a good question for philosophy to ask in this neighborhood. But I submit that personal identity is a mere given and a criterion of adequacy—any theory that does not allow for the sort of personal identity we take ourselves to have is a failure. We are much more familiar with the phenomena of autonomous self-conscious rational existence and being the sorts of people we are than any scientific or metaphysical stance that would tell us what this must be.

Instead of radically changing our conception of ourselves to make room for theory, we ought to reject theories that ask this of us. We must hence switch our perspective. Instead of beginning with ontological and metaphysical prejudices and then providing a reductive account of what identity *must* be, we should begin with a general understanding of identity and hold this against ontological and metaphysical claims. Of course we should be careful here—our understanding is so limited that we must not make rash conclusions as to ontology. Neither should we infer ontology based solely on phenomenological analysis. Rather we should simply accept our understanding of identity for what it is, doubt theories that make this impossible, and let ontology take care of itself.

So what am I doing? I seek not a reductive account but a deeper understanding. I make no ontological or metaphysical commitments or claims. Rather I aim to analyze and explicate identity in such a way that we come to *understand* it more fruitfully. So when I argue below that identity is constituted by a web of roles, I am offering an explication of the ordinary phenomenon of personal identity aimed at a deeper understanding, not a religious or scientific theory of how this comes to pass. This may seem disappointing to many, as it makes no sweeping claims about the nature of reality (whatever we take to be the scope of reality to be). None, however, is merited. Theories too often arrive at fantastic and poorly argued ontologies or theories of identity because they cling to the idea that we can and must conduct moral inquiry in tandem with ontological inquiry. When this becomes confusing, one or the other or both are given sweeping but dubious treatment, leaving accounts rich on provocative conclusions about ontology or ethics or identity but poor on understanding.

It is better to step back. I seek understanding of our moral condition and look to identity to find this. And I seek to understand our sense or moral identity not by giving a reduction of it but by giving an explication of it. Viewing identity as a vast web of roles we occupy with various dimensions and relations permits a better understanding of ourselves. If I am right about this, something of great value has been achieved. I seek not reduction but explication. No account from the ground up is to be offered. I do not see how such an account would bring understanding in any case. Rather I hope to explain various aspects of identity in terms of each other and thus explicate our previous implicit understanding. This may seem a conservative goal, but given the difficulty in this area is exactly what is needed. Reductive "accounts" are a dime a dozen and yet we usually fail to even understand what exactly human identity is outside of rash reduction.

On questions of ontology and metaphysics I wish to remain neutral, just as I seek to remain neutral as to substantive ethics. Though I criticize the approach taken by the predominant theories that seek to provide a grounding for morality, because I think they are not successful on their own, on substantive issues each can be made compatible with the approach I offer. I also favor no particular metaphysics but rather hold that the explication of identity I will develop is something that must be retained by any ontology. What this means for our ontological commitments, I do not know. My concern is to understand my way about these difficult issues and hence an explication of the phenomenon of personal identity will do.

Against rash reductionists who would insist that their ontological predilections rule out any robust sort of identity that I argue for, I reply only that the reality of such identity is much more certain than the tendentious metaphysics they assert.[1] I make no claim as to what ontology we must accept to explain identity, only that it cannot be explained away. Thankfully the ethical project of seeking ethical self-understanding does not need ontology. Rather we must explicate what it means to be the sort of beings we are and so come to understand identity. It is this project of ethics without ontology that I am engaged in, and it is this project that strikes me as the proper providence of a philosophical and ethical inquiry.

---

1 Similar in my view to a biologist who would claim that after his detailed research and theory construction he has determined that human beings do not exist because they are incompatible with his theory!

Where Do We Begin?

In *On Certainty* 471 Wittgenstein writes, "It is so difficult to find the *beginning.* Or, better, it is difficult to begin at the beginning, and not try to go further back."[1] I have set my task as an exploration of our moral condition not designed to produce any sort of theory but rather some understanding of a dimension of human life that can be very perplexing. Moral dilemmas are my proposed way to do this. But where do we begin in such an inquiry?

Most modern ethicists begin with a certain imported picture of what sort of beings we are exactly. Hence the current popularity of both evolutionary and theological ethics, depending on one's other views about the nature of things. We create a naturalistic or theological picture of what we are and then reach conclusions as to what could possibly be the case for morality. I view these approaches as extrinsic in that they look at morality from outside our moral condition as we find it and instead construct a moral position, or reject its possibility altogether, based on other views and theories they hold to be true.

My approach differs. I don't want a comprehensive theory and seek instead a beginning within ethical thought and practice. An acceptable moral theory must make sense of our primitive understanding of our moral condition. If a theory about human nature or the ontology of the world leads to a moral theory that is wildly at odds with our moral understanding, or makes it impossible that there could ever be a moral dimension to human life, then it is a failure, at least in the sense that it is missing something that we seek to explain and understand.

The proper beginning for developing a deeper understanding of our moral condition is our moral intuitions and our primitive sense of what our moral condition is. I start here because we must start where we are. All too often people make the mistake of trying to go further back, thinking that they can take a God's eye view on the universe and from the outside develop a basic theory that dictates all of the rest. But there is no such view available as a starting point for inquiry. Such theories depend, essentially, on rich views about what must be the case that also must be developed by where we are. We must start with the moral being pressed by ethical problems, sensitive to moral norms, and asking what sort of person one ought to be. In doing so no ontology is presumed or imported and none follows. The project seeks understanding.

If someone tells me that morality is unreal because his physics and ontology doesn't account for it, I will agree if the claim is that it is unreal in the realm of the physical things his inquiry is talking about it. But I will

---

1 Wittgenstein *On Certainty* 471.

add that his conclusion does not show in the least bit that there is no moral inquiry to be had. There are physical phenomena we seek to explain and there are moral phenomena we seek to explain. That a favored explanation of the former doesn't account for the latter doesn't mean that we shouldn't seek to understand the latter at all. The trouble is with the word 'real' and the seeming implication that if something is real, we must be able to go see it and touch it. Again, I'm not interested in ontology in this sense. I want to find my way about, and to do so there is no other choice but to start where we are. It is silly to bring in a different sort of inquiry and declare that even though this is where we find ourselves in relation to morality, we simply cannot be here because a different inquiry doesn't account for it.

Hence insofar as an account of morality makes morality impossible or cannot make any sense of it at all, that account (again as an account of morality) can be rejected as either doing something else or seeking a moral theory but abjectly failing to provide one. But note that by saying this, I am not endorsing a move in the other direction, from an internal account of moral phenomena to robust conclusions about the nature of things. I decidedly am not saying that we can use our moral theories and understandings developed intrinsically to go out and determine any ontology or physics. Thus I reject that argument which, in its simple form, moves from moral intuitions to the need for a source, to the existence of a God as such a moral source. Indeed I think such arguments fail on their own merit. But more generally I think that it is a confusion to develop an ontology out of our moral condition just as it is to take a prior ontology and determine against all intuition what our moral condition must be. This is not to say the two sorts of inquires are totally isolated from one another but rather to say that to do one, we don't need to do the other, and shouldn't make quick jumps between the two.

So I also reject what philosopher Charles Taylor calls the Best Account Principle.[1] It holds that whatever provides the best account of the phenomenon, in the present context moral phenomenon, must be accepted. So not only can we reject as at best incomplete theories that cannot make sense of morality as we find it, but we can endorse what turns out to be the best account on the table as true and draw all sorts of conclusions from that. I have two problems with this. First, as above, I see no reason to automatically license an inference from the best account we have at present to a particular ontology or other theory. Second, there is no reason that we

1 Taylor, Charles, *Sources of the Self*, 58; I agree with Taylor that metaphysical and epistemological considerations cannot force us to reject common phenomena, like conscious and normative thought but disagree with the next step of accepting the best account of those phenomena regardless of any extrinsic considerations. Taylor seems to oscillate between the weak reading I endorse and the strong reading I reject because it allows us to assert a robust account simply because it is the best we can think of.

need to accept any account or theory at all. It may end up that no theory provides an account that we can endorse and we suspend judgment. This is why a theory is not my aim. My aim is to understand why we are confused and why we are led to these problems and hopefully to provide an explication of our moral condition that helps us better deal with and understand the challenges that we face as autonomous self-conscious rational beings. In this task the beginning is simply where we are as beings reflecting on ourselves and asking who we ought to be and what we ought to do in life.

The Role of Intuitions

Moral dilemmas and ethical reflection generally rely on moral intuitions. They present situations in which moral intuitions that are appealing produce contradictory results. When a theory is involved, and these theories are often driven by some intuitive appeal, moral dilemmas use the theories to produce a decidedly unintuitive result. But why should we pay any credence to our intuitions?

The simple answer is that in this realm they function as a sort of raw data, part of the beginning we see when we start where we are and try to develop an ethical self-understanding. Plus, what else are we supposed to rely on? We do in fact have natural or cultivated reactions to what is morally correct in particular situations. Moral theory is developed out of these intuitions as a way to crystallize abstract moral principles. Sometimes these principles may lead us to reject intuitions, but this does not make intuitions suspect across the border. Imagine a moral theory that had absolutely no intuitive appeal and almost always led to unintuitive results. Would such a theory be acceptable? I think not. It might be internally consistent but that is really all it has going for it. It might be viewed as a nice construct with an internal elegance, but we would have trouble calling it a *moral* theory.

But perhaps we can find more. Imagine someone develops a theory that is not a moral theory and has some appeal in another field. Then this person reasons from that theory to a particular moral theory that in the end rejects intuitions but, importantly, still offers a moral theory. This person doesn't conclude that moral theory and moral nature is a charade but rather that it is real, and we just have it wrong. For example, instead of saying that our nature means that we seek self-preservation and power, and morality is unreal, this person would say that by nature we seek self-preservation and power and that this entails that true morality dictates we seek these at expense of all else, even though our moral intuitions are deeply offended by this.

While such a position is coherent, it is difficult to hold. The problem is that such a person is using the term "morality" but is doing so in an odd and unrecognizable way. We have a grasp of the concept in ordinary life, and it doesn't really help any inquiry to use the same word but deny that grasp as having any relation to it. Hence the difference between the two characters above is less than may meet the eye. In the end the view is the same, only the words being used are different. Both deny our moral sense and natural position, as we take it to be, as utterly without merit. One just wants to keep on talking using words we recognize.

Above, I've explained why I think such theories are ancillary to my discussion. Essentially my project is an explication of our moral position, not a development of an ontology or metaphysics or even a robust moral theory. Moral space is real in the sense that we find ourselves in it. By saying it is real, I do not imply there is anything real in the sense of what is real in the world as physics or biology, etc., talk about the world. I simply begin where we are as autonomous self-conscious rational beings with a moral condition we seek to understand. A theory that rejects this altogether or can't make sense of it is either irrelevant to my discussion or can be rejected because it fails to account for the obvious. If we stop obsessing about ontology, we might develop a little understanding about the condition we find ourselves in to begin with.

It is not the case that intuitions are sacrosanct and must be respected. Some may be wrong or misguided. But what I am saying is that intuitions are important in moral inquiry in that they give us something to work with. Hence theories and understandings in this domain must make sense of our intuitions by countenancing most of them and offering a better understanding of why some intuitions lead us to incorrect or confused conclusions. Intuitions are data, but they are not infallible.

The Moral Being

I am concerned first and foremost with the moral being, that is, humans who are bound by moral norms of both the ought to do and ought to be varieties. I begin here because this is an ethical inquiry, and hence I must accept and begin with my sense of a moral being who is engaged with moral questions. Throughout I will speak of this being to be an autonomous self-conscious rational being. This is not a full account but an explication of what matters about us in a moral inquiry. A few words about each category should help frame my approach and perspective.

An autonomous being is at least sometimes free to act and be a certain way. This opens the possibility of normative appraisal of all sorts (epistemic, moral, pragmatic, aesthetic, etc.) because there is a choice that one is responding to as an agent. This does not require that we are always free to act, just that we sometimes are. For example some people may be compelled to do certain things that are beyond their control. Heart beats and breathing are examples. So is a reflex that is tested by a doctor. Addicts are those who are internally compelled to act in a certain way, whether it be to ingest a certain drug or gamble or whatnot. These are people who feel trapped, in that they do not want to do what they are nonetheless compelled to do. This is not to say responsibility does not attach for any of these sorts of activities, just that in a particular frame they are not free, though there may be freedom to avoid or escape from that frame altogether. Moreover, these cases show that freedom is not binary but comes in degrees.

Immediately the stress on autonomy runs up against the modern penchant for mechanic naturalism, whereby all there is a series of cause and effect, and free will is an illusion within naturalism. This picture of the physical world as machine leads in two different directions. First, there is the theistic turn. Since the physical world is mechanistic and doesn't permit norms or freedom, but we know that these are real, there must be a God and we must have souls, etc. So, for example, we have Descartes (at least as he appears on the surface) who views the world as a machine, and animals as even lacking consciousness, but holds onto the mind or soul or thing that thinks as what is essential to humanity. On the other side there are those who see no room for freedom or norms, and just accept this as sober truth.

Both should be resisted. From the perspective of natural science of course the world is mechanistic, but this is because that is the frame of natural science, and it takes us outside of what we are studying to look on it in this way. Moral inquires (and many others as well) are different. We are by necessity inside the object of study and we cannot get out. We cannot both posit a view from nowhere, from which we can make claims and offer reasons and judgments, but then conclude that we are by nature mechanistic or that there must be some ethereal realm.

My project is one of explication, and as humans who live in this world, we experience freedom. Perhaps some science may tell a causal story, but we are constituted by an important part of that story; we are not on-lookers who somehow come to look at us from the outside.

Humans are also self-conscious beings. Chemicals and rocks and the like simply react. Trees and plants react in a different way, and we deem them alive. Animals react to the world but are also conscious of it.[1] They experience the world and feel, for example, pain.[2] Human beings are conscious as well.

---

1 These categories are useful though I do not find them to be as rigid as they may seem: between mere things and life there are grey areas, as there are between animal and plant life. Likely the same holds between human and animal life. Categories are helpful but not rigid—they represent points on a spectrum.

2 Mechanistic accounts of the world can run into trouble here: Descartes, for example, located all conscious phenomena with the thinking thing or soul and this was possessed only by humans and thus animals were machines

But the key feature of human beings in the present context is that we are not only conscious of the world but conscious of ourselves as well. We are self-conscious and so can think not only about the world, but think about it and ourselves at a much more abstract level. Animals (and some human behavior fits as well) may communicate in the sense of giving signs. Humans have acquired language, with complex grammars, that allows for the expression of thoughts that are complex and of which there are infinite possibilities.

Being self-conscious is an essential ingredient of morality because it allows for reflection on courses of conduct and the constitution of one's life. It allows for inquiry and justifications and explanations that fit into a rich fabric of who we are and how we live. Conscious beings can respond to rules that are ingrained by nature or by training. Self-conscious beings can do this, and they can investigate and adopt or reject various rules. This possibility makes these rules rich norms, and norms are essential for moral life.

Human beings are also rational in that we offer reasons and engage in inquiry and argument. Rationality means that we are able to give good and bad reasons (or refuse to give reasons at all) for beliefs we hold, actions we take, character traits and roles we have, and forms of life that we live. I do not mean to trace the contours of justification—that task is massive. I only want to point out that we, as human beings, are engaged in the practice of inquiry and giving and asking for reasons. Moral inquiry looks to what we ought to do and be, and as such it is important that the moral agent be a rational agent that can engage in normative inquiry involving justification and explanation.

None of this is meant as a "scientific" account of the human being (whatever *that* is). Rather it is our self-reflective perspective on ourselves. Man as machine pictures tend to dominate inquiry at present, but when discussing morality this perspective cannot do. Our moral condition is essentially ours. The man as machine metaphor takes an outsider's point of view that we gain in self-consciousness. But moral inquiry is essentially within the self-conscious perspective and so it is a mistake to attempt to look from the outside in. There is no outside from whence to look. We must approach the subject in terms of what it means to find oneself in the world as an autonomous, self-conscious, rational being. This essay is an attempt to develop a way to think about what this means in terms of a moral condition and deal with moral dilemmas, tensions, and problems—not with solution, but with at least a better understanding of our situation.

that could not feel pain. Most find such a view incredible.

CHAPTER THREE: MORAL DILEMMAS

Introduction

Moral dilemmas come in different sorts and are used for different purposes. An acceptable general ethical understanding of them should account for or at least explain each sort of moral dilemma. It is unhelpful to ignore one sort to address another. If only one sort is dealt with, then it is clear that the theory is opportunistically employing a moral dilemma to a particular theoretical or dialectical purpose rather than giving a theory of moral dilemmas that seeks to solve or at least help us understand them. In various ethical debates, it is often the case that moral dilemmas are used only for a particular rhetorical purpose in order to presumably defeat a rival theory. Its use is dialectical and there is no attempt to deal with moral dilemmas generally as a problem for an ethical theory or a phenomenon that is part of our moral lives and that we should attempt to better understand. An acceptable account of moral dilemmas must apply to all types, not use one type to a certain end while ignoring others. It is important to begin, then, by sketching each general sort of moral dilemma: pedestrian dilemmas, theoretical dilemmas, and critical dilemmas.

What is Not a Moral Dilemma

I will turn to each type of dilemma momentarily, but I must first be clear as to what I am *not* talking about. Often we find ourselves in situations when we are forced to choose between a course of action we know to be morally correct and a course of action that will bring us great benefit. Cheating on a difficult exam or perhaps stealing office supplies from an employer are examples of this sort of situation. There are many others. While such situations may be stressful and may involve dilemmas, they are not properly *moral* dilemmas. In these cases there is a clear moral answer and we are tempted to act unmorally for personal gain. We know that cheating is morally wrong but are tempted to do so anyway because the test is important. There is no moral argument to be made for cheating in this case. Likewise there is no moral argument to be made for stealing office supplies, though it may be quite tempting.

Now, there are important philosophical questions to pose here that have great historical providence. Many Greek philosophers were very concerned with whether or not the moral man was better off than the unmoral man. This question is whether or not it is good, in an instrumental sense, to be moral. But, as noted above, this question is quite different from the issue I am primarily interested in. I am interested in what exactly one should do and who one should be as a moral agent. Moral dilemmas arise within moral space and create problems therein. The issue is not whether or not to be moral but instead what exactly it means to be moral when we are forced into a situation in which there is no clear answer.

In a moral dilemma, at least two mutually exclusive actions have a clear moral rationale for them or there is simply no moral answer at all. It is not that we are tempted to be unmoral but that there is a moral conflict regarding which course of action we ought to take. There are certainly dilemmas of practical reason pitting moral reasons versus other sorts of reasons and forcing us to confront the question of why we ought to be moral if the sort of "ought" we are concerned with is not the moral ought. These are not the sort of dilemmas I am concerned with here—I am concerned with cases in which morality itself seems to demand two different incompatible actions. While such dilemmas are local to morality, they are far more threatening in that they purport to bring out a collapse of morality itself.

This point, once made explicit, is fairly obvious, yet it goes quite unacknowledged, so much so that in ordinary parlance and popular usage moral dilemmas are mistakenly thought to take this form. For example, in his book *Ethical Ambition: Living a Life of Meaning and Worth*, Derrick Bell presents the dilemma we often face between doing the right thing, resulting in material harm to ourselves, and doing the wrong thing for personal gain, ambition, and success.[1] His framing example is his own choice to leave the faculty of Harvard Law School in protest over the lack of any women of color on the faculty, the failure of that institution to conduct faculty hiring as he wished, and his impression that he was not being given due deference in

---

1 Bell *Ethical Ambition: Living a Live of Meaning and Worth*; though I pick on Bell here for his framing, it is quite a nice and no doubt instructive book. My quibble is with how he presents the issue he is dealing with.

faculty meetings. This decision cost him a great deal of material benefit and led to much uncertainty in his life, especially given that his wife was quite sick at the time. Now, I do think that Professor Bell was faced with a sort of moral dilemma, but it is not of the sort he presents. In his analysis the choice was between right and gain, and he is virtuous—in fact, a hero to some—for having followed right. The lesson to others, especially law students, is to do the right thing even when faced with material loss.

Bracketing the value of this overarching lesson, the issue is not framed as a true moral dilemma. It may be a dilemma of sorts but it is not a moral one. In fact, it can't be for Bell's point to carry—he *needs* morality to line up on one side of the issue for his analysis to go through. Hence it behooves him to analyze the situations so that they are not proper moral dilemmas but rather dilemmas between morality and expediency. We certainly do face such dilemmas in life, and in fact I think more often than not they are moral dilemmas if analyzed differently, but presented as such they are not moral dilemmas at all and shall not be my topic here. For a dilemma to be a *moral* dilemma, there must be a clear moral case on both sides, not a conflict between moral rightness and base temptation or mere material gain.

Pedestrian Dilemmas

We face moral dilemmas nearly every day, though we seldom face the sort of stark and monumental dilemmas discussed in theory and literature. It is important to begin our analysis with those lesser dilemmas that make up normal life—what I shall call pedestrian dilemmas. By calling them pedestrian, I do not mean that they are easy or without stress. Quite the opposite: they are some of the most stressful encounters we have day to day. Rather, I only mean to point out that this variety of moral dilemma is everyday in the sense that we face these sorts of dilemmas all the time.

What are they? Usually they involve conflicting duties or obligations. Often they are situations we get ourselves into inadvertently by promising more than we can fulfill without knowing the consequences of the promises when we make them. They sometimes involve unforeseen circumstances arising—one activity taking longer than we thought, an emergency situation, etc. They may also simply involve conflicts that are foreseen but cannot be avoided. We tend to get ourselves into them by accident or foolishness, but sometimes we find ourselves in these sorts of dilemmas for wholly extrinsic reasons.

Pedestrian moral dilemmas are situations of this sort in everyday life and they are often not given a great deal of thought by theorists. I take them to be conflicts between duties such that one must act against one duty in fulfilling another, but in so doing one does not forfeit deeply held ethical principles or ethical traits of character. The conflict between duties makes such cases dilemmas, while the latter limitation makes these cases pedestrian. Theorists do not dwell on this sort of dilemma because by offering a theory in which there is an overarching good, they believe they easily solve these, to their mind, false dilemmas.

Other moral dilemmas are more difficult because their theory is forced to conflict with some intuitions, and so they may sometimes address those, but pedestrian sorts of dilemmas are not worth the ink. Neither do these sorts of dilemmas get much literary or dramatic treatment. No one wants to watch a show or read a book in which a character must choose between keeping a promise to finish the work one was assigned by the boss or keeping a promise to meet a friend who hasn't been feeling well. These dilemmas don't entertain or shock, precisely because we face varieties of them so often.

Here are some examples. You promise a friend to help her move and your boss that you will finish a project that day. The work is clearly taking longer than you expected, and you must either break a promise to your boss or to your friend. Both courses of action have a moral case to be made for them and yet both cannot be done. Promises are not essential: one can face a similar dilemma when a good friend is appearing in a play but work is taking longer than you thought; even if you have made no promises, being a good friend and being a responsible employee require incompatible actions.

Or imagine that you must decide whether or not to take care of your aging mother or work at a food bank where you have worked at every Saturday afternoon. You must either forgo a longstanding charitable commitment or fail to uphold a filial duty. Suppose a friend confesses to a crime or sin against another, in confidence, and you are later asked about it. Do you tell? There seems to be both an obligation to the truth and an obligation to one's friend. Or imagine a case when you are asked a question you know the answer to but also know that the truth will be quite hurtful for no good reason. Do you tell a white lie to achieve the best outcome, or do you tell the truth despite the harm it causes? Moral arguments can be made for both: one has both a duty to the truth and a duty to avoid causing needless harm.

These sorts of situations may seem to be the height of inanity—they appear somewhat inconsequential simply because they are so familiar. There may be some conflict brought out in such cases but it is not of the sort that should really worry us. Still, I think they are important and worthy of theoretical interest. They can be quite confusing, stressful, and trying. Certainly, being caught between two promises that cannot both be fulfilled is disconcerting. No matter what one does, a promise is broken, and it seems one has acted unethically. We may be able to resolve these dilemmas, but they are nonetheless pressing. The same sort of desperate feeling can attach to cases in which a white lie can save a lot of hurt feelings. We seem to have competing obligations, both of which cannot be fulfilled. This happens all the time, yet the fact that such situations are commonplace makes them no less important.

The initial treatment of them is to dismiss them as dilemmas. Rather than a failure of our ethical system, we are faced only with confusion in the bustle of everyday life. Moral knowledge would show us that these "dilemmas" are merely apparent and that there is a very clear right and wrong. They are trying only because the weak masses lack true moral understanding. Moralists will take such cases and clarify them so that there is one clear answer. To them the dilemma is only apparent and, through right character and reflection, is easily resolved by appeal to some antecedent view as to the order of duties. So in the case of competing promises, it might be argued that some sorts of promises trump others or that the promise made first trumps the later promise, or vice-versa. Generally it is argued that one should explain the situation to one party and beg excuse from the promise. When this is possible, it is certainly an advisable course. In the case of white lies, it may be argued that one's duty to the truth is more important, that it is not one's job to protect others, or on the contrary that one shouldn't create needless controversy.

While the situations can be clarified away, an interesting thing happens in this process: often the situations can be clarified in variant ways that imply different actions. Moralists will disagree as to the correct way out of the supposed dilemma. This is to be expected, as disagreements will be commonplace, but it does call into question exactly how productive moral clarification is in these cases. Actually this is quite embarrassing—the dilemmas are dismissed as mere products of moral ignorance, yet when those with supposed moral knowledge approach them there is no agreement as to the correct course of action. The dilemma, then, seems more legitimate than most allow. These sorts of moral clarifications may help but I do not see how they eliminate the supposed dilemma if different approaches lead to different conclusions. My point is simply this: moral clarification does not resolve the apparent dilemma but rather transfers the real dilemma from the first-order problem of what to do in this case to the second-order problem of how to think about what to do in general. Here we end up in similar arguments, and upon reflection, with a parallel dilemma. This suggests that pedestrian dilemmas deserve more serious consideration than is ordinarily given.

We write them off because we assume that ethics is not dilemma prone and hence these dilemmas cannot be real challenges. What they show, if anything, is that we are dilemma prone because ethics is so hard. There is one superior duty in all of these cases and no real conflict; we just go awry in determining what this is. Essentially, one who takes this line must hold that one side of such dilemmas is fundamentally confused. In an enlightened moral state the supposed dilemmas are as clear cut as any other case.

Yet this is phenomenologically off base. When in the thrall of pedestrian dilemmas we seem to have competing duties, and even once we make a decision, we feel regret at being unable to do the other action as well. Such regret persists beyond moralistic clarification. But as such the dismissal of such dilemmas by claiming they arise from ignorance is hasty—we may deal with them, but the fact that we do so with regret belies the fact that they are not merely epistemic failings but part of a larger "failing" of our ethical system. Ethics and moralizing do not grant us knowledge so that everything is clear and stark, but they help us to make choices that are tough and regrettable. Hence it is worthwhile to seriously inquire into pedestrian dilemmas when doing ethics.

Theoretical Dilemmas

Whereas pedestrian moral dilemmas are commonplace but not often treated in serious inquiry, theoretical dilemmas are thought experiments developed for the express purpose of testing theories. They are artificial and manufactured and have only tenuous analogical relations to moral reality. Pedestrian dilemmas involve conflicts between duties in ordinary life. Theoretical dilemmas differ in that they are constructed to involve explicit conflicts of deeply held and intuitive ethical *principles*. Real moral life is complex in that there are always various considerations and complications in play, and so, when trying to determine whether an abstract theory captures something right, focusing on ordinary life often just confuses the issue. By getting rid of extraneous complications, theoretical dilemmas work to provide examples we can deal with in the context of testing a theory against intuition.

Now I don't want to imply that I believe that the artificiality isn't a problem with these dilemmas. I think it is, but exactly why that is so must wait until an approach is developed. Basically, the problem isn't so much with the dilemmas but with the idea that we need or can have some ultimate, clear moral theory that answers all questions. But these dilemmas reside within that project and so should be taken seriously if only because that particular project is taken quite seriously. An approach to moral dilemmas must be able to understand what is going on with these dilemmas, even if doing so reveals why the project they are so important to is itself misguided.

The situation that leads to theoretical dilemmas can be understood as follows. In ordinary life we find ourselves confronted with moral problems. These might be outright dilemmas and tensions. We naturally look for ways to solve these problems to determine who we ought to be and what we ought to do. This leads to moral theory and the development of ethical principles. By engaging in moral inquiry, we hope to discover the truth and then be able to solve the problems that confront us. Theoretical dilemmas are important because they are ways we test and refine moral theories and principles. Because we think we need absolute principles, when theoretical dilemmas can be formulated they are a problem. In understanding these dilemmas we must hence either show that they can be solved in an acceptable way by a particular theory or develop an understanding of our moral condition such that we don't need a solution and can rather understand how and why they emerge without leaving us lost and empty.

I was first introduced to this sort of dilemma with a thought experiment given in a high school course on comparative government (I do not recall the exact pedagogical purpose). This is the dilemma I introduced in the first chapter: you venture upon a sacked village held by a strongman about to execute three randomly chosen people. You protest and the amused strongman gives you a choice between killing one yourself and watching his men kill all three. What do you do?

No matter how one answers or what one does, a terrible wrong occurs. Two intuitively plausible ethical principles are in direct conflict. First, do not personally cause harm, or, more specifically, do not kill people. Second, act so as to maximize the good (or more particularly minimize the loss of life). Moreover, there are further questions to be asked. Suppose you decide it would be best to kill the one yourself to save the other two. The principle here seems to be that it is the end result, and not the means used to achieve it, that determines the correctness of the action. You must be involved in the actual killing in this case, but you do so excusably because it is done to save two who would otherwise die as well. But now suppose there are two prisoners. Would you kill one to save the other? Or suppose the strongman says that one must die, and that if you do the killing, then you may decide which, while if he does the killing he will decide which. Suppose there are two young children and a very old man. Would you still be justified in involving yourself, even though the net loss of life is the same? If not, why not? It seems the end result is better if you get to choose than if the strongman chooses, and if the means are not relevant in such cases then there should be no question. What if the strongman lets you choose between killing your beloved companion and the three villagers? Can you refuse to kill the one you know to save the three you do not, when you were quite willing to kill one to save two? What if the strongman lets you choose between killing yourself and letting the three die? These sorts of difficult questions can, and tend to, proliferate endlessly.

Now suppose that you decline to involve yourself. You reason that though a terrible wrong is committed and three people die, you have kept yourself out of the situation as best as possible. The guilt is wholly on the strongman, not you. Your duty is to ensure that you do no immoral actions, and killing someone with your own hands is clearly an immoral action. From this perspective, the rightness of the means trumps the benefit that results in the end. But is it really possible to remain uninvolved? Is it that the world has rather forced you into the situation, and denying involvement is akin to denying what you see because you wish it not to be so? What if it was a choice of whether or not to kill one to save three? Four? Five? A million? At some point it seems that this abstract principle is lunacy. If one is willing to sacrifice the principle at some point, then what is the exact number? And why this number? Why is it OK to kill one to save seven but not six? What sort of sick calculus is being employed here?

These questions multiply quickly. The fanciful story involving the strongman is a dressed up way of asking the simple question of whether smaller evil done by one's own hand is better than greater evil by another's hand or vice-versa. Such questions test ethical principles that are supposed to apply universally. By gerrymandering the situation just right, we can manipulate intuitions such that one or another principle is embarrassed. If we are critiquing a means-based principle, we make the ends suitably terrible if proper means are followed, while if we are critiquing an ends-based principle we bring the variant ends close and stress the disparate means involved. The idea in such examples is not to deal with actual life directly. We do not face such stark situations but only those roughly like them—for example, whether or not we should militarily intervene to stop genocide—and initially it may seem that such examples are entirely irrelevant to ethics. This misses the point. Theoretical dilemmas are meant to address theories that in turn deal with everyday life. By vastly simplifying situations, we can better analyze ethical theories and then take these ethical theories and apply them to actual life. In a way, we can see the move to theory arising out of pedestrian dilemmas, and conflicting intuitions and theoretical dilemmas, as tools with which theories are tested and refined.

At present the most commonly discussed theoretical dilemma is the trolley example.[1] It has many variations but the basic idea is as above. Imagine a trolley speeding down a hill with no one on board. In its path are three people tied to the track. There is no way to stop the trolley but you

---

1 The problem was introduced by Philippa Foot in "The Problem of Abortion and the Doctrine of Double Effect." It is much discussed in the literature. Recently it has been studied in the social sciences as part of an endeavor to understand the processes by which moral judgments are made, for example in the work of Joshua Greene (see *Moral Tribes* for an accessible discussion of the various permutations of the trolley dilemma, and much else besides).

are standing at a switch that will divert the trolley onto a track on which only one person is tied up. What do you do? Do you intervene to cause the death of one or do you watch passively as three are killed? As above, the hypothetical can be adjusted to shift our intuitions.

There is another variation that is also interesting to note. In this case there is no separate track but rather you are standing on a bridge over the track with a very fat man. If you push the fat man onto the track in front of the trolley, it will stop in its tracks and kill only the fat man, while if you do not the three others will die. Do you push the man onto the track? This may seem to be the same as the first case, but is interesting because in empirical research it turns out many are willing to flip the switch to divert the train but unwilling to push the fat man onto the tracks. This difference arises despite the fact that the salient features are identical. It seems that physical contact or proximity to the person being sacrificed changes our ethical intuitions.

In one sense, this interesting empirical tidbit is entirely irrelevant to prescriptive ethics. It is an interesting note for sociologists and the like, but for philosophers the task is not to gather intuitions but to develop theories that tell us what *ought* to be done. Yet this should not mean that intuitions are ignored—we expect ethical theories to at least reconcile, acknowledge, and make sense of our intuitions. Some may well be rejected outright but are so rejected because they are confused intuitions, not because they are intuitions.

Theoretical dilemmas are important in the testing of various theories. They are resolved by the application of a theory in a way that clearly comes down on one side or the other and makes sense out of the dilemma as such. The former is simple—one can simply posit a rule that erases the dilemma. The latter is quite troublesome in that it is difficult to make sense of these situations in a satisfactory way. At some point we are tempted to take the odd results of the dilemmas to be a refutation of the theory. And, like above, there are ways to resolve these dilemmas on both sides and both can seem quite reasonable and compelling, usually because the argument for one resolution is motivated by the poverty of an opponent's theory. The dilemmas can be tweaked so as to pump up various ethical intuitions, but the problem is that our intuitions as to which principle is correct will change based on the way the dilemma is presented. In order to motivate a favored principle, a theoretical ethicist can present the dilemma in such a way that it embarrasses an opponent. But then an opponent does the same and quickly we reach an impasse if we take the dilemma itself seriously. In theoretical dilemmas, we find ourselves moving from a moral dilemma of intuitions to a dilemma of incompatible principles. This is particularly embarrassing because the move to principles was supposed to help us with pedestrian dilemmas. But it turns out that we can develop thought experiments that pose moral dilemmas for these theories as well.

This is the deep problem of theoretical dilemmas: because our intuitions vary and we can find ourselves oscillating based on the way the dilemma is presented, supposedly sacrosanct ethical principles that form the basis of ethical theory can be called into question because they can be made to lead to intuitively absurd results. A theory must be able to explain why we are confused or simply bite the bullet and implicate intuition as morally bankrupt in some situations. An approach to ethics and moral dilemmas that claims no theory must also deal with theoretical dilemmas because it must be able to explain what is going on with them and why they can seem so troubling to us when engaged in ethical inquiry.

Critical Dilemmas

Critical moral dilemmas are a third category of moral dilemma. Pedestrian dilemmas are stressful and common. Theoretical dilemmas are non-existent in pure form but are designed to be impossible to decide because they engineer direct contradictions between core ethical principles. They play a key in role in evaluating and developing ethical theories. Critical dilemmas are excruciating and nearly impossible to resolve, but thankfully are rare. They involve a forced choice that is impossible to make.

Pedestrian dilemmas are conflicts between duties. Theoretical dilemmas are conflicts between principles. Critical dilemmas are conflicts between core ethical character traits—a choice arises wherein one must follow one duty in such a way that another duty is circumvented to such a degree that irreparable harm is done to one's character (or soul, or identity, etc.).

A rough way to think about them is that they are real, unlike theoretical dilemmas, but differ from pedestrian dilemmas in that they do not present a problem limited to what one ought to do in a circumstance but require one to determine who and how one ought to be as a person. In a pedestrian dilemma I can act against a character trait that I believe is morally good without forfeiting a claim to embody that trait. Critical dilemmas are so soul-wrenching because they are deep enough that the virtuous character trait itself is at stake.

There are two varieties to consider. The first involves the need to choose between two alternatives one cannot accept for the *same* reason. For example, imagine the case in *Sophie's Choice*, where a young mother is told only one of her two children can continue to live in the concentration camp while the other will be sent to the gas chamber and that she must choose.[1] Which child does she pick? In these cases the key point is that a choice is forced wherein

1 William Styron. *Sophie's Choice.* 1978.

the rationale behind and against each choice is the same. The same case can be made for sending each child. The world, through no fault of her own, has created an impossible situation and a seemingly chance decision must be made. Because such decisions are fraught with ethical implications, they present moral dilemmas.

These cases are very rare and in their starkness are much like theoretical dilemmas. They are not exactly theoretical dilemmas because in cases like war, and sometimes with medical care, they can arise. Moreover, unlike theoretical dilemmas, they do not present conflicts between principles. I shall have little to say about them and they are not often discussed in the literature. They can be ignored not because they are not awful—they are perhaps the most awful form of dilemma—but because there is no moral issue to resolve here. There is no genuine competition because both choices have the *same* moral case for and against them. We do not have a case wherein two principles or intuitions come into conflict with one another. Here the *same* principle and *same* intuitions reside on both sides of the dilemma. As structured, there can be no resolution.

The lesson of such dilemmas is that we are often at the mercy of the world and sometimes we end up in morally awful situations. We are humans, not gods. This is an important lesson to learn, but within the realm of moral theory and understanding there is little more that can be said. No matter what choice is made, a terrible wrong is committed, and in both cases it is the same wrong. They are dilemmas because of the way the world has conspired against us and no amount of philosophy can resolve them.

The more important variety for my purposes involves the outright conflict between two different and equally fundamental and indispensible moral duties or virtues. Pedestrian moral dilemmas involve conflicts of duties but the stakes are generally low and do not threaten one's moral character. Critical dilemmas differ on this point—the incompatible choices offered require one to abandon a central feature of one's moral character in a way that the damage caused cannot be repaired easily or perhaps even at all. Any such move seems impossible—as if it makes us a different person on account of what has been forsaken—yet we are faced with a choice. The dilemma is how to go about choosing how to be and what to do when any basis for doing so seems to be called into question because our moral being is torn between the options.

One famous example of this sort of moral dilemma comes from Sartre's discussion of absolute freedom.[1] For Sartre, it is important that we realize our authenticity through recognition of our absolute freedom as individuals

---

[1] Sartre's most detailed discussion is in *Being and Nothingness*. This example is presented in *Existentialism and Human Emotion*.

choosing our essence. Critical moral dilemmas provide cases wherein no moral system is capable of resolving the dilemma and the individual must ultimately choose without basis. In the example, we are to imagine a young man in France during the Second World War with an ailing mother. He has a choice. Does he stay with his ailing mother and take care of her or run off and join the French Resistance to the Nazis? Both cannot be done, yet both seem to be essential duties. The forced choice leads to an ethical crisis.

In these moments, we realize our freedom and have a chance at authenticity through adopting a mode of being that is wholly our own, unbounded by any outside constraint. So even though critical moral dilemmas are perplexing and frightening, they lead us to authenticity by leading us to the situation of absolute freedom. These dilemmas are not resolved by a principle but by individual fiat. If one does not agree with the existentialists' point of view, there is much to find wanting. It seems to posit a freedom through purely arbitrary choice, not choice for a reason that is one's own, which would seem to be a more comfortable sort of freedom. The idea is to point to self creation, but there is something uncomfortable about the idea that this is done from absolutely nothing at all. Absolute freedom is frightening for good reason, because it requires that we spin in a formless void without any basis at all. It would be wrong to think that one displays moral fortitude in such a case by merely choosing, because in a situation of absolute freedom, there is no self that is choosing, but rather a formless existence that by "choosing" comes to have a certain essence. Confronting absolute freedom means deconstructing our sense of self and any moral basis we may think we have and replacing it with a merely selected essence out of the void of being.

Moreover, there do seem to be better and worse choices in these cases. The dilemma is a crisis of morality but we seem to be able to think rationally about it. For example, any freedom experienced in such cases is not so absolute that anything can be done—it is not as if the man in the example can justifiably join the Nazis. Second, such cases are the exception, not the rule. Sartre sometimes seems to argue that such cases show something universal about morality, yet it is wholly unclear why this follows. To hold that this is the case, one would have to endorse the principle that any moral theory that cannot easily handle any possible case has no force whatsoever. Yet once made explicit, this principle is quite absurd. We do not reject winter coats as good and proper because they fail to keep us warm in the most extreme climates. In the same way it is unclear why we should reject ethical theories and principles that fail in extreme moral circumstances if they function well in ordinary circumstances.

It may be the case that morality breaks down in critical dilemmas and this reveals something important about our moral condition, even though morality does quite well in most situations and is just as constraining as before. Finally, when evaluating critical dilemmas we have trouble making a choice but we can argue about it, that is, weigh the relative merits of each choice and argue for them. Of course, being a dilemma, there are powerful arguments on both sides, but this hardly implies we are entirely at a loss for words. The picture of absolute freedom that is most plausible is that it is a situation in which there is nothing possible to say on either side— we are wholly frozen by circumstance. If our moral universe has collapsed into the void of meaningless on account of the dilemma, it would seem all argument has collapsed as well. But surely this is not what actually happens: we rather find in such cases that we debate back and forth and have altogether too much to say. Indeed, such situations are problematic not because we seem to be totally free to fix our essence but because we are so constrained by competing essences already in place. The existential analysis is rather paradoxical, on reflection. In reality these situations are morally over-determined, and hence it isn't nothingness but a surplus of meaning and value that we confront. The existentialist moves from a tension or contradiction between two essential moral commitments to a negation of all moral commitments and the discovery of authenticity in arbitrary choice arrived at in the situation of absolute freedom.

To be honest, I simply cannot understand why one would actually reason in this way seriously. If one must jettison a moral commitment that seems essential, the natural thing to do would be to weigh what is more important and save all that can be saved. The existentialist would have us react by jettisoning everything and then pulling something back on no basis whatsoever. It is unclear what is so liberating about such odd behavior.

Another famous example of what I would call a critical moral dilemma can be found in one reading of Sophocles' *Antigone*.[1] In this tragedy Antigone has a familial and religious duty to bury her dead brother Polyneices, whose corpse rots on a battlefield, but a civic duty not to bury him since the new king, Creon, has ordered that the body of the traitor is not to be touched. Both duties are important and Antigone must decide what to do. In this case it doesn't matter whether or not Creon is justified in making the law in question—the law is out of Antigone's hands and yet as a citizen she is still bound to it. The dilemma arises because of the particular situation she is in. Does she betray her brother or the state? She is set on honoring her brother and accepts the consequences of doing so. But as her sister Ismene's argument shows, the correct action is not clear—indeed there is no correct action. We can certainly debate which betrayal is preferable and this will no

---

1 Sophocles. *Antigone*. In *The Three Theban Plays: Antigone Oedipus the King, Oedipus at Colonus*.

doubt affect how we see Antigone, but the crux of the issue is that we see clear obligations on both sides and it would be best to fulfill both. But she cannot, and the consequences of either choice are dire.

In cases like Sartre's and Antigone's, the critical moral dilemma is apparent and the consequences massive. A particular choice must be made in extraordinary circumstances and the alternatives are mutually exclusive. But not all critical dilemmas are so apparent and they may arise over an extended period of time, rather than with a single choice. At base, a critical dilemma involves a forced choice as to who and how one is going to be. A particular action may be the way the dilemma emerges but the crisis involves norms of being, not merely doing. Put simply, pedestrian dilemmas involve conflicts of duties, theoretical dilemmas involve conflicts of principles, and critical dilemmas involve conflicts of character.

In a sense, we all face such critical dilemmas in our lives, even if they do not emerge in one single clear choice as they do in the examples above. Life is short and we must make tough decisions about who and how to be. Often we are pulled in multiple directions between various careers and lifestyles, or between family and work, or between ambition and leisure. We can have a lot in life, but we cannot have it all. We must make choices. Often, like the dilemmas that face us in making such decisions, the decisions happen implicitly and are not fully apparent to us.

Critical dilemmas are real for most people, though often they are not starkly presented. It is imperative that any ethical approach be able to understand how we deal with such cases. Ethics is the study of practical norms—both norms of action and being. The various moral dilemmas sketched here bring out tensions or contradictions among such norms. It may seem that in these cases our very moral systems are being challenged. We may need to clarify or reform them, or we may come to see that they entirely collapse and we are absolutely free. In any case, in order to find a comfortable perspective on our ethical condition we must come to understand them.

Conclusion

Moral dilemmas present tensions and hence it is a goal of ethical inquiry to understand them in each of their varieties. They differ, yet are similar in producing ethical conflicts. Pedestrian dilemmas present cases wherein one must act against one duty in acting in accordance with another. Theoretical dilemmas present cases in which one must act against one principle in acting in accordance with another. Critical dilemmas present cases where, in acting in accordance with one way we ought to be, we become something we ought not to be.

The distinctions are, of course, artificial in the sense that in reality they are not stark or precise. They lie on a continuum. Theoretical dilemmas shade into the other dilemmas in that we can construct cases that in rare cases might emerge. *Sophie's Choice* is such an example in that it appears far-fetched but we can imagine it being real. There is no bright line distinction between critical and pedestrian dilemmas, as what is at stake lies on a continuum. Nonetheless it is helpful to separate moral dilemmas into the three categories because it reveals how moral dilemmas can emerge, how they function, and what is at stake when we are dealing with them.

Being able to understand each sort of a dilemma in one ethical approach is desirable in and of itself. But it is also important for more general reasons. Moral dilemmas make ethical conflict explicit and hence lead us to explicitly confront issues and problems that are often easy to ignore. In seeking to deal with moral dilemmas, then, we will be led to confront other important ethical issues and by doing so come to a better understanding of our ethical condition.

CHAPTER FOUR: THE USE AND PURPOSE OF MORAL DILEMMAS

Pedestrian Dilemmas

Each variety of moral dilemma is put to a very different use. Pedestrian dilemmas are most often discussed by moralists or viewed as unworthy of attention and simply not discussed at all. Moralists are those without any deep critical theory or argument who nonetheless seek to offer popular adages and advice on ethical behavior. In relation to moral dilemmas an interesting dynamic develops. Rather than seeing the moral dilemma as the confrontation of two ethical principles or duties, it is rather cast as the confrontation of a proper principle or duty and some sort of base temptation in disguise. So, for example, in the case of the white lie it might be argued that one must tell the truth and that the thought of causing good by lying is an evil temptation that must be resisted. Oddly, this leads to a situation wherein telling the truth is *only* really exemplary in the face of such temptation. Ordinary cases do not display moral worth; only cases where one feels an opposing "duty" count as laudable.

This sort of train of thought should appear familiar, yet upon reflection it appears deeply confused. Surely causing good feeling is a laudable goal and we have duties to bring good feeling to our fellows. We certainly have duties to tell the truth as well. Yet on the moralists' approach, these two morally appropriate ends alone are not all that laudable. When they come into conflict, however, one moral end becomes laudable while the other takes the form of evil temptation. When two generally good actions conflict, magically, it seems, one becomes evil and the other becomes the essence of virtue.

Initially it ought to be thought that cases wherein one can tell the truth and cause good feeling are the most morally laudable because both duties can be fulfilled. When they conflict one must forgo one duty for the sake of the other and we are forced into a worse moral position. Yet somehow this all gets turned around such that when there is a conflict, a former good thing is unveiled as bad, and resisting its allure leads us to moral bliss. I think this happens because moralists by trade must have an overarching norm that determines the appropriate action in all cases. There can thus be no true moral dilemmas. Rather, there are cases when genuine and improper duty conflict. To admit both duties to be proper would undermine the fiction that they have a complete and pure moral system. Moreover, the drama that is the wile of the moralist is greatly enhanced when a dilemma is turned into a test of true virtue, and the moralist can swoop in on the confused masses and reveal the nature of virtue to us benighted mortals.

Hence, pedestrian moral dilemmas become cases where true and false duties meet. Choosing true duty is only morally laudable where there seems to be conflict, because false duty presents a temptation to overcome with virtue. When both can be met, the action does not necessarily stem only from true duty and hence is not as laudable. Moral dilemmas as instances of temptation become teachable moments and important as tests of one's goodness. Hence, for a moralist, pedestrian dilemmas are important because they are clear cases where true moral goodness can be demonstrated. Pedestrian dilemmas become important for them not because they represent a challenge to be met but because they provide cases in which their view is on full display and the moral fortitude they recommend is manifest.

Bell's case from the previous chapter is a nice example of this confusion. He faces a dilemma between leaving the Harvard Law School faculty in protest or retaining his job and economic security. Bell treats this case as a conflict between duty and expediency and holds it out as a paradigm case of living a life of meaning and worth because he chose duty at great cost—a nice job, money, and security at a time of family need. I argued above that if we accept his analysis, it is not strictly a moral dilemma at all. But given the previous point we should see that his analysis is suspect. There is a real moral dilemma here but because Bell thinks he has a clear answer to it, he transforms it into a clear case of duty vs. expediency. Yet it strikes me that Bell has a moral obligation to keep his job for many reasons—he will likely be a more effective agent of change on the inside and he certainly has familial duties that behoove him to retain economic security. Indeed, given his increased reputation and the material gain of a book deal that he receives by leaving his job, it is even unclear where exactly expediency stands. As a well-established member of the legal academy employed by Harvard who publicly leaves for political reasons, it is doubtful that he is going to have any genuine difficulty finding a job with generous remuneration at another school. On reflection it isn't clear he was risking so much, given his job prospects, but in order for his point to carry he exaggerates the risk he took in terms of practical loss and the moral gain his decision brought. But it isn't so clear where either expediency or morality stand in his particular situation.[1]

There is a moral dilemma in Bell's case and it strikes me as an extreme pedestrian dilemma because two (actually more, but two to keep it simple) duties come into direct conflict. It could be seen as a critical dilemma as well, but I hesitate because it is unclear to me that there is as much at stake as Bell implies and because it strikes me there are easier ways out of the situation. But given Bell's aim in his book, it is not expedient to analyze it as a moral dilemma in the straightforward sense. Instead he must transform a genuine conflict of duties into a battle between true and false duty and hold that it only shows character to fulfill true duty at the expense of false duty. Rather than being tragedies, moral dilemmas become opportunities for virtue.

That there is something suspect about this can be seen in the following question: would it not be better for Bell to find a way to work for change on the law school faculty while still providing economic security for his family? I'm not convinced that this was not possible in Bell's case, though even if it were impossible we should still think that fulfilling both duties would be better than fulfilling one at the expense of the other. It wouldn't make much of a book, but virtue need not be exciting (and most often is not). Making tough moral choices isn't a constitutive of virtue in and of itself. Indeed a propensity to actively seek out tough moral choices may be a vice, while conducting one's life in a way that these tough moral choices are not necessary may be a genuine, though perhaps boring, virtue. Finding one's way out of a very difficult situation is a virtue, but it is also a virtue to be able to stay out of those situations to begin with.

In the end, I don't much care what moralists do so long as we recognize them for what they are, but it is troubling that more serious academic inquiry tends to ignore pedestrian dilemmas altogether. This is done because it is thought that mere confusion is to blame in these cases. Perhaps, but even if

---

1 If we change Bell's position, the situation alters quite a bit. Imagine that instead of being a highly acclaimed legal mind Bell was an un-skilled worker at a factory, at a time when unemployment is high, who is drawn to quit in protest due to the hiring practices of his employer. Here, quitting will change nothing and there is no book deal in the offing. And Bell's career prospects are dim if he leaves the job. Expediency surely recommends staying in the job. But unless the factory is committing terrible wrongs, there is a very strong moral case for staying as well. Indeed, we might admire people who swallowed their pride and worked for a company they had ethical issues with, in a case where it was the only option to provide for a family. Bell is able to make his situation do the work it does as an example of moral courage partially because, though there are risks to quitting, he is reasonably well-assured of coming out okay in the end.

it is, the fact that it is quite difficult to make this confusion clear suggests they ought to be more important to theorists. The fact that such dilemmas are ubiquitous is also important. They don't fit well into standard ethical theories and yet are a clear part of ethical life. This suggests that something is being missed by the way we approach ethical theory.

Theoretical Dilemmas

Theoretical moral dilemmas are used in both empirical psychology and theoretical ethics. In the former they are used to discern how we do in fact think about morality, while in the latter they are used to test theories. The latter project concerns me more. Theoretical dilemmas clearly have a role here but we should be cautious about how they are used. They relate to real situations only analogically. We never face situations that are quite as stark as the ones posited and even those that are vaguely similar would not work in the way necessary. To do the destructive work they do, it is important that theoretical dilemmas be easily modified to extenuate problems in any theory. This is somewhat proper but also worrisome: we may expect too much of an ethical theory if we expect it to deal seamlessly with any possible case; merely helping us in reality may be all that is necessary. We must treat theoretical dilemmas with care. They are easily manipulated to bring out one sort of intuition over another and to play a certain dialectical role. They function as what some philosophers call intuition pumps—carefully designed examples that work to pump up an intuition beyond its proper force and confuse the issue. For any ethical theorist with a theory to undermine or establish, they can be quite powerful because they can be manipulated to make those theories lead to very unintuitive results. This is why they are used so often in academic exercise. Yet this is also why we should tread carefully around them.

Moreover, given that such cases do not really occur, the power of our intuitions regarding them is suspect. Often the way cases are presented may lead us to different answers and in any case intuitions are mere guesswork. The proper use of intuitions is a difficult issue. Currently they are generally held to be quite important, but it is always open to a theoretician to argue that she finds our intuitions suspect and confused and thus rejects them as evidence for a theory. We generally do not want theories that are intuitively absurd, but neither do we want theories that merely attempt to describe intuitions (it is hard to see why such a thing would even qualify as a theory, let alone a good one—popularity is not a criterion of truth). Theoretical moral dilemmas work by bringing out variant intuitions. Yet it is plausible to think that our intuitions are formed in response to ordinary cases and for the purpose of responding to these cases. There is no guarantee that the proper role of intuitions in daily life entails a proper role for intuitions in abstract theory while responding to wholly artificial cases. Our intuitions may be especially confused here because the case is contrived. The benefit of ordinary intuitions is unclear when considering cases that by definition are entirely extraordinary.

Though we should tread carefully because of these questions regarding the proper use of theoretical dilemmas, I do not think this merits outright rejection of them. Presented in the right context they have an important role to play. Often we discuss them as entertainment or simply to argue about with friends. This is fine but should be taken with a grain of salt as mere entertainment. Their proper use occurs in theoretical contexts. If we do have a theory, or several competing theories, it is wholly proper to develop hypothetical cases to test that theory. This is the whole point of a thought experiment—the theory claims to be able to deal with all cases and hence we develop cases that bring out the tensions and weaknesses of a theory. Thus we can find ways to get at the key issues and have structured debates. Though we should be careful about intuitions in such cases they do serve a definite and important purpose.

Notice again, however, that this purpose is quite narrow. Theoretical dilemmas are only developed and confronted in a particular theoretical context to be used to various particular ends. They aren't taken to be problems that need to be addressed prior to inquiry but as ways of achieving a particular goal once in the process of inquiry. Hence we should be quite skeptical of the use they are put to; we must always consider whether or not the dilemma could be modified to the opposite theoretical purpose. Ideally we would have a theory that began by taking theoretical dilemmas to be a problem and tried to understand them rather than several theories that used them when it was to their benefit.

Critical Dilemmas

Critical dilemmas are usually only put to use in those parts of philosophy that introduce them. For example, Sartre's dilemma sketched in the previous chapter is generally only discussed in reference to existentialism, either to show the truth of the claims made by it or to challenge those conclusions. The same limitation also applies to theoretical dilemmas: they are really only put to use in reference to the project of analytic ethics. In the theoretical case this is to be expected since they are merely theoretical dilemmas, but in the case of critical dilemmas it is a bit puzzling. These dilemmas are rare but real and so it would seem that any approach to ethics ought to have something to say about them. Yet they do not.

For existentialists, of course, they are important and they reveal something essential and profound about our moral condition. The idea is that they present a situation in which no theory can provide an answer, and a choice must be made on no basis at all. By choosing, blindly choosing indeed, because the point of the situation is that there is no right or preferable choice, we experience absolute freedom because we create the moral law and give it to ourselves (we do not discover it and then give it to ourselves, as in Kant). We choose arbitrarily in this absolute freedom, and to live well is to fully accept that freedom and that choice. The dilemma, then, is incredibly rare, but is the crux of our ethical position.

The situation is actually a bit comical. Those who pay attention to such dilemmas seem to make much too large a deal out of them, using them to undermine all ethical theories and to reveal our essential human condition as absolutely free. But not only do the conclusions drawn follow only tenuously but critical dilemmas seem altogether too important in such theories, given that they are rather rare. On the other hand, in other approaches to ethics, there is no discussion of such dilemmas seemingly because they are rare and because they do little work for such theories. This is worrying. Though rare, they are extremely challenging and should at least be addressed. We should be able to understand how we got ourselves into such dilemmas and what they mean even if we cannot resolve them through theory.

Critical dilemmas may seem to have only local use because the starkness with which they are presented makes them seem contrived and rare. Further, the conclusions drawn from them may seem wholly absurd to someone not in the thrall of the favored theory, and hence they appear unimportant. But if we retreat to the essential question of critical dilemmas, we can see they are of the utmost importance. Critical dilemmas are situations wherein we must make a choice about what sort of person to be. We are pulled in multiple incompatible directions and must choose which way to go. Such situations are part of what it means to be a human being—we must balance, and sometimes forfeit, values and aspirations and make hard sacrifices.

Framing these situations as critical moral dilemmas demands that ethical theory provide some way to deal with these sorts of vital questions of life. Choosing who and how to be is fundamentally an ethical question—we at least seek—though if the existentialist is right, cannot find—a way to determine the objectively correct way of being. Ethical theory ought to help us in this endeavor or at least understand what is going on. Critical dilemmas ought then to have quite general importance to ethics.

On reflection, it is rather scandalous that these dilemmas aren't more widely discussed. If indeed they are genuine—and if they aren't, that takes some showing—any ethical theory ought to have something to say about them. It would be absurd to think that the only possible use and importance of such dilemmas is to bring out the existentialist's absolute freedom. No matter what one thinks about our ethical condition as human beings, there ought to be something worth saying about these fundamental moral dilemmas.

What is Sought in Response to Moral Dilemmas

It would be beneficial in relation to each sort of dilemma to have some mechanism to resolve the problem we find ourselves with, and it is essential that we at least be able to understand why we are led to the dilemma in such a way that it enlightens our moral condition rather than threatens it. How is this to be done? What is needed is some grasp of the grounding of morality such that we can come to see more clearly the way moral dilemmas function. If we could understand the origins of norms and their power, then we could approach moral dilemmas with a procedure for resolving or at least understanding them. In large part this is exactly what theorists seek to do generally in ethical investigation, but moral dilemmas bring out exactly how difficult the task is. Indeed, looking at the way each of the types of dilemmas is treated, we can see how we can become disappointed in the approach once we realize that what is really needed is an understanding of our moral grounding.

Pedestrian dilemmas are usually treated with adages but not given the sort of robust grounding that would establish the favored solution as superior. A competing moralist can offer another adage to a different conclusion and we quickly become confused again. To sort out the competing claims, we need to investigate the basis of the adages favored by each moralist and quickly find ourselves with the task of grounding morality generally. If we could figure out how norms are grounded we would be in a better position to evaluate the power of variant norms and then return to the pedestrian dilemmas likely able to resolve them and at least able to understand why it is they present such dilemmas for us. The latter result would not give us a clear answer but would at least remove the confusion that accompanies pedestrian dilemmas. Indeed, the deficiency in many treatments of pedestrian dilemmas is that we are given a supposedly clear solution but without a way to understand why we find ourselves in the dilemma to begin with. A proper understanding of the grounding of ethics must at least explain why we find ourselves so dilemmas prone. Otherwise we will return again and again.

Theoretical dilemmas are created within the project of testing various ethical theories and so clearly relate to the project of grounding moral norms. We develop them as direct challenges to particular moral theories and as ways of bringing out the deeper differences between competing theories. In order to resolve them we need an ethical theory strong enough to explain away the opposing intuitions and so remove the dilemma. To do so we need, as theorists, to go beyond the original theory and come to understand the normative basis of ethics in general. Such an understanding would allow for a robust justification of a particular theory and derivatively a proper way out of a dilemma. Though theoretical dilemmas seem to require resolution rather than understanding, we can also see how a proper grasp of the grounding of morality would permit at least understanding. We might come to see how various norms have a hold on us and then see why in these hypothetical cases we are in the grasp of competing norms that lead to this dilemma. We may not be able to resolve the dilemma, but we would see why we were in it and could better dismiss such a dilemma as merely theoretical.

The same holds in a different way for critical dilemmas. In these cases we face a critical choice about the course of our life—mutually exclusive alternatives are central to our moral character. What ought we to do? Clearly, in order to answer this question we will need a robust understanding of our moral condition. As above we naturally seek a grasp of the grounding of norms such that we can return to the critical dilemma and discern what ought to be done. Now, interestingly, this is not what has been done by those most interested in these cases. For existentialists these cases bring out the way in which there are no grounded norms in such cases and force us to confront our absolute freedom and make a choice regarding our essence. Hence they do not seek grounding in these cases but understanding of how grounding fails, such that we come to realize our authenticity. Thus it is through the failure of the grounding of norms in such cases that we are led to an individual grounding of norms in personal choice. Though this task is somewhat inverted from the natural move to seek to ground various norms in order to discern the correct action, in the end both are investigations of the grounding of norms. In the existentialist's case understanding of the dilemma is sought through which resolution is found in our authenticity. But again we are really seeking to grasp and understand something about our moral condition and the grounding of moral norms.

Conclusion

All of this may seem quite obvious—faced with a dilemma, we ought to investigate it in order to understand the grounding of the views, intuitions, principles, etc., that lead us into it. This pertains to all inquiries, not just ethics. The important point to grasp for my purposes is that, though the different types of moral dilemmas are used by different groups to different ends, it is entirely natural to pursue the same sort of inquiry in response to them. What we should want is a unified understanding of the grounding of moral norms such that we can resolve or understand and be at peace with each of the variety of moral dilemmas. Present treatment, insofar as it even occurs, suffers from the compartmentalization of each type of dilemma into different inquiries even though what is needed to respond to or understand them is the same. Treating them all is not just a hodgepodge of different projects but in the end one larger project that manifests itself in different ways. If we could understand the grounding of norms, then we would be better prepared to evaluate the proper action in pedestrian cases. We could make our theories immune to theoretical dilemmas by dissolving them. And we would know how to think about critical dilemmas in such a way that they do not loose mere anarchy upon our moral world. For the remainder of this essay, I aim to begin such a unified approach.

It should now be clear just how important and fruitful study of moral dilemmas can be. Each sort of moral dilemma leads us to seek a more robust ethical grounding and a deeper ethical understanding in its own way. The issues that they concern are not merely local to specific puzzles in ethics but concern important and crucial ethical questions. These questions are often merely implicit in theoretical ethics, and moralizing and moral dilemmas present cases in which they are made explicit and tensions become apparent. For example, they provide a rationale for seeking moral grounding that otherwise may seem like a stale exercise: in life it turns out we do run into ethical problems that naturally lead us to further critical inquiry. The unified study of moral dilemmas, then, is important not just because they present problems to be solved but because in confronting and understanding moral dilemmas we inquire into key aspects of the human ethical condition.

CHAPTER FIVE: ATTEMPTS TO FIND MORAL GROUNDING

Introduction

To provide a unified approach to moral dilemmas we must investigate the grounding of moral norms. This is a massive and massively difficult task. Yet it is the natural response to a moral dilemma. We face a problem in ethics and this leads to an attempt to dig deeper and find a solution. How is it that ought to do and ought to be norms are grounded? Which norm on this analysis takes priority in the case of the dilemma? These are not easy questions—indeed theoretical dilemmas are constructed to test and challenge theories that attempt to ground norms and so it is to be quite expected that they resist theoretical treatment, at least of the traditional sort. Nonetheless these questions are important. If we avoid them, then we will be left needing to dismiss the importance of moral dilemmas outright, and, though this is a popular response, it can hardly be satisfying for one who has been touched by them and takes them seriously.

Of course the grounding of moral norms—and norms generally for that matter—is a question that is often pursued for its own sake without even paying attention to moral dilemmas. If we want to assert a principle that one ought to do x or be y, then when doing inquiry we try to ground this principle in something more secure. This leads to a regress and we get appeals to self-evidence, intuition, or some extrinsic view about the world. Much of my criticism will target these sorts of moves. I place this examination within the context of moral dilemmas because of my methodological commitment to start where we are. The quest for grounding, absent any reason in our lives to seek it, is driven by the desire or some ultimate view from nowhere (or God's eye view) that I eschew. But if in our lives as moral beings we are led to the sorts of dilemmas I have sketched above, and our intuitions and extrinsic views create problems, then it is natural to look for grounding even though we have not begun with a methodological presumption that we can and should take a view from nowhere. Understanding why we are naturally driven to these theories can help us understand why they are ultimately unsatisfying.

There are a variety of ways to approach the grounding of norms. In this chapter I briefly survey four approaches that seek a theory of a particular sort that can provide answers to moral dilemmas by providing grounding. Each promises a theoretical grounding constituted by moral principles and I argue that each fails to deliver this and does not really deal with or fully understand moral dilemmas. This is not to reject the approaches wholesale, only to reject them as theoretical solutions to the problem of grounding norms. I then argue that they suffer from a common problem: either they trade away understanding for grounding or, in offering a grounding that we might understand, offers something either in need of more grounding or unable to ground moral norms—put otherwise, what is offered is not both ground*ed* and ground*ing*.

Based on these arguments, in the next chapter I offer an approach centered on identity as the most plausible because it is something that is in principle understandable and can provide a normative fact of the sort that is grounded and yet grounds norms. The identity approach is compatible with the other theories surveyed here, but it is an important change not because it refutes and rejects them but because it reorients our understanding of the grounding of morality, focusing inwardly on features of the moral agent rather than outwardly at the world.

Here I merely survey approaches to grounding to bring out what I take to be the general problem. Each approach is developed in enlightening and brilliant ways by various thinkers. I do not sketch or selectively refute those theories here. I do believe that the general problems I develop, as well as the key deficiency in these accounts I attribute to them, do in fact apply to each of the detailed theories that have been given. Perhaps I am wrong and some ethicist has provided a nice knock-down argument that would allay my skepticism about the project. I'm certainly open to the possibility. But as I argue here, the basic problem with theoretical approaches suggests that we ought to think about taking a different approach altogether.

Criteria for a Successful Grounding

There are at least three criteria a successful grounding must meet. First it must be clear that what is pointed to actually grounds norms: *a*. It must clearly relate to the norms and *b*. It must not be in need of grounding in the same way the original norms are. If what is offered fails in either way, then we have not grounded the norms at all: *a.* simply asks that there not be a tortuous gap between the norms to be grounded and the ground offered; *b.* asks that the grounding actually be grounded. Put another way, what is offered as grounds must be both grounding of the norms in question and grounded in order to be proper. This is a basic requirement for any sort of grounding, epistemic, ethical, and so on. It simply must be the case that what is offered is not subject to the same deficiency that required its offering and that it relates to the claims that are to be grounded appropriately. Though this criterion is quite simple and straightforward, it is surprisingly difficult to meet.

Second, the grounding must be something that we can understand. If what is offered actually grounds norms but does so at the price of making norms wholly beyond our understanding, then we no longer are conducting inquiry into ethics but declaring such inquiry impossible, or at least largely beyond critical examination. Some may be comfortable with an ethical grounding that is beyond understanding. I am not, and I cannot imagine that one interested in inquiry of the sort conducted here could be. All this criterion of adequacy demands is that we can come to understand our ethical condition in a revealing way though our grounding, and hence that in grounding ethics we remain within the field of ethical inquiry. So if we want to conduct ethical inquiry we can only use grounds that are in principle understandable. To do otherwise is to change the subject. It may be the case that there is no possible ethical grounding that is understandable, but this then is an indictment of ethical inquiry of this sort as a whole, not a position within it. In the final analysis one may end up in such a place and may be comfortable with this, but we should view this sort of appeal to our lack of understanding as a dismissal of ethical inquiry into moral dilemmas and its replacement with a sort of blind faith.

Third, a grounding offered must be able to account for the dilemmas. This need not mean a clear solution. Rather it is necessary that the grounding offered makes sense of *why* we find ourselves faced with dilemmas and helps us at least understand how to deal with dilemmas. Indeed, it is perhaps more important that a grounding of norms explain why we find ourselves in dilemmas than tell us how to get out. It would be best to find both, but unless we can at least achieve understanding of the source of a dilemma, we will be left with a lingering doubt regarding the supposed ground given.[1]

---

1 Moral theories sometimes suggest that moral dilemmas are not really possible. This strikes me as akin to a physicist who proposes a theory of motion and then, when we ask him to tell us how we got to a certain place, informs us that it is impossible that we are where we are. I'm stretching here, because the comment really is claiming that we are just confused about where we are, but we should at least get some explanation of why we are so

This should hold of all types of moral dilemmas, not just one. With these criteria of adequacy in mind we can now turn to four popular approaches to ethical grounding.

Theological Approaches

Historically, the most prominent approach to grounding norms has been theological. In this approach, a maxim is to be preferred because it is divinely ordained. How do we tell what is divinely ordained? Such truths come from God or the gods as divinely ordained and are not open to doubt. Though this sort of reasoning will not convince an unbeliever, it is internally consistent and cogent. Prophets and priests can be sources of the divine code. Perhaps a certain book is held to be the word of God and prescribes various norms. These norms are grounded because they are in the book. We know that the book is valid because it assures us that it contains the word of God, and as the word of God it is valid.

There is some obvious circularity here, but what is one to expect? Another book? What good would that do? At some point, the search for grounds must come to an end, and why should that end point not be here? The situation develops into a stalemate: one who is not inclined to accept the view sees no reason whatsoever to accept it, while one inclined towards the view doesn't see how anything more could be offered. At some point, there seems to be a need for an intrinsically valid criterion, and to one who does not accept this criterion the reasoning of one who does will be viciously circular. But the other can also return the favor by querying the criterion used by the doubter.

Massive dispute about just what is divinely ordained is embarrassing, no doubt, but does not outright refute the theory in question. One in the grip of the comprehensive view forwarded by the theological perspective that is preferred finds all of the grounding she needs in that perspective, and though others may disagree, there is no question in her mind that those maxims are beyond dispute.

The real deficiency here is that any such theory will not be able to give us the understanding we seek in moral inquiry, because in order to work, one must put a stop to the questions that propel that inquiry. It is the second criterion above that a theological approach fails to meet. If we can grasp divine purposes, then we should be able to understand the norms without simply pointing to the gods, but if we cannot, then we are left with a seemingly arbitrary maxim. An opponent may not refute us, but insofar as part of our ethical project is an understanding of norms, we will have failed.

Either we can understand *why* God favors a norm, or not. If we can

confused about the situation we are in.

understand why this is so, then it is this further rationale that is doing the grounding, not God. If God favors a norm because it brings about the most happiness, as a rule, then the norm is grounded in its bringing about the most happiness, not the favor of God. The favor of God is an intermediate step to the ultimate grounding of the norm. But if we cannot understand in principle why God favors this norm, then we cannot understand the grounding of the norms, and insofar as we are conducting an ethical inquiry we will have failed, because there is nothing really to say in that inquiry. This is a straightforward failure of the second criterion above. So long as we are doing ethical inquiry, we must stick to claims, theories, and grounds that are at least in principle understandable. If we point outside of this world to a grounding that we cannot understand at all, then we have ceased to do ethical inquiry. This is exactly what happens with most theological groundings of ethics. Insofar as they are understandable, then the move to the theological is an intermediate step, and insofar as the theological is not an intermediate step, the grounding is not in principle understandable.

The point is simple but can get confused. We believe that killing an innocent person is morally wrong. Why is it wrong? We might cite a passage of scripture or what we have been told by a prophet or felt in our soul as the divine law. So why is it the divine law? Often, we say because human life is valuable and we harm another, etc., etc. But at this point we are moving away from the theological grounding. God isn't doing the heavy lifting, the feature that God favors is. The value of human life is the reason God favors it and the reason killing is wrong. But then we can question this, as we questioned the original norm. Either something we can understand is offered, or ultimately there is an appeal to the divine that does not revert back to a reason it is preferred but is grounded just because it is divine and there is nothing more to be said. It is precisely the fact that there is nothing to say that makes this sort of grounding beyond understanding within a moral inquiry of the sort I am engaging in.

The problem is not that God is inadequate to ground ethics, in that by *definition* God is such a being that is adequate to do this work. This is why appeals to the divine are so historically popular in grounding ethical truth. But when we try to understand this grounding, this strength turns into a weakness in that because God stands outside of our comprehension and as such can ground ethics, we cannot understand how and why this is done. The appeal to the theological, then, is ultimately a rejection of ethical inquiry in that we cannot understand the basis of ethics beyond a shrug of the shoulders and an appeal to God. Certainly there is still serious work to be done in explicating the ethical system divinely ordained, but the sort of inquiry moral dilemmas leads us to is one that cannot be seriously engaged in.

My objection to theologically-grounded ethics is not that it is inadequate but only that it pursues ethics of a different sort, because the problem of grounding has only limited salience—in that any system of theological ethics is founded upon a stipulated grounding that is beyond inquiry. This may, in the end, be the only way to ground ethics (and a theist may well insert God behind any grounding in other ethical approaches), but we must recognize that this is not an answer to the problem of grounding made within ethical inquiry but a different frame of inquiry altogether. Grounding is ultimately put beyond the scope of critical inquiry and understanding.

This line of argument against appeals to the divine is evident in Plato's *Euthyphro*.[1] In this dialogue Socrates encounters Euthyphro on the way to court. Euthyphro is about to prosecute his own father for murder and claims he is taking this surprising step (for that culture) because it is pious. Socrates questions Euthyphro regarding the nature of piety, seeking instruction. Such instruction would certainly be helpful for Socrates in his own upcoming trial. Euthyphro goes in circles, at one point claiming that the pious is what is loved by the gods. Socrates next wonders why the gods love these actions. It seems that this is so because the actions are pious, but now we have gone in a rather tight circle!

More abstractly, Socrates poses the following dilemma: are actions pious because the gods love them or do the gods love the actions because they are pious? If the former, then we have no real understanding of what it is that makes an action pious—any action is pious if the gods love that action, and we have no further analysis as to why they love that action. But if we claim that the gods love some action because it is pious, then we are still left with the question of what makes the action pious, the original question of the dialogue. Theological explanations thus either leave us with a grounding we cannot understand in principle or lead us immediately back to the original question of grounding.

Note that this problem with theological explanation is quite general. Consider the cosmological argument for the existence of God. This argument in its crudest form is simply that something had to be the first cause and this is God. What caused the Big Bang? Only God could have done it, and so God must exist. Immediately a skeptic will wonder what created God. Why is it that the cosmos needs this sort of explanation but God does not? If an explanation for the cause of God is offered, then God is really not doing the ultimate explaining of the cosmos. But if it is simply asserted that God is of a different sort and requires no explanation, then we don't really understand God. Further, we might wonder why we can't just assert this of the cosmos

---

1 Plato *Euthyphro* 10ff.

itself and skip the divine step for the sake of simplicity.[1] Of course we are uncomfortable with this—when searching for any sort of grounding, we want something secure. The divine is tempting because it points out of this world. But the price of doing so is large, since it removes the subject beyond inquiry. In ethics we end up with only the task of extrapolating the divine mandate, without understanding why it is so ordained. To an inquiring mind this cannot be satisfying.

When doing ethics as an inquiry, we seek both grounding and understanding. The theological perspective cannot do both. It provides grounding at the expense of any possible understanding because it points to another world entirely. It is only because this grounding is inscrutable that it can serve as grounding. As soon as some rationale for divine favor is given, then we are off again wondering about that rationale. At some point an arbitrary end in the transcendent must be offered, but now we cannot understand why our norms are so grounded in a satisfying way for the purposes of inquiry. My point is manifestly not that theological morals or moralizing ought to be dispensed with, but only that theology is in principle unavailable to a theoretical ethicist in the current inquiry—as soon as we move to the theological plane, we give up on the project we embarked upon.

I am not disparaging religion, or even theology, but only pointing out that in the present endeavor it is unavailable to do the needed work. One can adopt another sort of grounding within this project and still have religious beliefs. For instance, if the grounding of norms is the fact that they display feature x, one can also hold that God favors x as well, but within the moral theory x is not grounded by God's preference for it. My point is limited to how we claim moral norms are grounded; it does not make any evaluation of other beliefs.

A proponent of theological ethics will likely simply argue that this is so much the worse for my project, not his. So be it. I seek to understand moral dilemmas and to do so must understand the grounding of norms. Theological ethics can offer a grounding, but it is not one that we can properly understand since it is not of this world. It will hence be unclear how exactly we are to understand moral dilemmas, even if we are given solutions to them that are divinely ordained, because we will not understand why we found ourselves faced with dilemma and why we ought to act as told, other than the catch-all explanation that God or the gods so ordained it. In such cases the theological ethicist will only engage in moralizing, not ethical inquiry. If my project has any hope, it must avoid theological grounding for norms.

---

1 Or, like Spinoza, equate the two.

Consequentialist Approaches

Consequentialist approaches argue that proper ethical norms are grounded in some feature of the consequences of the actions in question. For example, utilitarianism holds that we ought to act on maxims that bring the greatest good to the greatest number. The question remains as to what is good. Unless we understand this, any theory remains ungrounded. Indeed on a very general understanding of "good" the doctrine says nothing at all, since it is simply a placeholder for what we ought to do, the question we are posing in the first place. The utilitarian often introduces a sort of pleasure principle whereby we aggregate pleasure and then act so as to maximize it. Pleasure is enjoyable and we naturally seek it. Bentham, the founder of the school, equated good with pleasure and hypothesized a measurable unit he called "utils" that would standardize pleasures so that the calculus could be done.[1] So in discerning what ought to be done, we look to the overall pleasure of everyone or everything in some specified set. Immediately, however, three problems emerge.

First, such a principle would seem to promote massive pain for a minority if necessary for greater total pleasure. This strikes me as wrong. We have intuitions about fairness and about the rightness of actions in and of themselves that are contrary to the consequentialist approach. There are, of course, ways a consequentialist can deal with such counterexamples. For example, fairness can be defined as a valuable consequent and hence we can build intuitions into our consequentialism. Yet while the intuitive results might be retained, they are not retained for the reason we would like—fairness is ethically valuable in and of itself, not because it has some contrived relation to good consequences. Moreover, once we start complicating consequentialist theories like this, it becomes unclear that we have something workable or even something that holds onto the natural essence of consequentialism. We may end up modifying the theory so much that it is consequentialist in name only. Rather than providing a theory based on a concrete property like pleasure, we revert to using a property that we are supposed to be analyzing.

Second, imagine a drug that would bring constant pleasure—should it be given to everyone? A pleasure principle would seem to require this, but such a result is unintuitive.[2] We tend to value the reality of a state in terms of our place in the world and not just the state itself. We seek to earn happiness and pleasure, not to have it imposed upon us by a foreign agent—indeed a rich conception of true happiness is conceptually linked to the reality of what we take our life to be. Someone who is massively deluded can only

1 *See, e.g.,* Bentham *An Introduction to the Principles of Morals and Legislation.*
2 The example was first presented by Robert Nozick in *Anarchy, State, Utopia.*

think that he is happy; he cannot truly achieve the rich sense of happiness we seek in life. Yet if the consequences are all that serve to ground norms, this sort of desire is wrong-headed in total. How we get to a certain state of affairs or feeling does not matter—all that matters are features of the consequences themselves.

Third, it makes sense to query *why* pleasure is ethically good. If this is an open question, then it isn't clear that we have really grounded ethical normativity. This can be said of any analysis of the good. Pleasure is obviously good in one sense, but 'good' is used in a variety of different ways. In the current ethical context we refer to the morally good, and while it is debatable how exactly pleasure and moral goodness relate, it is quite a step to say that they are identical. Often we think that pleasure is depraved and morally bad, especially if it is achieved through objectionable means. We can avoid these problems by redefining the consequent, but in doing so we lose the concrete property that is supposed to be doing the heavy lifting.

If we are given some sort of principle of what is good, we can query why this is so. And we can develop examples in which the supposed good, like pleasure above, is intuitively not morally desirable. To deal with this, utilitarians develop complex theories in which the good becomes more and more refined so as to capture our moral intuitions. Mill, for example, works to refine the simple or vulgar utilitarianism of Bentham by differentiating various orders of good so that simple pleasures are not worth as much in the calculus.[1] The problem, however, is that by reference to the good as the basis for moral theory, the utilitarian achieves a momentary victory in that, of course, we should maximize the good in the sense that 'good' is what is morally right, but if this is the sense that is used, the theory hasn't produced anything at all. Difficulties are dealt with by smuggling moral principles into the definition of the good—which would be fine except that the theory is supposed to provide, not assume, moral principles. Once we give a definition of the good that doesn't make covert reference to the morally right, we can immediately look for a reason to believe that the property is in fact good, and the counterexamples emerge.

The theorist is left with three options, essentially. He can tell us that we ought to maximize the good consequences, wherein the good is what is morally right. But this isn't even a theory, because it doesn't add anything we didn't already have by definition. Or he can posit a simple definition of the good that we do have a handle on, like pleasure. The problem now is that for each simple posited good, we can look for more grounding and play intuitions against the theory. Finally, he can develop a detailed and complex account of the good designed to avoid the problems we found before, but

---

1 Mill, *Utilitarianism.*

now the theory is difficult to understand, and grounding becomes even more of a problem because it is unclear what makes the things in the theory good in the complex situations it considers, other than the need for the theorist to avoid embarrassment. But if this is where we are headed, it is time to reconsider the approach altogether.

As the school has developed, its adherents have pursued the third option. Mill, as mentioned, introduces levels of pleasures, though of course this gets rid of the simple apparatus of Bentham that provides a theory we can understand, even if it is intuitively embarrassing. Mill and others have moved to rule-based utilitarianism such that we should adopt general rules of conduct that, applied over many acts, maximizes happiness rather than looking at each act individually. The result is that intuitive principles and our recourse to rights can be incorporated.[1] But again this is just making things impossibly complicated in that we don't know what level of abstraction to form rules at, and it appears that every time we encounter a problem we just change the rule to get rid of it. The price of this move, however, is that we are left with an inscrutable theory.

The consequentialist faces a dilemma between the two aspects of the first criterion of a successful grounding, providing a genuine grounding and connecting this grounding to clear norms. We can accept that the good is a genuine grounding of maxims, but any theory can accept this. The question is what counts as the good. The consequentialist will offer analyses like pleasure and happiness. These can be taken in concrete or abstract terms. If they are taken in concrete terms, it will be easy to see how they relate to specific norms, but then it becomes an open question whether pleasure or happiness in these concrete senses are really good, which is to say genuinely grounded. The inclination we feel at this point—especially when faced with the sorts of puzzles found in the first two criticisms—is to retreat to an abstract sense of pleasure or happiness such that it is defined in terms of the good. Now we end up with a genuinely grounded grounding, but at the price of making it unclear how this grounding relates to concrete norms of action. It is easy to fulfill one aspect of the criterion in question but incredibly difficult to fulfill both.

This last criticism is the most important here. The first two criticisms present counterexamples that can perhaps be addressed by a more complicated theory, though the more complicated the theory gets the more likely it is that it will have forfeited its initial intuitive appeal.[2] The third

---

1 Bentham in *Anarchical Fallacies* termed rights "nonsense on stilts"; it is an attractive and fun quote, though I do not know why the folly of nonsense is worse when it is put on stilts.

2 *See, e.g.,* Hare, R.M. *Moral Thinking: Its Levels, Method and Point* for a nice development of a consequentialist view that attempts to address some of the problems sketched here. Hare's main move is to claim that our anti-

is a more principled problem. Moral dilemmas lead us on a quest for an understanding of the grounding of the norms that lead us into the dilemma in the first place. The consequentialist points to the goodness of the results but then must analyze goodness. If we are to arrive at a genuine grounding for norms, this analysis must occur in concrete terms that provide us a clear way to judge which consequences to pursue. Yet once this is done, how appropriate the analysis really is becomes a pressing issue. At this point the counterexamples mentioned above return full force and the theoretical dilemmas become more pressing. Consequentialist theories seem to need to approach the dilemmas dogmatically by rejecting one set of intuitions without leading us to understand why the dilemma appears genuine.

So in reference to moral dilemmas, there are two real worries regarding consequentialism. The first is simply that there seems to be nothing more than a dogmatic assertion that one side is correct in response to a moral dilemma. It would be better to be able to understand why we find ourselves in a dilemma in the first place and why it is so difficult. A consequentialist offers a singular and universal theory of ethical norms and hence there is no room for legitimate conflict. The only way to account for moral dilemmas is through epistemic limitations—we feel like we are in a dilemma because it is difficult to judge which action brings about the best consequences, but with full knowledge there would be no dilemma at all. This sort of response, however, strikes me as a failure to truly acknowledge the phenomenon of moral dilemmas—even were I to have full knowledge, I think I would still feel like I was faced with a dilemma; and I have a hard time believing that I would be entirely irrational in thinking so. To put the point another way, moral dilemmas as experienced do not feel like mere confusion. They present real problems and it is hard to accept a theory that must hold that there is a clear and obvious answer for the enlightened, without an explanation, beyond stupidity, for how we got into the problem in the first point.

Second, in offering a grounding that would deal with moral dilemma, the consequentialist relies on a conception of the good. This leads to an unpalatable oscillation between offering something grounded and offering something that serves clearly to ground something else. In the first instance,

---

consequentialist intuitions are a result of deontological rules of thumb (he does not like the term, but to my mind it is the clearest way to make the point without detailed exegesis) that we use in everyday life to simplify difficult consequentialist analyses. Apparent problems are created by developing unlikely hypotheticals in which the rules of thumb fail to track consequentialist results. So Hare accepts that his view leads to unintuitive results but has an explanation for why this is so. As will become apparent below I agree with some of his moves and his characterization of some moral principles as a sort of heuristic or rule of thumb. I differ, however, as I view consequentialist principles in the same way and look elsewhere for moral grounding.

we simply point to the good without substantial analysis. But then it becomes unclear how this abstract good relates to the actions we prefer and the norms we seek to ground. So we analyze the good. But having done so in some concrete terms, we oscillate to the other problem in that it isn't clear why what we have offered isn't in need of grounding itself, leading us right back into the original problem.

Deontological Approaches

Deontological theories face similar problems. These theories focus on duties and hence determine the propriety of a norm based on a certain internal characteristic of the act itself and the motive behind it. An act is moral if and only if it is in accordance with duty. The classic example of such a theory is Kant's categorical imperative: in one form acting only on maxims that can be universally affirmed and in another form as acting so that everyone is treated as an end, not a means. Further, the only morally good thing is the good will—motive or acting for the sake of duty is the key issue in moral evaluation.[1] Kant is the classic example, but it is not necessary to this approach that we focus on the motive or will. The important point is that the goodness of an action follows from the nature of the act and not from the consequences that follow from it.

For Kant, in order to test a given maxim we apply the categorical imperative in order to discern whether it is legislated by reason. If indeed the maxim passes this test, then it is in accordance with duty. A good action is one that is in accordance with duty and done out of duty. Other deontologists might disagree about how to test maxims but the form will be the same. Properly grounded maxims are those that are in accordance with duty. Consequences or heavenly sanction are irrelevant to the grounding of maxims.

Taken abstractly, one can easily agree with such theories, but in order to truly ground our norms we must be able to give an analysis of what our duties are. This is not easy. The categorical imperative, for example, has multiple formulations and suffers from counterexamples and lack of clarity regarding how to formulate maxims. One formulation is to act on only maxims that can be legislated universally. Another is to treat people only as ends and not as means. The tests share a core around the dignity and value of persons, but despite Kant's assertion they are not obviously equivalent. Moreover they are far from clear in concrete meaning.

The maxims that follow from the tests can be problematic. To take one

---

1 See Kant, Immanuel *Groundwork of the Metaphysics of Morals* for the clearest exposition of Kant's theory (which is not to say that it is clear). The sketch given here follows points from that work.

of Kant's examples, consider lying. According to Kant, it is a categorical imperative that one never lie. If it were made a universal maxim that we could lie in certain circumstances to our benefit, then the whole structure of truth telling would collapse and lying would bring no such benefit. Hence a maxim that allows lying cannot be universally affirmed and fails the test Kant offers. Lying, thus, is impermissible. But now think: suppose a crazed murder knocks on your door asking if the woman you have just hidden is in your house. Should you lie? Certainly! Yet according to Kant, the categorical imperative says otherwise.

To get out of this, we refine the maxims such that they refer to specific circumstances in a better way. For instance, the maxim is, "Don't lie unless the person you are lying to is going to unjustly harm a third party based on information contained in the truth." By doing so, we may be able to preserve our intuitions but the theory becomes unwieldy and there seems to be no way to determine *how* we are to formulate maxims. At what level of generality are maxims to be stated? Moreover, the end result of such tinkering is that we are hardly left with a theory at all and rather find ourselves with collections of highly specific maxims that simply summarize our intuitions. Rather than having a test, we end up fiddling with the maxims we put into the test to arrive at results that we already want. If this is what is going on, the theory isn't doing the work.

There is nothing wrong with talking about duties and focusing on the motives behind actions, just as there is no problem looking to consequences. Indeed the approach I will sketch will be put in terms of duties and will look to both motives and consequences. The point I am pressing here is that when we are looking for a theory that distills a grounding for moral norms based on clear ultimate principles we quickly find ourselves in trouble. One general test can be given, but it is very unclear what it means. As we spell this out we run into intuitive problems, as in Kant's problem with a seemingly morally permissible and even required lie. These are dealt with by adding more sophistication, but in doing so we allow our clear understanding of the theory to go by the wayside and we are left with something so complex that it is justified not by first principles but only because all of the ad hoc exceptions introduced to neutralize objections to the theory that was once so elegant. We begin by pointing to duty but have difficulty defining it with a test, in that the theory is supposed to provide solid grounding for duty. Once we have a test, we end up with some unintuitive results, and moreover it is hard to know how to state the maxims that are going to be put into the test. We fall back on an intuitive sense of duty to motivate the theory, but are quickly embarrassed by the fact that we were supposed to be defining and theorizing this duty to begin with.

The underlying problem is that while we may have grounded maxims in duty, it is now unclear how we discern proper duty. This is similar to the issue above: we either seem forced to leave duty unanalyzed and hence forfeit understanding and connection to useful, concrete norms, or we analyze it but then open ourselves up to further questioning regarding why *that* is really duty and why such duty is really morally good. The trouble, again, is with fulfilling both aspects of the first criterion for an acceptable ethical grounding. In order to provide something that is truly grounded, we talk abstractly about duty and define it so that it is automatically anchored in the good. In one sense of "duty," of course, I ought to do it because what I ought to do is what we call my duty. But in order to connect our grounding with actual concrete maxims that a theory seeks—that is something more enlightening than duty meaning simply what we ought to do—we end up offering an analysis of duty that leads to counterexamples and opens the question as to why the analysis given is really grounded. A concrete test of duty can be given, but then we face the problem of showing that its results are grounded without relying on the normative concept being defined. In deontological theories "duty" suffers from the same problem as "good" in consequentialist theories. It must be given two sorts of analysis, one that makes it clearly grounded and another that makes it clearly ground concrete maxims. But the trouble is showing that these two analyses are the same, so that we have a theory of the normatively-laden concept.

Additionally, the deontologist isn't easily able to provide an understanding of moral dilemmas. When they are addressed, it is by mere fiat without a deeper understanding of the power of the dilemma. Dilemmas arise because of competing duties. It would be desirable to come to understand how these duties relate and how duties can contradict one another. For a standard deontological theory, however, this is not possible because universal principles do not lead to contradiction. So when we are faced with a moral dilemma, it is only a *seeming* conflict of moral duties. If we were properly enlightened, there would be no conflict at all. Thus an epistemic account of the phenomenon of moral dilemma is the only one possible: there is one ethically correct resolution but our failure to properly understand our duties leads us to confusion. Yet the initial acceptability of any epistemic analysis is quite suspect because moral dilemmas feel quite real and can be quite trying. They are not just the product of confusion easily removed by theory. Indeed the deontologist seems to be saying that once his view is presented and we gain the knowledge we were lacking, moral dilemmas disappear. But they do not; we are still troubled and torn by such situations and scenarios even if we know a particular ethical theory.

Note that the deontologist can make a move to a transcendent realm and indeed Kant often seems to do so by grounding his system on the noumenal self.[1] Doing so escapes the problem at hand but leaves him in the same predicament as theological ethics. A theory is properly grounded and grounding because it is so by definition when we point to the supersensible realm that is beyond our access. But at the same time that grounding is removed from the realm of human understanding and we are left with an ethics that cannot be fully understood within critical inquiry precisely because the exact grounding move is deemed inaccessible. We are led to the same problem facing the advocate of theological grounding, except that instead of relying on a God that is beyond us to do the heavy lifting in grounding, we are relying on a self that is beyond the scope of inquiry to do the grounding.

Virtue-Based Approaches

One other major approach to normative ethics at present is virtue ethics. These theories ground the goodness of an action in the virtue of the actor. So the basic normative property is virtue possession and other norms follow from this. The predominant norms to be favored in a dilemma would be those that are consonant with the character possessed by the virtuous man or woman. We begin by identifying virtuous people, extrapolate the virtues they possess, and then extrapolate maxims that capture these virtues. These then are the proper maxims. Though in many cases they may identify the same maxims identified by the deontologist or the consequentialist, the important point is that the grounding is entirely different. Instead of holding those who follow the good maxims to be good people, virtue approaches begin with good people and move to good maxims. The order of explanation is thus inverted in an important way. When looking for grounding, then, we conduct a very different sort of inquiry. When asking whether an action is morally correct, a utilitarian will ask whether its consequences produce the most good, a deontologist will ask whether it is in accordance with duty, and a virtue ethicist will ask whether it is one that accords with a certain virtue or one that a virtuous person would do.

The question of grounding is somewhat difficult on this theory. Presumably maxims are, in the end, grounded in virtues. But what are these? Well, they can be listed: honesty, courage, wisdom, moderation, etc. But why these and not others? In one sense, the question isn't coherent: taken in a quite normatively-laden sense, they just *are* good ways of being. But then

---

1 I find Kant a bit vexing on this point. The noumenal realm is present but how much work it needs to do is not entirely clear. My view here is that a Kantian *moral* system can be reconstructed in its most essential parts whether or not the noumenal realm is given an important place in the theory.

what does it mean to be, say, courageous? Here we can get a description but find familiar trouble: once we get into the details we lose sense of the clearly normative sense of the terms because when we start describing actions, we can question whether they ought to be done.

Take courage. It is good to be courageous, but what does that mean in practice? Well, the soldier who charges in battle at the enemy is being courageous. It is cowardice to remain behind. But that alone will not do. It isn't always a virtue to charge into battle. We can say that courage is often a virtue but sometimes a vice, but now we've lost any grounding to maxims because courage isn't a pure virtue; rather, appropriate or wise courage is the virtue that does the grounding. So we back up; sometimes it is courageous to charge into battle, sometimes it is not. One who charges into battle when it is not courageous to do so is foolhardy, and this is a vice. It leads to unnecessary and pointless death and reflects a juvenile understanding of courage. But then, how do we tell when an action is courageous as opposed to being cowardly or foolhardy? It is between the two, and yes, we do have an intuitive sense of what actions we generally solemnly approve of and call courageous. But if a virtue is going to be a grounding of the sort we seek in ethical theory, we need something more than rough intuition. In the end we are back to the normative sense of courage that we use perfectly well but have difficulty articulating outside of ordinary discourse about the virtues.

This approach may give us answers but again does not provide understanding. What are the virtues and why these, rather than others? This question cannot be answered by other theories in ethics because then they would be doing the work—we would have another sort of theory stated in the form of a virtue theory, not a genuine virtue theory that stood on its own. The only answers are intuitions, or to stipulate someone as the virtuous man and examine him to see which virtues he embodies and which maxims he follows. But we seek more, yet given the form of the theory, no other grounding can be found. We must either reconcile ourselves to this seemingly meager grounding or look elsewhere, accepting that there is little grounding to be had in virtue.

In fact, we find ourselves in the familiar conundrum captured in the two aspects of the first criterion of a successful grounding. Virtue in an abstract sense is clearly appropriately grounded. Everyone can agree with this. But the virtue ethicist holds that we conduct ethical theory through an initial analysis of virtue and then derive the good and duty from this. In order to offer an acceptable ethical theory, we must link virtue to concrete norms by a more definite analysis. Once virtue is analyzed or the virtuous person is identified, however, familiar problems emerge. First there are likely to be counterexamples wherein we ought to act against such virtues (e.g., lying to an aspiring murderer about the location of his proposed victim if we hold truthfulness and honesty are virtues). Moreover, in providing a concrete analysis we invite the question of how this concrete analysis really captures the abstract sense of virtue we begin with: once the concrete analysis is given, it becomes difficult to show that it is really grounded in the way necessary. We shift between the abstract and concrete senses of virtue in an attempt to satisfy both aspects of the first criterion but have difficulty finding a stable analysis that is both grounded and grounding of concrete norms.

Not all of those who practice virtue ethics find themselves in this sort of problem. They are perfectly happy to think and talk about the virtues without providing a detailed theory of what constitutes them. I have no objection to that project. But it is not the project of providing a grounding to maxims that we are so often after in ethical inquiry. When virtue ethics is given as an answer to that question, it is hard to make much progress because we depend so much on our intuitions and general normative sense of the terms in question.

Furthermore, even on a basic intuitive understanding of the virtues, we can easily cast various virtues on both sides of the dilemmas. We are left without a solution or understanding as we really have just restated the dilemmas as contrasts in virtues. In moral dilemmas, both actions seem attractive and embody a virtue. It is unclear how we are to discern what to do and which virtue is superior. We can look to the virtuous man, but who is this? And do we really think that the virtuous man would not see any dilemma in such situations? If not, he seems foreign, as if operating in a different moral universe. Quickly it seems that our ability to provide proper grounding runs out and we must provide a dogmatic solution. Even if we accept this, however, we are left baffled as to why it is that we found ourselves in dilemma in the first place; that is, why it is that two seeming virtues could contradict one another in this case.

Conclusion

In this chapter I have briefly surveyed four families of moral theories that seek to provide grounding to moral norms. Initially each can appear plausible, but after critical examination problems emerge. First, insofar as what they claim is something we can understand, we are left trying to figure out what the ultimate principle means and why we should accept it. As we fill in the content of the principle more concretely, an open question emerges as to why the basic concept of the theory—good, duty, virtue—is an acceptable grounding when filled in as suggested. To deal with this problem, as well as seeming counterexamples, theories become more complicated, making ad hoc moves to track intuition that end up undermining the coherence of the theory.

Moreover, each of these approaches fails to truly provide an understanding of moral dilemmas. They aim to provide ultimate principles that are grounded outside of, or extrinsic to, our moral condition. Thus the only available account of why we are prone to moral dilemmas is epistemic. The theories claim that there are clear solutions to moral dilemmas, but have trouble explaining why it is we are so troubled by them. They must claim that we are benighted. But they all think we are benighted in different ways and must assert that only they have a grasp of our true moral condition, and that this true moral condition is one quite different from the one we believe ourselves to be in. While this is no refutation of the theories advanced, the claim the moral dilemmas are the result of confusion alone is an odd tack to take. At least, we would hope some explanation of our confusion would be provided, but rarely is such explanation offered. We are left with a gulf between our moral condition as the theories claim it is upon enlightenment and our moral condition as we find and experience it.

Note that it has not been my argument that these theories should be entirely rejected. I am not arguing that God can have no place in ethics or that there are fatal flaws in consequentialism, deontologism, or virtue theories that require that we reject them wholesale. I do not claim to have refuted them or to have established that they are fundamentally wrong—they each have their place and importance and each offers insights into our moral condition. Rather, I hold that these theories have deep problems and are not satisfying when we ask for a grounding principle that is understandable and is both grounded itself and grounding of other moral norms. When we confront moral dilemmas and think critically about our moral condition we seek grounding, and in response to this query the proffered categories of theory cannot do the needed work in a satisfactory way—they cannot provide the sort of grounding we are after in the moral inquiry we have been naturally drawn into. They may, and I believe do, bring important insights into ethical thought when it is done within an approach that looks at moral grounding in a different way. Identifying that different way is the next task.

CHAPTER SIX: IDENTITY AS GROUNDING

The General Problem

Each of the above theories is considerably more complex than I have allowed and by no means have I offered a full discussion. In each case, particular objections can be addressed by considerably complicating the given theory in order to account for varying intuitions and objections. In one sense, such complication defeats the purpose of offering one general theory in that theoretical virtues like simplicity and comprehensiveness are quickly forfeited, but it is not my aim to offer decisive refutation of all possible theories. Rather I only hope to suggest some very general reasons to be dissatisfied with the predominant approaches in relation to moral dilemmas.

The same issues keep arising with each of the families of theories. First, once we provide a grounding for moral norms, we face a dilemma. If left unanalyzed, then it is unclear what is meant. But once it is analyzed, it becomes difficult to show that what has been provided—good consequences, duty, virtue—is really ethically good. A substantial argument seems necessary here, and yet if this is so, we are off looking for grounding elsewhere. This basic problem is concealed, to some degree, because the terms used—good, duty, virtue—taken in a very general normatively-laden sense, are able to ground "ought to do" and "ought to be" norms because they pick out what we ought to do or be in life. But then, the theory defines the terms using an extrinsic account that in the end loses track of the initial intuitive appeal and leads to the search for more grounds that we can understand.

This problem is illustrated well in an essay by Bertrand Russell, partly because he isn't really aiming to offer a philosophical theory in ethics.[1] His underlying ethical principle is that we should act so as to maximize the good. The philosopher's error is to think there is a fundamental theory that captures this principle. But unless we can say what the good is, we haven't said anything: he formulates his principle in a consequentialist way, but any position could be stated using the principle by changing what counts as the good. Russell declares that what is needed to complete his account is a list of goods and evils, but that he will not do this. The result isn't much of anything, though I doubt Russell was aiming for much more.

Second, we can frame moral dilemmas such that both choices embody the good given. The theories are then required to be quite substantial and detailed in order to deal with these problems. Providing such theories is a difficult task. The second criterion of adequacy for ethical grounding leads us to reject theological approaches and stick to grounds we can understand. This is by no means a refutation of theological approaches to ethics; rather it is a clarification as to exactly what such approaches can and cannot do and what proper role they can play. They cannot give us a readily understandable grounding, but in seeking such grounds, as the other theories do, the first criterion of adequacy is difficult to meet. In offering an unanalyzed account of the good, right, or virtue, we have something that is clearly grounded, but it is difficult to connect it to concrete maxims. Once we connect it to concrete maxims, it turns out that it is unclear it is still grounded in the necessary way. And even if we could solve this problem, we seem no closer initially to a way to understand the moral dilemmas and hence satisfy the third criterion of adequacy.

The present conundrum can also be understood through the naturalistic fallacy in ethics. In seeking grounding for norms we often fall into the naturalistic fallacy introduced by G.E. Moore.[2] Norms compel action in some way and can be cashed out as maxims of the form, "you ought to do x." With any such maxim it seems proper to query *why* one ought to do x. Often answers point out that x is good or is in one's duty, or brings pleasure, or is in accordance with the categorical imperative, or is what a virtue requires. But why does this action fit one of those categories? We can give a descriptive answer whereby those terms are defined to include those actions, but then we lose the original normatively-laden sense of the terms that we are after. The naturalistic fallacy in ethics is an attempt to capture the normative with the non-normative. Theories that stress duty or other normatively laden terms avoid this, but at the cost of leaving the content of the theory undetermined.

---

1 Russell, Bertrand. "The Elements of Ethics." *Philosophical Essays.*
2 G.E. Moore. *Principia Ethica.* Hume makes essentially the same point.

So if we give an analysis of the good in pleasure, duty in the categorical imperative, or virtue with conventional wisdom, then we are pressed to show that pleasure, the categorical imperative, or conventional wisdom is in fact morally proper. Here we retreat to the normatively-laden senses of good, duty, and virtue, but these then are left without a clear analysis. A gulf between the ethical terms and extrinsic accounts has been opened and it is only concealed by equivocating on the key terms in theory. The naturalistic fallacy arises when one tries to capture an *ought* with an *is*. This is just what happens when we seek grounding for our norms. We might usually be comfortable without such grounding but moral dilemmas create situations in which we are not. In seeking grounding, offering further maxims doesn't make the issue as concrete as we need it to be, while pointing to some fact that is not normative leads us into the naturalistic fallacy.

Proponents of theological ethics often argue from this problem along the following lines: morality is real: in order for morality to be real, we need normative facts: and the only source of such facts can be God. Again, I think this works as a grounding but at the expense of taking morality out of the realm of human understanding. Those who doubt theology for various reasons can accept the naturalistic fallacy and conclude that there are no moral facts and that morality is just a matter of relative opinion. But this just rejects the possibility of interesting moral inquiry (as opposed to scientific inquiry into the bases of such judgment). This, again, is a way to go but it runs into difficulty because we do confront moral questions all the time and they dominate our lives. Moreover, all inquiry is normatively laden and if we banish the normative as illusion, then the arguments that led us to this conclusion fall as well. In any case, the argument moves too quickly from the claim that there are no moral facts "out there" (like there are quarks out there) to the conclusion that there are no moral facts.

Most ethical theories that engage in critical inquiry try to split the difference, claiming that they can offer analyses of moral terms that are robust and quasi-scientific. But, again, this move often trades on dual senses of terms like 'good' and 'right' in which we can describe them a certain way and then segue quickly into their normatively-laden normal uses.

Even among those who seem to take the naturalistic fallacy seriously we find this problem. For example, Sam Harris argues that science, though not the crude evolutionary just-so stories about morality, can give us a theory of human values. His basic claim is that moral truths are truths about human well-being and that inquiry into the brain can provide these truths.[1] The wiggle word here is "well-being." Ordinarily we use the term to signify what we ought to be and do. But that isn't to provide a scientific account of

---

1 Harris, Sam. *The Moral Landscape.*

morality, whatever "scientific" is, here, or even any sort of account at all. So it is crucial that we understand what is meant by the term. However, Harris simply says that he has a clear idea of it and yet cannot define it. Roughly he seems to think that we have some ideas about what sorts of things promote well-being and then we can correlate these sorts of things with various brain activities and thereby get a scientific account of morality. His argument is that "well-being" resists definition but is indispensible and hence can be used as the basis for a scientific account of morality, thus overcoming the naturalistic fallacy.

I must admit I don't have a clue what is going on here. Sure the concept of "well-being" is indispensible—just like concepts of "good" and "duty" and "virtue" are indispensible. The argument from the naturalistic fallacy doesn't say we shouldn't use those terms. Some people who wish to dispense with moral inquiry altogether may make that conclusion, but it does not follow directly from Moore's point. Rather the point is that while we can use and need such terms in moral inquiry, they cannot be adequately captured by a merely descriptive definition, for example one that ends up referring to certain brain states, precisely because there is an open question as to whether achieving that brain state is something we ought to do. The only way to get to that conclusion is to reason that we generally actually do value such and such brain state and so it ought to be achieved, but this is just the statement of convention.

As will become clear, I don't think such reasoning should be entirely off limits. What I object to is the thought that we can note the indispensability of normative terms like "well-being," state some descriptions of things that we often think are part of this, correlate this with something that sounds scientific, and then state that we have a scientific theory of morals. The heavy lifting in this chain of reasoning is done by the indispensability of the normative sense of "well-being" and then the quick transition to a descriptive approach. Rather than overcoming the naturalistic fallacy, the argument embraces it: because we use the normative terms and we can't precisely define them, we can just give descriptions of what we think fits there and call it an account. We need the concept and thus need the account, and the only respectable account is anchored in descriptive science of some sort, and hence there must be such an account. What is missing here is an argument that we must have an account of morality and it must be of the sort favored by the theorist. We don't deny morality as importantly unreal if we say that we can't give a full theory of it or if we say that a theory of it won't end up looking like one of the natural sciences.

Moral language is normative and cannot be translated without loss into purely descriptive terms. Some use this point to argue that the only possible way moral language can be important and meaningful is for there to be a good that makes it so and conclude with a theology. Others use this point as a reason to reject moral language as important for a philosophical account, leaving it as an expression of opinion to be studied descriptively in various ways. Others try to provide a descriptive account that they believe properly scientific but do so by using concepts like good, duty, virtue, and well-being in slippery ways. Those terms retain their normative sense on the surface, but when defined concretely by the account this normative sense gets lost. By using the same word and being obscure about what is going on, we end up with an apparent science of morality.

But we don't have to make any of these responses. We can, and should, view an account of morality as one that should be given on its own terms without trying to reduce those terms to what is considered scientific explanation and without importing extrinsic ontology and theories.

The fundamental problem is with giving an extrinsic account of morality. The project of grounding begins with normatively-laden terms like good, duty, and virtue. Moral space and terms seem unclear because of dispute and dilemmas and so we look to define the terms in a more concrete way using extrinsic theories. But this is just the problem. A gap is opened between the extrinsic theory and the normative force of morality. The theories seek to obscure this problem by using the same term (such as good) in two different ways. It seems to capture the normative force characteristic of moral space because "good" is a term with normative intonations but then it is defined concretely in terms that we can raise normative questions about.

This suggests that grounding is impossible and that morality is an illusion or a mere construction that is fundamentally arbitrary. We seek grounding and so look for an extrinsic theory that is more secure than the moral norms we seek. Yet once we do so—and do so honestly—we quickly find it seemingly impossible to bridge the gap back into the sort of normative claims we need. My task here is to resist these dire conclusions without offering an extrinsic theory.

The way to do so is to begin within our moral condition as we find it in order to understand it, rather than to look for an external construction. Instead of trying to place morality within a grand metaphysics or theory of everything, we should seek to explore the contours of moral space as it appears in order to gain a grasp of what it is and how it might be grounded. This means looking to our nature as moral beings, or our moral nature, not looking to human nature on some other plain and then trying to construct a grounding for morality.

The situation seems to be as follows. In seeking a proper grounding for norms, we find ourselves failing by not really grounding the norms or not connecting our grounding to the norms. If we offer further maxims when grounding norms, it is hard to view them as grounding in any way at all since the original question will simply repeat itself. But if we point to something concrete that may seem grounded, then we become baffled in connecting it to the norms we were trying to ground in the first place. The way out of this conundrum is to find something that is both factual and normative—this is what is needed to fulfill both aspects of the first criterion of adequacy given above. Being factual, it can ground the maxims properly, but being normative, it can relate to the maxims clearly. The problem is that the idea of a normative fact may seem outright incoherent—the naturalistic fallacy seems to show that the search for one is confused. Yet in order to provide a legitimate grounding for norms, such a normative fact appears necessary. What could play such a role?

The Identity Approach

This problem is quite difficult. The best way to address it is to change our orientation to thinking about how norms are grounded rather than trying to develop a new theory of the old sort. Old theories suffer from the same structural problems and hence we need a new approach to understand the problems of ethics. Generally we look for something wholly *external* to ourselves to ground ethical norms, since the thought that it must determine how we ought to act leads us to conclude that it must be external. Otherwise it would just be subject to our whim. We want grounding and so look for something entirely objective. If we look to ourselves, there is no chance of finding grounding at all, for it seems that anything goes, which in ethical inquiry is the same as saying that nothing really goes at all. The fear is that if morality is not objective and externally grounded then it is arbitrary and unmasked as unreal, that is to say, not anything like our ordinary sense of morality at all, because we have lost the strong normative force that is essential to our experience of our moral condition.

So we look outside for grounding and the theories above do just that: looking to God, to utility, to our abstract rational nature, or to objective virtues. Once this is done we find ourselves trying to explain how some natural state of affairs or fact could really constitute what it means to be good. We could point to an alternative world and take the theological route, but then we lose any grasp on the good that would bring the understanding we seek. When we move to ground norms externally, we find ourselves in the unhappy situation explained above. Any fact we grasp in the world seems to be itself in need of grounding or unable to ground norms in an appropriate way. God can do so, but only because God can do anything, and looking to God provides a grounding by forfeiting understanding and explanation. Yet to ground norms it seems necessary to look outside of ourselves. Without external grounding, morality is a charade, but once we look for grounding we are either left asking more questions as to what grounds the supposed grounding, or with a gap between a mere natural fact and a moral norm that is supposed to be objective.

This move to the external is the wrong way to begin moral investigation. In grounding norms we should not look for something in the world but ourselves. Norms are grounded in who we are—our identity. We ought to act according to such a maxim because of the person that we are. No further grounding is necessary. Given a certain norm we are looking to ground, we should look at whether it conforms to who we are in some way. If it does, then we ought to act such a way because we are such a way. Some aspects of our identity may rely on other aspects of our identity, but eventually we end by simply pointing to a fact about ourselves that is not chosen at whim but is essential to and constitutive of who we are—though these facts are about us they are objective and beyond personal control because we did not choose them and cannot escape them.

How Identity Deals with the General Problem

I shall explain what I mean by identity in more detail in the next chapter and then make a number of points about it in Chapter Eight. Then I will give some examples of how the approach works before returning to moral dilemmas. The approach given, I then address the deep worry that by relying on identity we are pushed into a formless relativism. Before moving on, however, notice how well this simple reorientation deals with our problem. We seek a grounding for our norms that is robust enough to understand and deal with moral dilemmas. In doing so, we need a sort of normative fact. Identity can meet this need. We ought to do x because we are y. We can get an *ought* out of an *is* and hence end the regress because we end in something concrete about ourselves. Yet since the fact is one that pertains to our identity, it is normative in form. It is not a mere state of affairs but constitutive of who we are—being an x means being bound by a set of norms. Human beings are normative animals through and through. When pointing to identity, I mean identity as a normative fact. In becoming autonomous self-conscious rational beings with a certain place in this world, we are initiated into moral space, and it is who we are as human beings that is the foundation of this space.

I do not suggest that in order to have moral value one must occupy this space—otherwise only fully-minded humans would have moral value, and this strikes me as obviously wrong. Rather my point is that in becoming who we are, we become party to moral space, and that the peculiarities of who we are serve to ground ethics. Having ethical worth and being bound by ethics are not the same, a point that is clear enough but surprisingly easily missed.[1] I am concerned with the latter and I suggest that in becoming self-conscious rational human beings we become party to moral space in virtue of who we are. Identity is comprised of normative categories—ways of being that we ought or ought not exemplify in virtue of who we are. There may seem to be a regress of ways of being lurking here, but eventually we hit bottom and our spade is turned, in that we simply are a certain way in virtue of who we are. It is these basic facets of identity that I hold grounds ethical norms. They can do so because they are facts and have normative import.

What the Approach Offers

I am offering an identity approach to the grounding of moral norms, not necessarily a replacement theory that rejects all of the theories considered above. Indeed consequentialism, deontologism, and virtue ethics are all compatible with an identity approach.[2] A consequentialist would hold that in virtue of the sort of moral beings that we are, we ought to act so as to maximize the good. The deontologist would argue that in virtue of the sort of moral beings that we are, we ought to act in accordance with duty. And the virtue ethicist would argue that in virtue of the sort of moral beings that we are, we ought to exemplify certain virtues. What has changed, however, is that the approach to grounding leads to identity, in that in discerning the form of the theory that is favored the ethicist looks to the sort of moral beings that we are. Hence what I am offering here is not meant to refute various ethical theories but to suggest a better way to approach the question of ethical grounding so that we can better understand moral dilemmas and our human ethical condition.

But this is bound to seem too simple. I isolated the trouble other theories run into by arguing that they seek external grounding in facts but then cannot bridge the gap back into norms that bind us and provide a rich moral life. Then I simply stated that identity is a moral fact that is internal and thus can do the work. If it was this easy, then why do we have such trouble in

---

1 To take a simple example, it is certainly sensible to think that trees or animals have intrinsic moral value though certainly we wouldn't say they are members of moral space and are bound by norms. This isn't to say that they necessarily do have such value, we can certainly make sense of views that deny this; it is just meant to show that we are dealing with two very different things. Indeed we could conceptually go the other way and hold that autonomous self-conscious rational beings are part of moral space but do not have any moral value. Such a view would be perplexing and novel, but it is a logical possibility.

2 It is neutral on theological matters as well, should one wish to add a religious flourish to the approach.

ethics? Why are we so tempted to search for external grounding?

The answer is that I am changing what we ought to be seeking in grounding when doing ethics. This theme runs throughout this essay: I am not providing a theory but an explication of our moral condition as we find it. There is an interesting project that looks at how we come to be in that situation, but I think the mistake is trying to justify that situation in foreign terms. I am not positing a Platonic realm akin to the natural world in which there are moral objects and the like.[1] And neither am I importing a metaphysics from the outside and saying that this is all there is and we must build morality and identity out of it. The question as to what there is causes innumerable headaches. Bracket it. Begin with the phenomenon of moral experience: asking what duties you have, what you ought to do, how you should treat others, what you ought to do with your life, etc. These are questions we do face. If we want to understand our perplexing moral condition we should begin with them.

Another way to put this point is that we go astray when we think that moral laws are like laws of nature that the "hard" sciences provide us with. For most of history all theories of the world have been teleological: the natural state of something is the way it should be. So, for example, the ball falls towards the center of the earth when I drop it because that is its home and it ought to be close to it unless disturbed. This approach to nature fits well with taking morality to be a similar sort of object of study.[2] Norms govern nature and we ought to be the way nature wishes us to be. This doesn't make moral inquiry easy, because we still have to figure out what our natural state of being is (and the Greek philosophers were all over the place on this), but there is no problem with seeing morality grounded in nature.

We no longer conceive nature as governed by norms in this sense. Physical laws are abstracted from data and generalize how objects behave. There is no underlying presumption that the laws are somehow ultimately good. But we cannot strip norms out of inquiry into our moral condition without undermining something essential about it being a *moral* condition. So while the past struggled to figure out what the true natural state of man

---

1 And I don't think Plato was up to this either. We've, for better or worse, become captive of a picture of the real in which the physical is all that counts. So Plato seems silly because we picture him walking about looking for the Forms. He would have found this absurd; his picture of what it was to give an account of the real was different and he was dealing with different problems. Indeed, 'real' is a wiggle word of the highest order, seemingly simple, yet difficult to pin down in a satisfactory, rigorous way. Often by attaching a particular sense to it, for us the sense used in modern physical science, we can come to the conclusion that the great thinkers of the past were misguided fools.

2 The parallel is best seen in Empedocles, whose physical forces are love and strife.

---

was and from that thought they easily had grounded morality we have a non-normative understanding of the natural state of man and struggle to add to that or build out of that any semblance of morality as we conceive it.

So we posit a soul that is decidedly not natural and leaves us with little understanding. Or we start with pleasure as something that natural feels good and so try to build morality out of that. Or we come up with some core essence of man, for instance Kant's autonomous rational being, and argue that moral law follows from that. Or we simply reject any pretence to objectivity in morality and embrace a soft relativism in which anything goes. But truly accepting that conclusion is difficult because it guts all norms of value, and yet in our lives we are normative beings and have normative reactions. It can't be escaped because we are human beings.[1] We can proclaim there are no norms, in theory, but in living we respond to them and guide ourselves with them. A life lived on the adage that there are no norms that bind one is in fact one in accordance with norms, adhering to what one believes follows from such a claim and often seeking to act against predominant norms to exemplify one's views. But this of course is responding to norms founded on the rejection of traditional norms, not the end of the moral self, which is not a self that responds to particular norms deemed moral but that operates in moral space, responding to a type of norms generally that pertain to who and how one ought to be and what one ought to do. And if we could eschew all moral notions, we would no longer be dealing with something that we could see as a full-fledged human being because it would not be in moral space—we can recognize differences in the contours of moral space but it is hard to picture someone who was an autonomous self-conscious rational human being and yet did not responds to norms in a way at all similar to us and shared no intuitions with us.[2]

Focusing on identity as the ground of norms erases the analogy between natural science and moral inquiry because we aren't looking at objects or even abstract entities like the soul. We are simply looking at facts about the sort of person we are and figuring out the sort of norms that are embodied in our identity. We are x, so we ought to do y. But why ought we be x? Often we can answer: we ought to be x because we are z. The question repeats. Eventually we hit a wall; we can't provide more justification. The answer

---

1 This is one lesson that can be learned from Dostoevsky's *Crime and Punishment*—we can commit ourselves to an unmoral act to somehow show we are beyond morality, but our moral sense remains with us.

2 Indeed of those who near this state we talk of their ceasing to be human and treat them as extremely mentally ill. They have such a deformed conception of moral space, if they have one at all, that we do not locate them in it. At the extreme such unfortunates should not be viewed as having a different moral space but rather as failing to enter into moral space at all. What they have is so deformed that it is unrecognizable to us as a *moral* space.

is simply that we are z. This seems unsatisfying. But such angst is caused by trying to go further back. At some point we just are a certain person and to keep on looking for more behind the curtain removes the identity from the picture all together. At this point, who is the questioner? Who needs the grounds? The human conducting the inquiry has disappeared because to her the question cannot make sense. We of course could take the external point of view characteristic of natural science and then everything becomes mysterious, but the whole point of moving from theory to explication is that we shouldn't take this step when trying to understand our moral condition.

One might point out that there are lots of ethicists in history who have pointed to identity. Kant is a clear example in basing his ethics on the idea that man is an autonomous rational being. From this he argues that the moral law is a law one gives oneself and that it cannot concern the particularities of our situation. It must be a categorical, or unconditional, imperative. This follows from reason because we are all rational beings. Above I have defined humans as a moral beings as autonomous self-conscious rational beings, and this seems quite similar.

There is, however, an important difference. Kant's project is to determine a theoretical, absolute moral law based on the essence of humanity. That is, for him identity grounds norms, but only one facet of what we take to be identity is important: autonomous rationality. This is what gets him a theory that, though problematic, has an elegant coherence to it.

My talk of identity is much looser, as will become clearer in the next chapter (as will how this approach differs from a more Kantian use of identity). I want to understand our moral condition as we find it, not abstract one essence as the only relevant one. For me particular facts about us are morally relevant. And of course things we all share are morally relevant as well. This may not produce a theory, but that isn't such a terrible thing.

In my understanding what is really important about being an autonomous self-conscious rational being is that being such puts us into moral space. We share it with other such beings, though again that does not entail that only such beings have moral worth. It also creates some of the structure of that space, the bedrock that cannot be shifted because to question it would destroy that space. Yet that is not all there is to identity: other facts about us—some chosen, some by accident, and some involving a little of both— shape the geography of moral space as it exists for us. There may be variances between groups and between individuals. It may shift over time. Some facts are so essential to who we are that they cannot be removed. Others can be easily tossed or taken away. The result is a pluralistic and rich structure to morality, but not one that is arbitrary or ungrounded in a deficient way. Or so I shall argue.

Conclusion

Identity is a promising grounding of ethical norms because it is able to escape the problems that engulf other theories. It clearly fulfills the first two of three criteria given above. The first criterion is that the grounding serves as a proper grounding in that it relates to the norms and is not in need of further grounding itself. Because identity allows a transition between an *ought* and an *is*, it can do this. There is no need to search for further grounds after one points to one's identity that cannot be changed—one simply is such and such way, and would not be if not that way. There are valid questions as to whether one should be one way rather than another, but these can be deferred until the full picture is available.

The point at present is that identity is not in need of further grounds in the way that is offered by other approaches usually are. It is also clearly connected to norms in that identity is grounding of them—one ought to follow a maxim because one is the sort of person that follows that maxim. The second criterion asked that the grounding be something we can understand. I will explain what I mean by identity below, but initially it should be clear that because the grounding is *our* identity, it is something we can have a grasp on and can understand. The third criterion was that it helped us understand and perhaps solve each variety of moral dilemmas. This will be my topic in the tenth chapter, after I explain identity more fully over the next three chapters.

Review of the Argument So Far

This chapter has quickly dealt with a number of issues, and a review of the argument so far is in order before continuing. Moral dilemmas are important because they lead us to seek ethical grounding, a task of quite general interest. A proper grounding must fulfill three criteria. First it must be both grounded and grounding. Second, it must be understandable. And third it must provide an understanding of each sort of moral dilemma. There have been four predominant approaches to ethical grounding: theological, consequentialist, deontological, and virtue-based. It strikes me that none adequately fulfills the third criterion (as evidenced by their selective use of moral dilemmas), but this issue has been peripheral to my central argument.

Focus on the second criterion—understandability—leads to a rejection of the theological approach. Insofar as the divine is doing the relevant work, it is in principle not understandable. In the project of theoretical ethical inquiry, theological grounding has no place. This may be a refutation of the project of theoretical ethical inquiry, but that is an issue beyond the purview of this essay. The lesson here is that in seeking an understandable grounding we must stay in this world and deal with things we can in principle understand.

The other three approaches do this but each get into trouble with the first criterion: that the grounds offered be grounded and grounding. In each case what was offered could be analyzed loosely or concretely. When analyzed loosely it was clearly grounded but had trouble doing any grounding because it had no clear relation to actual norms. When analyzed concretely this was no longer a problem, but as the various objections rehearsed above showed it become unclear what was offered was truly grounded. The problem that emerged was that in grounding norms we could have something grounded or grounding but not both.

This problem is captured in the naturalistic fallacy and the way out is to find something that could move from an "is" to an "ought." Identity can do this, though how successfully it ultimately is depends on the rest of the argument. Initially, however, it deals with both objections that have framed my argument. Because it is a matter of who we are it is understandable, at least in principle because we can inquire into who and what sort of things we are in autonomous self-conscious reflection. And because as human beings we can ascribe normative properties to ourselves it can move from fact to norm because identity constitutes a sort of normative fact. I conclude that in seeking a grounding for ethics that fulfills the criteria set out above an identity based approach is the most promising. How fruitful it can be in producing understanding and theories or accounts remains to be seen, but at least we have a beginning of sorts. Rather than starting with a presumption ass to the sort of theory that must be had and then looking for a beginning it is better to start where we are and see where that can take us. If we don't get very far we will at least still have a better sense of our limitations in ethical inquiry and why it can be so hard and confusing.

CHAPTER SEVEN: AN EXPLICATION OF IDENTITY

Introduction

Norms are grounded in identity: what one ought to do and how one ought to be is rooted in who and what one is. But what is identity? There are several dangers here. First, it may seem I have simply replaced one difficult question with another. Unless it is understood what identity is and how it comes to be, I have really only answered the grounding question with a placeholder. This would be the same mistake that the accounts rejected above make when they point to intuitive concepts of the good, duty, or virtue and claim to have a theory. Further, by pointing to identity as a grounding of norms I seem to have fallen into the common blunder or explaining the rather unclear with the entirely unclear. Without a better understanding of identity, the suggestions of the previous chapter are vacuous. Identity solves the problem identified in the quest for grounding, but unless more can be added, this solution is hardly enlightening.

Moreover, pointing to identity as a source of normativity leads to a familiar oscillation in ethics. Identity either seems wholly externally determined or a product of self-creation. If the former, then we become separated from our norms and do not feel responsible for them or genuinely accountable to them. As we press this view, we cease to see them as norms that we are responsive to and come to view ourselves as machines operating according to certain laws. If *that* is what we are, then it is inappropriate to talk about norms in any rich sense— rather we have deconstructed norms and unmasked our pretences to virtue and condemnation of vice. But if the latter, then anything goes and in such a case there do not seems to be genuine norms at all. Norms are supposed to be ours in the sense that we choose to follow them, but not so much ours that we can choose them at will. Put another way, moral norms must be laws that are unlike brute physical laws but also not self-created rules without external bounds. This is, again, the trouble with needing a normative dimension that is objective. The banishment of teleology from nature has created a gap in the kind of beings we are: both part of nature and a being with true purpose—that is, purpose that is not arbitrary but is both objectively valid and within our power to choose.

A response to the first worry must also deal with the second—we need a robust understanding of identity such that it is no mere placeholder and shows us a way out of the oscillation between normative totalitarianism and anarchy, or imperialism and insulation. In this chapter I explain what identity is and thus address the first danger. The burden of this chapter is to show I have not merely offered a placeholder. The three following chapters fill in more details by making a number of general points about identity and roles, offering more concrete examples of how the identity approach works, and then returning to moral dilemmas. The penultimate chapter returns to the second worry and argues the identity approach can avoid the oscillation between insulation and imperialism—that norms are either wholly self-created and relativistic or wholly externally bound, absolute, and singular.

The task of providing an explication of identity is not the task of giving some sort of reductive account or dissolution of identity. That has its place, but it is not here. Generally in philosophy talk of personal identity is a "how possible" question. How is it possible that I have a personal identity that persists through time? Usually this question is based on a puzzle that emerges because of various accounts of what there is—for example if we hold that there is only a series of conscious states in time then it is difficult to understand how there could be such a thing as an identity that persists *through* time. The question can be turned on its head to argue that the idea of personal identity we are trying to explain is false—we have no such personal identity.

My task is rather to understand what we take personal identity to be—that is to figure out what is it we are trying to explain with these other sorts of accounts. And as this is not an ontological endeavor for me I am not concerned with arguments that there is no such thing as personal identity as such—I neither affirm nor deny such a thing. The inquiry begins with the phenomena of identity—I am a person and am trying to figure out who I am, how to understand myself in the most enlightening way possible as an autonomous self-conscious rational being conducting moral inquiry. Hence the aim is to explicate how we might think of ourselves in a way that expands our understanding of our moral condition.

Identity as a Web of Roles

So what is identity? My basic account is this: identity *is* the web of roles one occupies. I am the web of roles that define my life. When I reflect upon myself and who and what sort of person I am, I am drawn to the sorts of roles I play in my life, as a family member, friend, philosopher, citizen, human being, etc. This is how we describe ourselves to others—not as some ethereal, formless ghost that has mysterious substance absent any roles at all. Remember, here we are not concerned with ontology or metaphysics or anything of the sort. Our question is how we should conceive ourselves as ethical beings; how we should come to understand ourselves as beings in ethical space, which is a space we find ourselves in during the course of our lives. The question of life, Cicero's question of who and what sort of person one ought to be, is one that naturally confronts us and is made pressing by the need to find meaning and peace. To begin to answer the question, we must reflect on our identities, and this means understanding who we are as we find ourselves in ethical inquiry. And here the best way to understand ourselves is by turning to roles for an explication of identity.

Identity is multi-faceted—there is not a single role one occupies but rather a large number of them. Identity is difficult to understand because of this. We are not merely one sort of thing but rather a great many together and all at the same time. When we attempt to reduce ourselves to one essential characteristic that is alone important, we lose a full grasp of ourselves and end up with theories and approaches that cannot capture the turmoil of being an autonomous self-conscious rational being. Indeed if we attempt to make identity just one simple thing then we end up losing anything that makes us, as individuals, who we are and are led to totalizing ethical theories that inadequately capture our thrownness into the world and leave us with an account of identity we cannot fully understand. Or, to put it better, no real account of identity at all because some abstract, unexplained thing, a soul for instance, is simply posited as the entirety of our identity. This is fine, so far as it goes, but to engage in critical ethical thought and get a real account or explication of identity we need an account of the soul and what it is about our individual soul that makes us who we are. And this is just the question we began with.

Roles are singular in that they are rather simple, having relatively clear possession conditions and consequents. To occupy a certain role means fulfilling criteria and being bound to behave a certain way and have various attitudes and beliefs. Identities are complex because they involve many different roles bound together in various sorts of relationships with one another. When we think about duties we or others have, we tend to simplify and talk of only one role. This is a mistake. We are the people we are because of the multitude of roles we take on and how we balance and harmonize these various roles. I take roles to be a basic category, a simple place one takes in a larger whole. They describe one's particular position in the world along a specific dimension. Identity is complex because it is constituted by many roles.

The roles that make up our identities can be familial, political, intellectual, social, professional, communal, cultural, aesthetic, spiritual/religious, natural, etc. One may very well have multiple roles in the same category and I do not mean these categories to be exhaustive or definitive—rather they are exemplifications of the sorts of roles that may form and shape one's identity. These roles together make up who one is and stand in various relationships to each other. Identity is not just a lump of roles but a complex and fluid structure or system of roles. Some roles may shape others. For example, I may be a member of the Parent Teacher Association (PTA) partly in virtue of being a father. Or I may be member of a political party because of some deep seated values that constitute part of my role as a political and social being. Some roles are subordinate to others: I may be a parent first and a friend second. And certainly roles interplay with each other a great deal: my political role is shaped by other roles I take myself to have and vice-versa. A brief explanation of some categories of roles should make these issues clearer and is the best way to exemplify what exactly roles are and how a web of such roles constitutes a complex identity.

Familial Roles

Familial roles are a good place to begin because they are easy to understand. They form some of the most important parts of our identity. One may be a son or daughter, husband or wife, father or mother, cousin, grandparent, brother or sister, etc. Some of these can be avoided: one needn't ever get married or have children. Others cannot: everyone is a son or daughter and other roles like brother or sister and cousin are not in one's control. Each of these roles involves how one relates to other people and is shaped by a special societal and cultural type, the family. How exactly one's family is constituted may vary. All may be genetically related or there may be adoptions and the like. Further, depending on one's circumstances, one's familial roles will be shaped by the proximity of others—different sorts of roles apply to extended vs. nuclear families.

Each of these roles is an important part of who one is and brings with it various obligations. For example, being a parent means one ought to act and be a certain way, paradigmatically acting in accordance with a deep duty of care and concern. Children and siblings have similar normative constraints placed upon them in virtue of the role they occupy. The exact shape of the role and the accompanying norms will depend on the exact family and situation. For example, one's role as a son in relation to a particular parent will vary depending on how that parent has fulfilled his or her proper role as a parent—filial obligations are lessened and maybe even abrogated if a parent has been entirely absent or abusive. Though the way the role works will vary our family roles are nonetheless important parts of who we are and ground various ought to do and ought to be norms.

When we think of ourselves, we tend to think of ourselves as members of a family and related to others in a certain way within this unit. This is reflected in how we describe ourselves to strangers. Our place in a family gives us a set of roles that constitute a portion of our identity. Since many of these roles cannot be escaped or can be shed only with great effort they form an important and central part of who we are—often we cannot imagine ourselves as not being part of a family, which is to say that our familial roles often form an essential aspect of our identity. Obligations are hence stronger close to home. Notice that this solves a problem hinted at above, that of the locality of moral affections and sensibilities. Intuitively we have deeper obligations to those close to us than to those far away. Yet on many ethical theories this is mysterious—everyone is equally valuable as a person and so it would seem that our ethical obligations have no tolerance for geographical closeness or blood relation. On an identity based ethics this problem disappears quickly. Familial roles form an important part of who one is and hence one's obligations related to family are much deeper. This doesn't entail that we think one group of people more objectively valuable than another but only that from our place in the world our obligations are shaped so as to make family more important. By stressing familial roles as an important part of identity we can capture intuitions and practice.

Political Roles

Political roles vary from society to society. In modern societies most individuals will have the role of a citizen.[1] I take this to be the primary political role. It entails certain obligations and political rights within the political system. Some of these are formal while others are not. For example, in the United States, citizens have various formal obligations associated with law abiding behavior, jury duty, licensing, etc., and rights as delineated

---

1 Though historically it is not true that most members of a society are political citizens. Political roles in virtue of membership in a community are actually easier to understand in ancient societies in which there is more stratification. It would be no oddity in the ancient world to be a man with no country. We often take for granted what it means to be a citizen in a way our forebearers did not.

in the Bill of Rights (including jury duty) and elsewhere (e.g., voting).[1] Less formal obligations include political participation, voting, patriotism, etc., as well as a generalized duty to contribute positively to society politically and otherwise. Different countries will have different sorts of citizenship. In fact, because political systems vary greatly, what it means exactly to be a citizen varies as well. But the general point is that the role of a citizen gives one a particular legal standing in a society and brings with it obligations to be a positive part of that society and to support it. It also generates prima facie adherence to the laws and codes of the land. Resident aliens and visitors take on roles with similar dimensions. Because one is a citizen (or whatnot) one ought to act in accordance with the law independent of any enforcement action the state may take against one. Being a political member of society is an important part of who one is and engenders many norms.

Other political roles include those created by leadership positions. In the United States these include elected and appointed offices that have responsibility for the conduct of government. Obviously not all citizens have these roles. But if one finds oneself with one, there are important consequences. One now has various rights and duties associated with the state, such as the right to lawfully detain citizen and the duty to apply laws fairly. These positions are generally a privilege because they allow one to be the agent of policy and a great deal of public trust is invested in them. They allow those occupying them to shape society to various degrees but also bring obligations that may put a great deal of pressure on them or require unpleasant activities (e.g., a sheriff's duty to evict tenants). Soldiers play a similar sort of role: they have the duty to follow orders and act as a vessel of the corporate individual that is the country.

There are other political roles as well. For example, membership in a party or other political organization produces a role of its own that fixes part of one's identity. Additionally, membership of a political society as a citizen might be a quite robust role: one may act and think a certain way because one is an American citizen or Roman citizen beyond the explicit duties and rights entailed in such a role. Often national citizenship suggests a certain character and set of values that becomes part of one's identity. Finally, particular political views may often fix an important part of one's identity. This is especially the case if one has extreme views—if one is a communist in America today a large part of one's identity is as a communist whereas merely

---

1 Rights and duties can overlap, as in the case of jury service. As a citizen one has a right to serve on juries—this is a powerful form of democratic governance. One also has the duty to serve when called, as a part of political society. Voting is similar, except that in the United States there are no formal sanctions for failure to vote. Such sanctions are employed elsewhere, and in any case there can still be a duty as a citizen that isn't formally sanctioned when breached—one has just failed to be a good citizen.

being a Democrat will entail a good deal less about one and likely constitute a less essential facet of one's identity.

There is certainly a great deal more one could say about political roles. Roughly these roles delineate the place we take formally within a society, that is, the place we take in relation to a formal whole that is the state. These are formal roles in the sense that they usually have sort of legal structure composed of rights and obligations. The exact shape of these roles will depend on the nature of the state one is a part of and on the particularities of one's position in that state. Some states will have richer conceptions of citizenship than others and some people will be more politically involved than others. Nonetheless, to some degree we all are political beings with political roles. These roles, with others, shape who we are and how we ought to act and be.

Intellectual Roles

One's intellectual roles can also be an important part of one's identity. There are at least three general types of intellectual roles. First, one's actual education gives one a particular role as college educated, high school educated, etc., that become an important part of how one sees oneself and how one is seen by others. Education shapes the sorts of jobs one considers, the sort of friends one has, and the class one takes oneself to belong to.[1] Even where one was educated can shape one's view of oneself and determine how one acts in various circumstances. This is especially true of the college educated—being a graduate of a school shapes one's obligations in terms of charitable donations, advocacy, and even comportment in the public sphere. Further, being a graduate from a certain school creates a relationship with other alumni of that institution that can lead to various obligations and amity between various people.

Second, one's learning and expertise leads to a role as a source of knowledge and information for others. This in turn brings various statuses and obligations. If I am knowledgeable about history, I occupy a role that leads others to defer to me in those matters and that asks me to share my information truthfully with others. Knowledge is part of who we are. Even common knowledge can shape common roles. Particular knowledge asymmetries do so more clearly because they set us apart from each other.

---

1 The educated have often taken on the role of being educated. This meant being familiar with certain ideas and works and being able to converse about them with knowledge. I leave that out here because the trend in education has been away from this such that those who are educated cannot be expected to be able to converse on a set of subjects simply in virtue of being educated. The role has not disappeared, but now involves less intellectual overlap.

When I am knowledgeable about a subject that many are not I take on the role of an expert in that subject and may take this to be an important part of who I am—so much so that I work hard to maintain my expertise.

Third, one's actual views on any number of questions are often an important part of who one is. As in the case of political roles this is most evident among radicals: if one has a certain radical intellectual view (e.g., that modern science is deeply misguided) this becomes an important part of one's identity. What you think and how you view the world helps fix who one is as a person. For example, if I am a proponent of string theory in physics then I take on a certain role within that community and at large. Positions in the debate over evolution in this country may be even better examples. By believing or disbelieving in evolution I have occupied a role of some import that makes up a small part of who I am. It may have consequences for who I associate with, how I vote, and especially how I think about a great many other issues. Any contemporarily hot intellectual issue will have this effect—merely by having a certain view one takes on a not unsubstantial role as someone with that view.

Social Roles

Social roles are a broad category but should be relatively easy to understand. Membership in a social group or a relationship confers a certain role. Friendship is perhaps the best example—I am partly defined by those friends I have and how I ought to interact with them. These relationships are an important part of my identity. Friendships come in various shapes and sizes and bring with them a great deal of normative baggage. One can depend on friends in a certain way and expect certain things from them. At the same time one has certain obligations to friends that one does not have to others. How deep these obligations run and how essential this role is to one's identity will depend on the friend. One's relationship with a life-long friend is quite different than one's relationship with someone who is a casual friend and the corresponding roles differ as well.

In the role of friendship we also see why those close to us are more important to us than those far away. It is essential that we distinguish between being important to us and being important sans phrase. Everyone is important sans phrase and valuable as a human being. But this does not entail that everyone has the same importance to us. Friendships generate bonds and obligations. We can both expect more from friends and owe more to them. These obligations arise because we take on those role and our friendships shape our identities. I am many things, some of which are friends to certain people. Losing my friendships would be losing an important part of myself.

Class can also be an important social role, especially in societies with definite class structure. In America, for example, being middle class is an important role for many people and defines how they see themselves. They buy certain types of goods, vote certain ways, and associate with certain people. Their social position fixes much of their attitudes about themselves and the world. Social roles are like political roles in that they are a matter of how one fits into society but differ in that they are not formally defined and often are much more local. Friendships are an important part of the social roles on plays yet these relationships are private and local in a way that political membership is not.

Communal Roles

Communal roles overlap with social and political roles. These sorts of roles are ones that fit into civil society. Thus various communal organizations, volunteer associations, participation in local events, etc., can all be part of a role one takes in the community. Perhaps groups like the Elks and Eagles are the best examples, though there are certainly others like the PTA. Many neighborhoods have governing groups that in may give identity to members. Local affinities not connected to citizenship also fit here. One may be defined by being a Southerner, an Oregonian, or a Bostonian. These roles all can be an important to a person's identity.

There are two different dimensions of communal roles. The first relates to specific organizations that serve a purpose in the community. It need not be a volunteering role but importantly these organizations have some purpose and ask something of their members. By belonging to such an organization one takes on various obligations and rights. The second sort of communal role shades into a cultural role. It involves being from or living in a particular place and hence belonging, in some sense, to a particular community. This creates a particular bond and shapes behavior. The best way to grasp this sort of role is to imagine what happens when someone is away from home attending school or on vacation. In such cases the differences emerge and one sees how much one's community shapes how one thinks of oneself and how one acts. The experience can be shocking in some cases, but reveals that an important part of who we are and how we structure our lives is linked to local communities of which we are a part.

It is hard to overstate the importance of civil society and communal roles. Political roles are usually rather formal and prescribe adherence to set laws and extend certain rights given formal, legal guarantee. Communal roles are much more fluid and touch on many different situations. Political roles constitute how one is in relation to society as a whole as a public being. They are hence generally more formal than communal roles in that communal roles do not rely on explicit statements and structures, rather arising within the practices of a community. Communal roles constitute how one is in relation to a particular community and how one behaves in areas of life beyond the strictly political. The difference is one of gradation and not kind. The same holds in distinguishing social roles from communal and political roles. Each captures a roughly different way in which one is partly defined in relation to other human beings and structures, whether it be in relation to the state or public thing, a particular person or group of people, or a community organization or loose group.

Cultural Roles

Cultural roles also make up part of one's identity—indeed often when we talk about identity cultural identity is what we really mean. One's language, tastes, customs, etc., all make up an important part of who one is and hence may very well ground norms of conduct and other norms of being. I may act a certain way because I belong to a certain culture and this may be all the justification I need. The second sort of communal role discussed above related to one's actual place of primary residence. Cultural roles are often tied to this but differ in that they relate to one's particular form of life. I may very well be of the southern culture though I have never lived in the south. Exiles are clearer cases of this. One may be of Iranian culture even though born in the United States, and further this need not involve genetic origins in Iran though, of course, it often will. In such a case one's communal and cultural identity do not line up. Such a person might be a citizen of the United States, from the Midwest, and a member of the Iranian culture. Certainly other sorts of communal and social roles as members of the exile community and group would be in play as well. My point is that culture is not necessarily tied to place.

My belonging to this culture may be inherited or learned and may be a more or less important part of who I am. We will most clearly notice the importance of cultural roles when we look at cultural minorities. When one belongs to such it a group it becomes apparent that it is a vital part of who one is, and it becomes clear how one acts differently on that basis. Below the surface, however, similar things happen for majorities as well. I perform many actions in a certain manner and proceed in certain ways because off my cultural heritage. Simply being of such a heritage is enough to ground such norms.

Affinity Roles

Related to cultural roles though worth separate comment are what I term affinity roles. These are roles that one takes on because of an interest or devotion to something or some activity. Hobbies are a clear example.

Imagine I collect baseball cards seriously and hence am quite devoted to the practice. I may identify myself with others who do the same and this practice is an important project in my life and one that I value greatly. It shapes how I structure my life. I may have many hobbies or I may have only a few. And people vary greatly in how important an affinity is. For most these sorts of roles are quite unimportant. For example, for me running is a hobby but not a serious one. I generally like it and try to stay in shape. I don't do it just because I like it—some days I run only because I'm a runner and that is what runners do most days, even when they don't really feel like it. Running is a habit, but I don't do it on these days merely out of habit—it is not as if I suddenly find myself running because that's just what I do every day. Rather, because I've chosen to be a casual runner, I've taken on obligations to run fairly regularly. If I fail to do this, then I lose the role and part, though for me a minor part, of my identity. So if I took yesterday off and don't really feel like running today, I will still likely run because I know that, as a runner, I ought to and I will feel guilty if I do not.

For me, and there are others who differ, running is not something that I stress about myself and I am quite willing to forgo partaking in the hobby if other things come up. The role is part of who I am, but not importantly so. For some people hobbies can be crucial and serve to structure one's life and give one purpose. But looking in from the outside without that attachment, their lives can look absurd and impossible to understand precisely because something that for us is trivial is so crucial for them. Indeed an individual can have a profound crisis of identity if they are no longer able to partake in a hobby that is an important part of their identity. If I am in a car accident and am injured such that I can never run again I will be sad, but I will quickly move on, shedding a part of my identity that I can no longer live but doing so easily because it wasn't a core role. But if a marathon runner who trains nearly every day and races often is in the same accident and suffers the same injuries, losing the ability to run is devastating to the person's sense of self and he will likely become profoundly depressed for a time until somehow a new identity is forged and what was once essential, but became impossible, is replaced (e.g., by becoming a competitive athlete in endeavors still possible or a coach or something entirely unrelated but consuming of the self in a similar sort of way).

Another type of affinity roles can be found in being a fan of a particular thing. The most obvious examples are sports teams. Indeed there are those who place incredibly high value on their affinity for a sports team, or even just a sport in general, and structure their lives in large part around that team or sport. They buy apparel, they travel long distances, and they only associate with other fans. Indeed for some it resembles more of a religion than a leisure activity.

Whether this is good or not I'll leave for another day. The interesting point is that we have the ability to take on a role wherein something that may appear quite trivial to most (say a particular football team and its performance) becomes a major part of our lives. We come to devote a great deal of time and money to it because we define ourselves to some degree by this role and this devotion. We act, and believe that we should act, various ways because that is what a devoted fan does. Our self-image and satisfaction with life may be tied into the performance of the team or a player. This speaks to the need for important roles and projects in our lives. Affinity roles are interesting because they can vary so greatly in their objects and to an outsider the importance of the role can appear bizarre. But at the same time they can be quite strong normatively and constitute a part of what we believe to make our life worthwhile.[1]

Professional Roles

Professional roles are those that relate to our careers and jobs. I mean "professional" quite loosely. Our jobs don't determine who we are entirely, but they are an important part. This is evident in fields with professional codes of conduct and especially those that require a great deal of training. Lawyers and doctors, for instance, often derive much of their identity from their professions and the norms entailed therein. So do professors and teachers. Soldiers are an even clearer case. Indeed almost any profession fills in a large part of someone's identity. There may be cases when it does not, but those are likely cases where the job is *just* a job done in the meantime. In such cases professional aspirations, even criminal in nature, play the role usually played by the job a person has. This is one reason why the loss of a job or a professional setback or even retirement is so disconcerting for many. One has in essence lost part of oneself and there is a major hole to fill in. One doesn't know what to do with oneself or even who one is. Hence it is quite a traumatic experience for those who consider their professions to be essential to their identities or those who have practiced a given profession for most of their lives. For some it isn't so much not knowing what to do with themselves as no longer knowing who they are.

---

1 How deep such roles can be became evident when the Red Sox won the World Series in 2004: one heard elderly fans saying that they were just glad they lived long enough to see the Red Sox win. European football fans are perhaps even a better case for the importance of these roles. Within these roles we can also see the importance of solidarity (commented upon in the next chapter) in that, when have an affinity for something, we become part of a group and identify with it in an important way. Consider, for example, Red Sox Nation and teams that have a global fan base that see themselves as unified in an important way.

Profession obviously shapes who one is and how one ought to be and act. It is often a large part of our life's work. It may shape our political obligations, our beliefs, and even our families and friends in important ways. Within the community one's profession leads one to act in a certain way. This is obviously the case when on the job but even occurs when one is not on the job—those in the service industry, for instance, often take themselves to have obligations to others in the service industry when not working based on common profession. Professions that involve a specific set of skills often impart duties to use those skills when needed even when not on the job. Off duty police officers still respond to emergencies and when asked explain that it is part of being a police officer. Not responding would be a professional failing even if one was not on the clock at the particular time.

Moreover, in one's professional or economic capacity one is subject to many norms dependent on one's role. For example, if I am a businessman, my economic activity is part of who I am and my loyalty to the company— limited in the sense that it is in virtue of exercising my economic function that I am so bound—I am required to act in a certain way. I am an employee of company x performing function y and this is an important part of who I am that leads to various norms regarding who I ought to act in that capacity. Professional role can vary in importance, but for the economically active it is usually a very important part of who they are. Indeed the loss of a job through being laid off, being fired, quitting, or retiring can be extraordinarily distressing for some, even if they are otherwise economically secure and think they no longer want the job. Having devoted oneself to a particular productive activity, a real attachment exists with who one is for many people, and losing that can leave an individual lost, searching for purpose now that a central role has disappeared. He or she may seek a return to work, or find other roles through family, community organizations, leisure activities, travel, political involvement, etc., to fill the void left by the loss of a professional role. Note that this is not to say that such people liked their jobs—that is immaterial. Rather the point is that whatever the attitude of a person to his or her job, career, or profession it usually comes to become an important role for their identities and the loss of it, even if desired, raises problems of its own because of a void within the person's identity.

Aesthetic Roles

For some, aesthetic roles may also be very important. One's personal style and tastes in art, food, architecture, decoration, etc., all can make up an important part of who one is. Being a person of such and such tastes certainly grounds various particular judgments of taste but may do much else besides. Style is broadly how one goes about doing things—it is not just a matter of particular dress. It is an image and comportment. Hence for someone whose style is very important many behaviors will be grounded in their aesthetic identity.

What sort of art one prefers, what sort of cuisine one prefers, and what sort of music one prefers all shape one's identity. How important this is to a person will vary considerably. If I am a devotee of grunge music and attend every concert possible, this aesthetic role may shape a great deal. If I merely enjoy it, the role may be quite insubstantial. In most cases these roles will appear important among those who have cultivated a certain taste or style. One who simply enjoys something or is a fan will not take these roles seriously, though they may have normative import for him or her. On the other hand someone who is a fanatic or a member or high culture may take these roles very seriously and the normative import may be massive. Like many types of roles, aesthetic roles can vary greatly in their importance based on the value we assign to them into our identities.

Religious Roles

Religious or spiritual identity is of obvious importance. One of the most important roles we take on in our lives is fixed by our religious affiliation or lack thereof. Being of a certain religion entails certain practices and views. It colors almost all of one's life. Being very religious means that this is even more the case in that one's religious identity will dominate others. If I am an Episcopalian I take on a role that involves various beliefs and practices. I am bound to attend worship semi-regularly, profess faith, and contribute to the church. Just by being such a person there are norms attached to my behavior as well as norms attending to my beliefs. Often these norms constitute a particular worldview and way of life and if my religion is very important to me it may be one of the most important roles in shaping how I act and am.

Even if one is not religious, atheism or agnosticism are roles one might take on involving certain attitudes, beliefs, and practices (or lack thereof). For those who would call themselves spiritual the same holds. Various practices make up one's daily life and the thoughts one has in this realm ground various behaviors and additional thoughts. Religion is a major part of human life. Even by rejecting it or pursing it in an unconventional manner one is reacting to it and defining oneself against it. This is an example wherein *not* having various beliefs or engaging in various practices can constitute a role as well that places similar normative constraints on one as would be found in cases where such beliefs and practices are adopted.

The depth of one's religious identity will vary by person and time. For some it is impossible to imagine existence without their religion. Those without religion or of a quite different religion appear odd, a type of other that is foreign to one's moral universe in some way. If asked what life would be like without their religion, they may have some inkling but the person they describe may seem entirely foreign. Others will not find religion very important, though they do think of themselves as belonging to a particular group. It is just a peripheral given for them. Still others may change religions often and quickly. In such cases religious identity is quite important but not very deep. Hence the person jumps from place to place attempting to fill a hole in his or her identity.

Philosophical Roles

We should also add the related category of philosophical roles in the sense of a commitment to a general understanding of the world, approach to life, and/or conception of the good that forms the sort of framework for who we are. This need not be, and usually is not, explicit and known to most people. It takes work to figure out what our basic implicit understanding of the nature of things is. Figuring out deep parts of who we are and what we value takes a good deal of work. I add it to this section because religion often plays this sort of place in the lives of people. But it need not, other sorts of philosophical approaches can do this as well and in fact we can draw on other sorts of roles to play this part in our lives.[1]

A person's conception of the good, or what it is they are seeking in life, forms a very important organizing role. If I determine that the good life consists of devoting myself to study of some subject and become a professor I occupy that professional role but also a role of having that conception of the good, as one who believes the good life is studying that subject. This isn't just a professional role because many may have the professional role and yet differ in their conceptions of the good. Additionally, a conception of the good may unite people in a role who otherwise are quite different: devotion to the unfortunate can unite people in a variety of different professions who share little else in their lives but are constrained by similar norms in their lives because of their conceptions of the good.

Of course, most people have pluralistic philosophies on this score and are not sure what it is they are seeking, at least in a way that can be articulated. Nonetheless, these philosophical roles are important: a big part of who I am is being someone who has such and such approach to the world and views about what the good life is. Based on that basic and perhaps implicit, unarticulated understanding, I ought to be and act in certain ways.

---

1 Additionally, including them generally avoids the difficult problem of providing necessary and sufficient conditions for something being properly a religion.

Natural Roles

The last sort of role constitutive of identity that I shall mention is simply one's natural role as a human being. In virtue of being a human being one has automatically taken on a very important and basic role with its own set of practices and norms. Fully explicating this is a highly complex matter that I shall not pursue in detail here beyond the points made in the second chapter. Roughly I mean to identify a sort of normative nature such that simply in virtue of being a human being one is thereby constrained by various norms. This is easier to see if we look at humans as rational animals—being such means various norms of reason apply by nature. The Stoics were after this in their naturalistic ethics and I think that those who ground ethics in reason are often pointing to the same sort of idea. As a human being one is an autonomous self-conscious rational being. This in and of itself grounds some norms and is an important role that fixes one's identity. It is perhaps the most important in the grand scheme of things, though it is often forgotten because we think of our identities in terms of those things that separate us from others. On the view of human identity I take, what we share is perhaps even more important. Being an autonomous self-conscious rational being is what all beings in moral space share because it makes moral space possible. As such beings we are free, to some degree to act and be as we wish, even if this leads us to act inconsistently with who we are and wish to be and even if it leads to deep tensions in our identity. We are self-conscious in that we are not just aware of the world but have the capacity through language and thought to reflect on ourselves, to pose questions as to what we seek out of life, what we ought to believe, and who we ought to be. And we are rational in that we give and ask for reasons, respond to norms of reason as a part of our second-nature and seek not just answers, but justifications, explanations, and understandings. These basic features make moral space possible, but they are not wholly constitutive of it—other roles shape it in important ways, these basic features are simply keystones of our moral lives, albeit keystones we may reject in our action and identity thereby creating basic tension in our moral being. Natural roles are not exhausting of moral space, but they are an important part of it because they bind us to norms of being and action abstracted from our thrown situation and evaluated from what it means to be a moral being in moral space generally.

In referring to the natural role of a human being I manifestly do not mean a merely biological category. That category is not a sufficient condition in that biological humans may, for various reasons, be unable to enter moral space. It is likely not necessary either as we can imagine another sort of being that is not biologically human yet has developed rational capacities that lead to moral space we can recognize. That is my intuition at least, but the point isn't central: what is important is that the natural role we possess is that of being an autonomous self-conscious rational being and it is this that is important for ethical inquiry.

Of course human beings are surely the sort of thing we can talk about biologically and describe as such. But we should not confuse this facet of human beings with a full understanding of human beings. Listing various biological facts about human beings does not fully explicate what we understand human beings to be. One thing that is missing is the normative category of being a self-conscious rational being, exactly what I am after here. This may ultimately by physically grounded in biological facts in that in order to become an autonomous self-conscious rational being certain physical and biological processes and developments must occur but listing such facts does not explicate what it means to be an autonomous self-conscious rational being.

I am a human being and as such have various needs, interests, and obligations. I respond to reasons, show sympathy with others, desire certain ends, feel affinity with my fellows, etc. Much of this is based on shared humanity and the dignity that attaches to being a human being that I sense and thereby see in others as well. Now it is of course possible that I lack some general feature of humanity altogether and yet remain a human being. This would be the product of cruel nature or hard (misguided) work on my part to eliminate part of my natural identity. This, however, does not show that these aspects are not part of being a human being, rather they show the opposite. Subversion of such aspects is entirely abnormal and indeed *unnatural*. Hence possessing them is part of what it means to be a human being. Lacking them—for instance being unresponsive to reason entirely—is a grave deficiency and goes against one's natural role as a human being. At the extreme such a deficiency removes one from moral space as an agent. Short of this I may come to deform my moral space such that though I still occupy it, I can be described as evil and deformed in a deep way, living such a contraction with what it means to be human—to respond to reasons, to value humanity, etc.—that I can be viewed as inhuman and as such living a hopeless contradiction as I attempt and act as if I am not truly human when beneath the surface I am essential a lie. I am a warped, deformed, and pathetic autonomous self-conscious rational being, bound to being human but constantly rejecting myself as such.

Being a human being comprises a large part of one's identity. We usually work at more particular levels, but in a basic sense the most important part of one's identity is this natural role. It is what differentiates us from everything else in the world and brings us into moral space. It cannot be wholly shed and can take many particular shapes depending on other roles we inhabit. Still, this natural role forms the basis for identity and hence is normatively quite important.

A Comparison: Kant and Identity

Kant can be read as using identity to ground ethics and can be understood as looking to roles, or really a role, as fundamentally important. A quick comparison will be helpful in explaining the similarity of the use of natural roles, as well as differences related to other roles. For Kant, we begin to understand norms by isolating what is essential about us. This is roughly akin to what I've been calling the natural role of being an autonomous self-conscious rational being. Our capacity for reason is important to Kant and based on this he derives the categorical imperative, in one form acting only on maxims that we can will as a universal law. In another formulation this means treating people as ends alone, never means. The idea he is stressing is that moral action must be according to a law and it must be one we can give ourselves. In giving ourselves laws we use reason and it is this that we all share. Hence value is conferred on reasonable beings within the exercise of practical reason.

I have followed a similar path in stressing identity and the importance of being an autonomous self-conscious rational being. But there are several key points at which I differ. First, I do not hinge moral value on the capacity for reason alone. The capacity for reason is essential for operation within moral space, but it is not the only thing that can confer value within that space. For example, I think that human beings who because of disability lack the capacity to be an autonomous self-conscious rational being still have great moral value. This is not to say that Kant believes the opposite, rather because of such issues I do not want to equate the essential ingredient for partaking in moral space with the value of a thing within that space. It is easy to quickly make the two equivalent, but it is not necessary to do so. Doing so tends to create embarrassing problems in which people and things who/that do not partake in moral space have only instrumental value based on their use to those who do partake in moral space. Being clear about the difference opens a way to avoid such embarrassments.

Second, Kant is concerned with maxims and, indeed, the categorical imperative is a way of discerning maxims. I think we should go back to antiquity and take a broader view of the domain of ethics and practical reason. Maxims are important, but I think we need to look at ought to be norms as well and try to discern how we ought to structure a complete life. Kant's approach makes these sorts of questions difficult to formulate.

Third and most important, though I share with Kant the view that we need an objective basis for ethics and that a key feature is our identity as autonomous self-conscious rational beings, I reject the view that this essential ingredient alone can get us what we want out of ethics. Rather, we must take not just those aspects of who we are that makes us the same but also those that make us different. The basic difference here is that I reject the thought that we can somehow through pure reason establish a sort of foundation that could get us an acceptable and understandable ethical theory. Things are too messy and we have to begin with where we are, wrinkles and all. The result is that we are led to an ethical pluralism that is objectively routed because it is bounded by natural roles stressed my Kant and most ethicists and by roles that are socially constructed and essential for large swaths of people. Within these bounds and given our particular circumstances our challenge is to work out who we ought to be given the roles and the tensions and the problems we confront. There will be variance as to what constitutes the good life (unless we define the good life in such an abstract way that it lacks real content) and proper norms, but this variance is anchored and hence prevents the slide to formless relativism and eventually moral nihilism that, in the end, is moral suicide.

Kant is much more complex than this, but for those familiar with his work pointing out the similar basis but also key differences should provide a better understanding of my approach. Identity is important for understanding and grounding ethics, but it is not just what is essential and universal that needs to be accounted for in identity. A broad understanding of identity also needs to look at other roles that are not universal and may be changed. This will permit, as I shall argue later, a sensible objective pluralism anchored in what we share but extending ethics in varying ways because of perfectly acceptable differences in the roles that comprise individuals.

Conclusion

Identity is a web of these roles and will, as such, vary by person and even more so by historical time and place. Indeed the exact meaning of each sort of role (e.g., brother or friend) will vary considerably. And there are certainly other categories of roles that could be explicated: I am not offering a complete categorization but just some more details that make sense of how our identity is constituted. For example, I have not discussed race as a role even though in many times and places it has been thought to be a very important role. I leave it out because there are many debates about how to think about race that, though interesting, would detract from the thrust of my argument. And I have not discussed gender roles or roles related to sexual identity that can be and often are quite valuable and come with normative import. We can also think of ethnic roles and national roles as a category. National roles, for example, are not always like more ordinary political rules because a nation may not have a state or a state may not have a nation. My point is this: the above analysis just gives some examples of types, not some absolute set of categories.

Additionally, the categories overlap. A particular role may be thought of as a cultural role, a political role, a social role, etc., at the same time in that it has various aspects. This is fine; the categories are just ways to think about the sorts of roles that make up our lives. I do not suggest any definite and absolute system of classification.

Hence there are certainly other types of roles to be traced. The categories are not hard and fast or unchangeable but only heuristic devices for us to use to understand how roles function and constitute identity. My hope in this chapter is that the types of roles I have sketched have made identity clearer. Identity is composed of a systematic web of roles, some of which we occupy by necessity and others by self-ascription. They impose norms on us and function in many cases by delineating a proper sphere of responsibility for things we do in our lives and towards people and things around us or in the world generally. Next I turn to some general points about how these roles function.

CHAPTER EIGHT: GENERAL POINTS REGARDING ROLES

Now that some categories of roles have been sketched the approach I am proposing should be clearer. It is, however, far from complete. I shall not attempt to sketch a coherent identity composed of roles here, and indeed I do not believe doing so is within my power. Moreover, it would help the approach but a little, since what I am offering is a way to think about ethics in terms of identity and roles. An important feature of this explication is that identity is not static because roles change in both existence and shape and relate to each other in complex, shifting ways. An attempt to describe a particular identity at a particular time might shed light on what that person ought to do and be/become and what tensions that person faced, but wouldn't provide enlightenment as to how we should understand and think about our moral condition. Rather some general points about roles should help to make clear how they come to constitute identity and ground norms and explain how they work in life and in shaping the moral space we inhabit.

Roles are Both Factual and Normative

A crucial point above was that identity is a normative fact—simply being a certain way entails norms of reason and action. Roles make up identity and thus are normative facts as well. One is, in fact, in a certain role for some reason, whether it be by nature, by accident, by choice, or some combination. So, for example, I am a brother as a matter of fact because I have a sibling. I am also a human being, a skeptic, a son, a friend, a member of my community, a citizen of the United States, etc., etc. Each of these roles has a factual component based on facts about my life, even if those facts are just those that I ascribe to myself. For example, I have ascribed the fact that I am a skeptic to myself and hence occupy this role in virtue of that fact.

But, importantly, occupying these roles also means being bound by certain norms. Roles are not just facts and not just norms but hybrids of them and both are essential to the role. I am as a matter of fact a brother and being a brother means that one ought to follow norms involving helping one's sibling out when he or she needs it, etc. I am in the role of a brother and so I ought to act in a certain way. Roles are blended facts and norms. This may appear puzzling, but this is only because there is a tendency in modern thought to define 'fact' and 'norm' in such a way that they are by definition incompatible, which, predictably, leads to worries and confusion about how norms could be "real" or binding, etc. Of course that is a problem if we make them incompatible at the start of inquiry. If we stop worrying about ontology, however, and bracket our metaphysical prejudices in favor of seeking an understanding of ourselves as moral beings, there is no need to begin inquiry by positing a distinction that makes genuine norms altogether impossible. Too often we create a problem with our structure of inquiry only to seek fruitless solutions to it within that inquiry, causing much angst and confusion as we feel pushed to deny something, normativity, that pervades our lives and we cannot do without.

The point is easiest seen by trying to imagine just the fact or just the norms that go with it. So, for example, imagine a society in which siblings did not have any relationship and did not have duties to help each other out when possible, etc. Would they really be brothers? We can say yes, in a sense, but something is missing from our conception of what it means to be a brother. We can, of course, imagine *bad* brothers, but this is done against a background in which the norms are in play. In the same way, we can imagine when society attached the sort of norms we associate with brothers to people in relationships with others but the two are not genetically related or part of a family unit. We would say they act like brothers and indeed in our society we do use this kind of description of very good and intimate friendships. But if there was no relationships of this sort between those who were related we could not honestly say that they are in the role of brother—something important is missing.[1]

This does not mean that I am not free to disobey a norm that is partly constitutive of the role I occupy. I may choose not to act as a brother in some way. We generally say that this is not being a good brother. Often we can change the facts that constitute a role: we can stop being friends or quit a

---

1 The idea of blood brothers is quite telling here. Two people undertake the sorts of norms characteristic of the relationship and as a symbol of this mix blood with each other as a way to create a sort of factual, natural bond like that shared between brothers.

group we are part of, but the factual component of familial roles don't work like this absent very extreme cases when things go so awry that we might say "you are no longer a brother to me." And even there it is still metaphorical in the sense that the relationship is still there, we are just stripping it of as much as possible. Facts can create roles that carry with them norms. And indeed we can come to occupy a role by following certain norms that thereby creates, in part, the requisite facts (think friendship—it can be created between two people by acting like friends and conversely can be destroyed as a role simply be failing, perhaps unconsciously and unintentionally to act like friends).

How exactly the factual and normative elements that define a role blend will vary by role. The important point is that when we consider a role we can describe it both factually and normatively and that to get a full description we must include both. Merely defining a blood relationship without the normative import of that relationship would not capture the role and neither would just giving a set of norms without describing facts in the world that put them into context. This may all appear simple, but the essential dual aspect of roles is exactly what permits them to serve as grounding for moral norms.

Roles are only possible for beings in moral space and thus are part of what can be called our second nature. They are acquired and take shape in a society of autonomous self-conscious rational beings. They impose rights and duties on those who occupy them and thus are essentially normative. But they are also factual in that the possession conditions of a role are defined by objective facts about the world—a natural feature, kinship relations, past actions, one's locality, etc. For some roles it is in our power to change the factual conditions that are possession conditions for a role, for others it is not. I occupy the role of a member of the PTA in virtue of having a child at the school and by having joined the group. But it is in my power, if I so choose, to change those facts and abandon the role. And the role may be stripped from me if I fail to fulfill it. On the other hand I occupy the role of a son and it defines my identity in important ways simply in virtue of having been born. I cannot change this fact, though I can act against it by failing to pay credence to the norms that attach to that role.

Things can get complicated quite quickly here, but the simple point is the important one. Roles are facts about us whether or not we can change them. But they are normative facts in that within a role one is bound by various norms implicit in that role. This permits grounding of legitimate norms without falling into the naturalistic fallacy. It is not some mere feature of nature that we find when we look to roles. Rather norms are contained within the role itself. We can attempt to ask why one ought to be constituted by such a role but eventually we lose the sense of the identity we are querying in asking such a question—the "one" that is the subject of the query disappears if we call the roles into question. As such, we have arrived at a fact that can end the normative regress as it pertains to the identity that is defined in part by the role we are focusing on but in a way that can ground legitimate norms because the role itself has normative import. There is no trouble with the naturalistic fallacy because we are not trying to magically jump the gulf between fact and norm. Roles, and hence identity, are unified normative facts about a moral being, that is, a particular autonomous self-conscious rational being in moral space.

The Content of a Role Has Various Sources

Roles have content that is factual and normative. Where does this content come from? That is, given a certain role, say brother, how do we figure out what exactly it means to occupy that role, to be a brother? There is no one, singular answer. Part of the answer is simply nature: we just are certain sorts of beings, some as essentially part of being an autonomous self-conscious rational being. More concretely, some of the specific content of a role comes simply with having the concept generally—what exactly it means to be a brother isn't something that just is a universal fact, but in order to have that concept at all there are basic element that must be part of the content.

This does not exhaust the source of the content of roles that are important in moral reasoning and inquiry—this point is one where I am rejecting the traditional way of using identity to ground norms. The content of a role can be shaped by society. For example, our role of brother is not essential—it is a social construct of a sort that is part of the space that we are initiated into when becoming a member of society. Parts are of course natural in that there is usually a blood relation. But this is not exhaustive or even necessary—families are generally but not necessarily genetically linked. Our human society has this role and its meaning has been shaped within that context. We can imagine a society that lacked this role because the norms we hold essential to the role are not present. There may be a relationship of a sort but it is shallow in that there are no bonds of fidelity. This is not to say that it is unreal in any way, just that we must look to social reality to understand the role. It is real for us because we are essentially part of that society in that it has shaped who we are. The content of the role is not a stipulation but emerges out of practice that encompasses our form of life.[1]

---

1 Compare linguistic meaning: 'cat' means cat because we use it to play this role. This does not make it artificial but neither does it suggest that there is one true language of nature absent human practice. When Humpty Dumpty declares that 'glory' is a nice knock-down argument, the problem is that this has no basis in social reality. But that does not mean that we can criticize

Furthermore, an individual may give some content to a role. This is often done by reference to other roles in that as we shape how we are a brother, etc., what that means will be shaped by other roles that we inhabit. The norms that give content to that role will then in some ways be self-given. There are limitations as to how much can be self-determined, but some can. For instance, I cannot say that it because I am a brother and my brother is in trouble I ought to do everything possible to make his life more miserable. This is not being a good brother and might be extreme enough that we would say, in a sense, I am not really a brother at all. But we can imagine different norms being articulated by different people in a similar circumstance that governs how one ought to help one's brother or perhaps help by not helping at all.

Roles are Acquired by Being, Accident, and Choice

The content of roles is determined in several ways. Similarly roles are acquired in a variety of ways. Some are a consequence of simply being and cannot be escaped. These are the foundations of moral space though—and this is where I differ with traditional approaches—they are not exhaustive of its structure. To be a sort of thing that is capable of responding to norms at all, one must be an autonomous self-conscious rational being. For us one must also be a human being and part of a society and a language-user. These are all related and constitute roles that follow form being the sort of things we are. Usually this is treated as an essential nature and the font of morality in whole. I differ in that I see it as the essential structure but not the only structure available. How our moral lives are structured turns in large part on other factors and roles as well and the content of these inescapable roles is in turn shaped by contingent factors. There is a common core but it emerges in many shapes and the various shapes bear a family resemblance to each other.

Roles can be acquired by accident: consider roles like citizenship and many family relationships. One does not in any sense choose these, they simply happen because of facts about the world. Sometimes they can be escaped—I can disown my family or renounce my citizenship—but this requires a grand act of disavowal and has very serious repercussions in my life if indeed it is a real renouncement. No such act or really any act is required to come into these roles—they are roles that are thrust upon me by the contingencies of the world. Nonetheless they make me different from others and are an important part of who I am—I ought to act certain ways because of the circumstances that I am in and the roles that define me. Others may have different obligations but this does not make my obligations or these roles any less important: they are an integral part of who I am because I exist

him for getting the world wrong.

in a world not of my making.

Roles may also be chosen unconsciously, consciously, or semi-consciously. I choose a profession and this shapes my moral life in important ways. I come into friendships, choose where to live, what religion and politics to adhere to, etc. I can shed these roles on reflection or by drifting away. I can even choose, in a sense, to take on or abandon a role even though I do not wish to. If I move to a community I become part of that community and take on a communal role even if consciously I want nothing to do with it. I can minimize the role, but by choosing to be there I have in fact taken on the role even if I don't much like some aspects of it.

Of course the categories are not this clean and distinct—often roles come in a mixture of accident and choice. Consider religion: I am cultivated to be a part of religion through no real choice of my own. Some people make a very conscious choice at some point to stay or change. Some do so more unconsciously. Some may not ever be able to fathom being part of another religion because it has by upbringing become essential to their identities. Thus though it is helpful to see various ways roles get adopted we must remember that this will vary by person in some ways and be quite complicated.

The various ways roles can be acquired highlights the importance of human facticity: we are born into a world not of our making and acculturated in ways that are not of our choosing. We, as autonomous self-conscious rational beings, come to be and exist in a society. Many things well beyond us determine the roles we come to occupy. The result is that the norms that bind us in a situation will sometimes vary considerably by person because we occupy different roles. This should not be troubling—ordinary experience gives no credence to the view that there is one norm that always governs in the same way and can be stated clearly. It is theory, not experience, that drives a desire for such a universal master norm.

Roles are Particularized

Roles are particularized in the sense that the consequences that follow from the norms that define them are limited to a certain particularized class of things. In my role as a brother I have duties towards my siblings, not the world writ large. Even when we speak most generally in terms of the role of being an autonomous self-conscious rational being, my duties are not to the universe writ large, unless we use that phrase metaphorical to encompass how I ought to behave towards several defined classes (e.g., I find it hard to believe I have duties towards quarks in virtue of any role). Even if one wants to resist this last point, that basic role (and perhaps a few others like it) is exceptional. Most roles are particularized to certain classes of people or things and situations. Largely this is because roles are relational and defined by the class of things that have value in virtue of having that role. Indeed, the idea of a role generally places it in the context of a larger whole. When I think about my role as a citizen it is in relation to other systems, the government, the law, etc. Put another way, roles are functions that involve doing something in relation to some part of the world.

The upshot is that norms are particularized as well. A norm that is binding upon me is so in virtue of a role I play. That role is in reference to particular people or things or some class of them within which it takes form and has meaning. Thus the norm will have bearing in relation to and particularized within the domain of that role. This is quite different than how norms are often conceived—moral norms apply across the board. And in a sense they do, but the way they apply is fixed by the roles in play. Additionally, even in my broadest roles I am still particularized to a set of things in the world, not to the set of things at large. In being a human being I see myself as an autonomous self-conscious rational being and part of that group. Even here, the norms that generally follow will be particularized to them. We usually drop the particularization as unnecessary in broad cases, but it is important to note that it is still there and that in regards to other norms it may be quite important.

Roles Form a System, Not a Conglomeration

Identity is constituted by a web of interrelated roles. By this I mean that they form a structured system and have relationships to one another. Some roles are more important than others and will trump them when there is tension between the two. Some roles are defined by others or mutually define each other. The structure is both fluid and complicated. We change over time and wear many hats at the same time. It is beyond this essay to try to sketch an identity of related roles. But when we "figure out who we are" this is sort of the issue we are struggling with. The whole thing is made more difficult because we change over time in our roles, sometimes by our own doing and sometimes not.

What I want to point out here is that we should not think of identity as a heap or conglomeration of roles that aren't connected. If that were so we would lose track of the singular self that is constituted by those roles and would come to think of ourselves as different people in the same body. Rather they form a systematic and shifting web in which some are more central than others and they work to shape the exact nature of the others because they are all part of the same unified person. To put the point quite plainly: we are not Dr. Jekyll and Mr. Hyde in inhabiting various roles. That sort of case is exceptional and something has gone wrong with the person's identity. Indeed such an unfortunate can be said to have two identities that have little, and in extreme cases no, relation to each other.

It is tempting to think of roles like hats that we wear. But this is also rather misleading because there isn't a separate me that is wearing the hats. I am, in a way, the hats and I am a whole bunch of them all at the same time. Circumstances (e.g., what I am doing) affect how the roles relate to each other, but managing my life and my identity is the process of working on a system of a plethora of roles that is somewhat coherent but sometimes in great tension and that can change. If we do not realize the systematic nature of roles in constituting an identity we end up either resorting to an ethereal self that gives structure to the independent roles or end up with a disintegrated self that is a mere heap.

Roles are Hierarchical

From the point that roles form a web and not a heap it follows that roles are also hierarchical. Some roles by necessity are more important because we can't escape them without ceasing to be the same person: e.g., being an autonomous self-conscious rational being (escaping this would mean a sort of mental suicide). Others are more important because they form what we might think of as the core of who we are. They trump other roles when there is conflict and we are not ready or able to abandon them without losing a key part of who we are.

Some roles are fleeting and can be flaunted or cast aside with ease. Some jobs are like this. So are some friendships. The degree of attachment to roles of certain types will vary by person. For example, someone born in a town and having lived his whole life there may be unable to cast aside the role of being a member of that community (even if moved away he would still strive to be connected and follow all the news he could find). But someone who has moved around a lot and has only been in the town for a short period could easily cast aside that role because it is not as important to her.

Simply put, some roles "trump" other roles, though particularities of a situation must be attended to when making such judgments. When deciding what to do when different roles make adhering to their norms impossible in a situation judgments are made and are often easy. My role as a son is more important than my role as a member of the PTA, so if a parent needs a ride to a doctor's appointment at the same time there is a meeting of the PTA there is little difficulty for me to decide what I ought to do. Unfortunately, such decisions are not always so easy. And I may be confronted with situations when I must choose which role to discard or to act against in a very serious way. Life, and forging and developing identity, is a difficult endeavor, which is what makes it so interesting and challenging. Here I only wish to note a fairly obvious point—not all roles have the same force in a person's identity. The force that a role exerts will depend on the role itself as well as how the person has occupied that role within his larger identity in the past and how he wishes to do so now.

Roles Shape Other Roles

I am constituted, in part, by my role as a brother. That carries normative import. But what it means to be a brother, in my life, is not independent of the other roles that also constitute me. My religion, community, profession, political views, other family relations, friendships, etc., may all shape the way I am a brother and what exactly the role of brother means. This is not a point about cases where roles conflict with each other in which I must somehow choose whether to fulfill one role or another. Rather the case here is that the way I fulfill one role is partly determined by other roles. This is what I mean when I say that roles shape other roles. The point reiterates something mentioned above that must be kept in mind: roles as particularized "hats" we wear are good as a device of exposition but we are complicated and we are one person and so we cannot imagine that various roles are somehow isolated from each other.

So, for example, I am constituted by the role of being a father and also by the role of being a member of the PTA. The exact nature of my role as a member of the PTA will depend on what it means for me to be a father, how I live this role out, and what kind of father I am. This can be a two-way street. My role as citizen and father can shape each other. As a citizen I change how I think and act and what norms I am bound by in being a father and how I am a father. I may have more of a duty to vote for and advocate positions that protect my children's interests. In the same way how I raise my children— what I teach them, the model I set, etc.—is to some degree shaped by my role as a citizen. I am a citizen of the United States and as such have a duty to teach my children about the country and our history, should attempt to impart patriotism of some sort in them, and should model for them good citizenship, as I understand it. The way I am a good father depends on other roles I occupy just as those other roles are shaped in their content and their normative import in virtue of my being a father.

Roles are Overlapping

Roles are overlapping in the sense that in any given situation multiple roles will be in play. The world isn't simple. We are many things at the same time and it would be silly to approach a question as to what to do right now by just singling out one role. Rather we should ask which roles are in play and how they relate in that situation. Within life we are playing many roles at the same time almost all the time and must consider how they interact in various situations. An inevitable result is that roles will often be in tension with one another because they suggest different actions. A challenge of practical reasoning is to figure out how to relate and balance the roles in play and determine what the best thing to do is.

The point should be quite obvious when roles clearly relate to each other, for instance in the example I've been using regarding being a parent and a member of the PTA. But roles are overlapping generally. First, some roles are so central to our identity that they are always, in some sense, in play. Natural roles are most obvious here, but religious roles and philosophical roles often have the same feature. Familial and political roles also can have this feature in some instances. Moreover, roles that at first blush unrelated interact and overlap in many ways. If I am a lawyer I have a professional role that imposes the norm that I be on time for court. As a citizen or other part of the political community I am bound by a role that imposes the norm of following, to a reasonably close degree, the traffic laws. When I am running late for court the roles overlap and, in this case, conflict. The conflict makes the overlap clearer, but is not essential. In all situations of life we are subject to a variety of norms, whether in conflict or not, that flow from the many different roles we are constituted by and which are relevant, to varying degrees, in the situation at hand.

Roles are Contextual

Roles are contextual in that whether they apply will depend on the situation and how they apply will depend on the situation and the other roles in play. If I am a judge that role may be relevant in most contexts but will be very important in the context of sitting on the bench in court. It may minimally apply or not even apply at all when I am at home teaching my child how to read. The norms that flow from a role depend on what one is doing and are not universal in any totalizing sense. Additionally, as various roles come into play based on a situation the roles themselves are affected in how they apply. If I am forced into wearing two hats at the same time (and I almost always am) then the hats must be balanced and coordinated.

Note that this point can make sense of an oddity. How can one justifiably act against one's individual conscience? Imagine a judge who is opposed to capital punishment. In his political role in his community he speaks out against it but he nonetheless sentences people to death because in his role as a judge he is to follow the law. There is obviously tension here and the judge needs to work that tension out, but there is nothing paradoxical about this: different roles dominate in different contexts and thus different stances may be required. The challenge for such a judge is to figure out a way to understand himself as playing both roles in good conscience, that is, to make sense out of the tension between them and reach a self-understanding in which the two can co-exist without undermining each other.

The contextual nature of roles also shows how important our facticity is in ethics. Contexts are often not of our choosing and the roles we come to occupy are not always of our choosing even when they are not universal. Contexts push roles on us and the presence and power of roles varies with context and the facts. Hence moral norms are best stated in application, not abstraction, because the bases for moral norms are often quite context dependent.

The point, like many in this chapter, is simple but important because it opens a more nuanced way to think about ethics. Depending on the situation—where I am, what I am doing, what has gotten me here, what other people are doing, etc.—a role takes on different application and varies greatly in how forceful it is and even if it is forceful at all. We are complicated beings and our identities are brought into to play in different ways depending on context, hence what once ought to do can depend on the context. We must be careful here not to allow a disintegration of an identity such that one's roles and derivative duties and rights are segregated radically such that they have no bearing at all on each other. Though roles and norms will have different shapes in different contexts we are, after all, one person with one identity that we seek to make coherent and whole. My only point here is that we can hold onto this while still acknowledging that the shape and application of a role one is in some sense constituted by will change with context.

Roles are Fluid in Shape and Existence

Most roles are fluid and change over time. This is so on two levels. First, over the course of a life various roles may play more or less important parts as we change. Some roles may come or go or oscillate. This can be by choice: I may quit a club, change friends, change jobs, move, or change political or religious roles. This can often be done easily, though because roles are so connected often there are ripples throughout my identity when a role is dropped or added. It can also be by no doing of my own: a friend may decide to move on, someone may die, a company may close, an organization may fold, etc. This happens often as well and the important thing to note is that we are not fully in control of our own identity. This concerns not just the roles we acquire by nature or by accident (like being part of a family or country) but even given this how our roles change over time. Who we are is in large part out of our hands. There is also a middle ground in which I do not wish to give up a role but by my actions do in fact abandon it and lose it: this is what happens when I betray a friend and she moves on, when I get fired, when I am thrown out of an organization, etc. In these situations I have not explicitly chosen to give up the role but no longer maintain it because of my actions that have compromised it so deeply it cannot be repaired.

Moreover what it means to fulfill a role properly will change as facts and other roles change. So what it means for me to be a brother will change based on facts about my circumstances and my siblings circumstances and the other roles that I inhabit. I still have a duty to be a good brother, but what exactly that means will change in time. This is so because roles are related and overlap. We are integrated beings and we are our roles. Hence it is a mistake to picture ourselves as abstract nothingness that magically puts on and takes off hats. We, to continue the misleading metaphor are our hats and in some sense where them all at the same time. Hence though the balance of which roles are in play and how strongly will change what it means to be an *x* will be shaped by what it means to be the other roles that constitute who I am.

Roles are Often Defeasible, But Some Roles Cannot Truly Be Abandoned

Roles are also often defeasible—capable of loss or annulment—either by choice or by accident. It is, of course, possible to act against a role that one retains. I can fail to act like a friend to a person and yet still retain my role as a friend to that person. I have done wrong and I ought to make amends. But roles can also usually be defeated by abandonment or be deviating in fact so much from what is required normatively that one cannot occupy that role. Sometimes, paradigmatically with professional roles, there is a formal procedure that strips one of the role. This may mean getting fired or disbarred, etc. Some friendships may have official endings. Often the ending is a whimper, one simply ceases to act like a friend to another and the role fades away.

Roles can be defeated by choice, conscious or unconscious, or against one's will. It may be that one simply cannot live up to a role or has acted such that there is no rescuing a role that nonetheless one wishes one could retain. Friendship is a nice example: the role depends on reciprocity in part and so if I have betrayed a friend to the point that there is no going back then I simply cannot continue to occupy the role of friend to that person even if I regret my actions. The bond could be reinvigorated, but this requires work to re-create something that has been lost.

There are also roles, however, that cannot be forfeited. Being human or an autonomous self-conscious rational being are such roles. Memberships in certain communities may be such roles. Familial roles are such roles and some religious, professional, and academic rolls can become so ingrained that they cannot be abandoned. To act against them consistently puts one in a perpetual state of bad faith and disquiet. Even if one wishes to escape one cannot because the role in question is so much a part of who one is that to lose it would be to lose oneself. Note that what these roles are may vary by person: one person may be so defined by a religion that the role of being a member of it simply is no longer up for grabs. Others may not be so defined by it and so can abandon it by choice or by simply drifting away.

There is a difference between denying, in thought or action, a role and abandoning a role, or, put otherwise, between being a bad *x* and no longer being an *x*. Some roles cannot be abandoned; natural roles are the obvious case. Others can and such abandonment can be by choice or unwillingly. I may decide to no longer occupy a role by quitting or changing professions, etc. Or I may act in such a way that I no longer occupy the role in question, either by formal act of others or by simply failing to live up to the norms that are part of that role so much that I can't be said to even occupy it. But such failure need not strip one of a role. I can be a bad member of the PTA if I fail to attend and participate but can nonetheless remain a member. At the extremes I lose the role. They may not formally toss me out, but there is no longer any sense in which I am a member. And then there are roles that no matter how much I act against I cannot lose. By behaving in a vicious fashion towards my fellows and the world I am being a bad autonomous self-conscious rational being. But no matter how vicious I behave and become, I do not cease to be an autonomous self-conscious rational being. I cannot escape it and my actions result in appropriate moral condemnation from others as well as a fundamental tension, a perversion really, in myself.

Acting Against a Role Can be a Form of Bad Faith

We are autonomous as moral beings in that just because we possess a role does not mean that we will act in accordance with it and failure to act in accordance with a role doesn't entail an abandonment of that role. I am a brother and as a brother I ought to help my sibling out when she is in trouble. But that doesn't mean that I will. I inhabit the role but I can act against it. When I do so I have acted wrongly, in a particularized sense (the qualifier is necessary because it could be I so acted because not doing so would violate other more important norms and so in an all things considered sense I have not acted wrongly). That does not mean I am not a brother. I could, of course, attempt to cast off the role and my sibling could attempt to deprive me of it. But most often I retain the role and hence by so acting come I occupy that role in bad faith. I am a brother but have not acted like a brother. Thus I have lived a contradiction and my life is in tension. Dealing with the bad faith usually means making amends by apologizing and acting differently or explaining, if even only to oneself, why it was necessary to so act.

Minor transgressions usually pass quickly and the role is not compromised. Amends are made by acting rightly. More explicit action is needed when I continue to occupy a role and continue to act against it or have violated a core duty. Casting off a role is not bad faith. If I am a member of the PTA, I ought to attend meetings. If I fail, I have not necessarily slipped into bad faith because it is not a deep obligation and I can fail to uphold the norm from time to time. If I continually miss meetings, then I am living in bad faith because I continue to occupy the role of a member of the PTA but do not act like a member. I may get kicked out, in which case I am no longer in bad faith, but no longer enjoy that role as part of my identity either. If I decide I do not want that role or for other reasons can no longer hang onto it, then by failing to attend I have not violated the role of being a member of the PTA. I have done nothing wrong by not attending as I do not occupy that role any longer and so am not bound by the norm mandating attendance.

If I did something wrong, it is because there is another role I do retain (such as being an involved member of the community or an active parent) that grounds and ought to be norm for me. If that role continues to have the same meaning for me, then I am acting wrongly and am in bad faith in regards to that role, not the role of being a member of the PTA (because I'm not a member, I just ought to be because of the other role). Dealing with bad faith in this instance requires rectifying my behavior in regards to attendance and (perhaps) apologizing. This is to make amends and restore my proper standing in that role. Or it can require that I cease to be a member and leave it at that. This is to change roles that are predominantly a matter of choice. Or often it will require that I drop the role and that I make corresponding changes in the content of related role such that there no longer is an ought to be norm that I am violating.

The web of roles is quite complicated as we start changing them, but that is part of what it means to be a complex human being. We are almost always in bad faith because we are over-committed and unclear as to which roles are to be retained. The struggle for good faith means exploring who one is and who one ought to be and reconstructing one's identity to make it more coherent. Sartre and existentialists analyzed bad faith as failing to recognize and embrace one's freedom. This is right—that is one way to live in bad faith in that one is failing to take responsibility for one's life and is merely acquiescing in it. But we must add the sort of bad faith discussed here: denying and living against a role one retains and thus living a lie.

Indeed we can understand the sort of bad faith wherein one becomes lost in a role and thereby fails to embrace one's freedom or true self in terms of the identity approach. As complex beings we must work to forge a coherent, rich, and whole identity. Being lost in a role and thereby acting by hiding within the role is a form of bad faith in that it is the denial of other roles when one so acts, a failure to be and act as a unified person, instead seeking shelter by total absorption and acquiescence in a role.

Roles and Rights

Thus far there has been little talk of rights in relation to the account of roles. This may seem natural: the current discussion relates primarily to ethics, not political philosophy and thus we shouldn't expect to see talk of rights. That may be so, but I do not believe that political philosophy and ethics are clearly distinct. Additionally when we think about what one ought to do we often begin with an injunction to respect the rights of others: human, legal, etc. Moreover, given that we think of rights as following in virtue of who a person and I am arguing that morality is grounded in identity we should be able to find the origin of rights in the same area.

Rights can be thought of as entitlements in a context. One has rights in virtue of the roles one occupies and retains them so long as those roles are occupied. They are the flip side of the commitments that constitute the norms that follow from roles that I have been more concerned with. Roles are particularized to a certain group and are reciprocal in the sense that they relate me to other people. As such I am bound to obey certain norms in virtue of my role and they are bound to obey certain norms (which may or may not be the same) in virtue of their reciprocal role. Because roles are particularized and relational and hence reciprocal rights are reciprocal.

Rights are of many sorts. In fact, the failure to distinguish various sorts of rights causes all sorts of confusion in philosophy, politics, and law. I have rights in virtue of roles. Human rights are rights I have in virtue of my role as a human being. I would add that beyond what we think of as human rights normally there are rights to respect of autonomous self-conscious rational beings that follow from those characteristics. Political rights are those that follow from being part of a polity. These will vary depending on citizenship status and perhaps other factors. Civil rights are those that flow from being a person in a society.[1]

Legal rights are those which are articulated and affirmed by positive

---

1 In common parlance we often conflate civil and political rights, but there is an important difference. Members of society can have civil rights but no political rights—for example, women in Nineteenth Century America had civil rights but often lacked political rights concerning the vote and participation in juries.

law. As a legal person (i.e., a person within the meaning of the applicable law) within a society there is a structure of rights and remedies—though not all legal rights have remedies necessarily—that defines what it means to be a legal person. None of these areas need be co-extensive: I may have a human right that is not affirmed in a political right or civil right. In the same way I may have human, political, or civil rights that are not legal rights. Much confusion in philosophy, politics, and law flows from the failure to make important distinctions based on the many roles one occupies and that cannot or cannot easily be forfeited. By talking just about rights sans phrase we end up talking past each other and engage in fruitless, though extraordinary bitter, debates.

We should also think of rights in terms of other roles even though there is no relation to legal rights, or at least little relation. Professional roles grant rights as do familial roles. I am a brother and so I have duties to aid my siblings in need when I can. In the same way if I am in need I have the right to ask for reasonable aid. Parents have duties of affection and care for their children and rights to affection and obedience from their children. Friendship also works this way, though, because we tend to speak of rights so concretely and formally, it seems a bit off. This is so because the dynamics and existence of friendships can change quickly. Nonetheless I have duties to my friends and a right to expect and receive aid and support from them.

There is obviously much more to be said about rights, but thinking about them in relation to roles is, I believe, a good way to make progress on better understanding how they work. We talk of rights quite a bit, but the concept is slippery and we often fail to distinguish the sort of right we are talking about. There are many sorts that play out in various ways. Not all rights have the force of law behind them, but that doesn't make them something else. We can still talk about them as rights so long as we are careful to understand that rights are of various sorts. Here I only point out that it is quite natural to think of roles and rights together. Roles can be viewed as a set of commitments and entitlements, or duties and rights. Identity is constituted, then, by a system of commitments and entitlements that are indexed to various contexts.[1]

---

1 There is an important difference between duty and right aspects of a role that is worth noting. One has duties to other things and this may include things not active in moral space. One has rights, however, only in relation to things in moral space. So we can speak of animal rights in the sense that because of the value they have in moral space we occupy we have duties to animals but it does not make sense to talk about rights we have as against animals because it doesn't make sense to ascribe full-fledged duties to them. If a bear attacks a human we will euthanize it to protect humans, but we will not say that the bear has acted wrongly because it breached a duty and violated a right the human had. We may term the bear "bad" and say it isn't behaving as it ought to, but we will not use such language whole-heartedly

Roles and Universal Norms

Norms, I have argued, are grounded in roles. I ought to do x because I am y. I ought to be y because I am z. And so on. We all are constituted by a complex system of roles and thus are subject to a set of differing norms that vary by role and hence by situation. In chapter eleven I will address the theoretical worry that this leads directly to an unacceptable form of relativism whereby any act or role can be morally correct so long as one simply adopts the appropriate role.

But there is a related worry: if norms are grounded on roles and roles are many and context dependent am I not adopting a situational ethics in which there are no general norms that ought to guide one (even if they are not the same for everyone)? This is sometimes thought to be just as bad as relativism because it seems to allow people to act immorally by simply anchoring the advantageous to a situation and shedding moral obligations. Put another way, we like general rules that state universal norms. For example, many assert that the key universal norm is the golden rule, in one form do unto others as you would wish done unto you. Many religions and cultures have some form of this rule, yet if norms turn on roles then there is no place for it.

In a sense this is right and not altogether a deficiency. Three points will bear this out. First, I am looking for more than just norms of action, I want ought to be norms as well. Generalized norms of the universal sort can be stated like this, but they are quite vacuous. The most obvious one is "be a good person" but clearly this does not tell us anything. One might say "be the sort of person you would like others to be" but there is no such person I want all others to be. How I want others to be depends on a variety of factors about our situations. When we ask who and what sort of person one ought to be we can get some traction by looking at ourselves abstractly, but this is not often very helpful because so much does depend on our situation.

Second, though norms flow from roles and some roles come and go and shift in importance, I am by no means saying that there are no general, universal norms that are not always in play. I only have argued that many are and hence that some of the normative terrain will change with roles in my life. A proponent of a single norm cannot blithely charge that there are norms that are always relevant and thus the role account is doomed because that is not ruled out. Rather, she must show that this one universal norm is the *only* norm that is relevant.

and accuse the bear of breaching a duty it owed to the human being in question. Its badness is more akin to a malfunction than to a moral breach. But if a human mistreats his pets we will take the pets away and fine him and are comfortable saying that we do so because as a pet the animal had a right to proper care and that right was violated when the owner failed to fulfill his duties to the animal.

Third, in doing so we back into norms like the golden rule. Most ethical theories have similar norms: maximize the good, do your duty, treat people as ends not means, act only on universalizable norms, do as the virtuous man does, treat all others with dignity, etc. Note that above, however, where these claims got into some trouble was precisely when we started theorizing and trying to figure out what they actually meant. Once we made the norms concrete they stopped seeming so attractive. The same, I hold, is true of all universal norms in a way. Take the golden rule. How do I want others to treat me? Shouldn't I rather treat them as they want to be treated? But what if I know better? Often a roles-based understanding is incorporated: I wonder how to treat a person and to evaluate I ask if I were him and he were me what would I want? But in this analysis the roles are being maintained, I am just thinking about them in terms of a presumed equality of human beings.

This is not to say such universal norms are unimportant. They are good *rules of thumb*, abstract expressions of how to think ethically that when applied in context within the consideration of roles lead to more definite norms. They are good for moralists but just the beginning of an inquiry into who and what sort of person one ought to be. Furthermore, within the identity approach to ethical thought we should see ethical theories as offering rules of thumb of a sort. They offer basic rules, like maximize good consequences or treat other people as ends that are good guides to how we ought to act. But they mistakenly translate these rules of thumb into ultimate moral theories. Rather we should see them as general statements that can function differently from role to role and fit some roles better than others.

For example, it is no surprise that the early utilitarians were focused as much on the behavior of governments as individuals. For them the same principle applied. And reflecting upon the idea of the greatest good for the greatest number in terms of public policy it is much more palatable. The sensible rules are extended to individuals, but here we begin to get more worried and some of the arguments mentioned above have more bite. But we should question the assumption that the same norms will govern the two realms. When we put ourselves in leadership roles it is more natural to think in utilitarian terms, but when our roles are limited to our actions as an individual human being to other human beings these terms are less natural. We can, of course, apply them in various ways but in doing so we often shift the exact meaning of the theory, for example in the move to a more rules based utilitarianism that is more intuitive.

The identity based approach is compatible with the general, universal norms espoused by theorists and moralists. But it understands them in a different way. Norms follow from roles and hence the universal norms that are offered are either tightly linked to a certain variety of roles or the norms themselves are loose enough that there meaning can shift among roles. We should view them not as absolute moral laws, but rules of thumb that are helpful in working out how we ought to act and be given the roles we are playing in a situation.

A Comparison with Ancient Ethics

A similar approach to the one here that looks to identity and uses roles to analyze it can be found in a variant form in ancient ethics and in particular with parts of Stoic ethics. They also stress the importance of norms following from roles and who one is. In order to find out what one ought to do one looks to who and what sort of person one ought to be. Comparing this train of thought with the approach I am offering will clarify just what the approach is and why it doesn't constitute a theory of the sort we actually do find in ancient ethics.

One basic difference mentioned above is that unlike the Stoics modern ethics has, to understate it, difficulty attaching telos to nature. The Stoics— and all ancient ethicists really—find it natural and easy to talk about how we ought to live according to nature because this brings norms with it. Indeed the Peripatetics, Stoics, Epicureans, Cyrenaics, Cynics, and even the Pyrrhonists in their own way all can point to nature as the foundation to their ethics. To live how one ought is to follow nature and so the disagreements are not over the source of norms but rather what exactly it means to live by nature.

And certainly there is lots of disagreement. Aristotle outlines various virtues found in the good man and the natural means that define his life. The Stoics focus more on austere duty, that is, when they aren't obsessed with the mythical wise man who alone is good. Epicureans argue for a life of pleasure, but one defined by what we would term the higher pleasures of pleasant conversation, healthy diet, etc. Cyreniacs adopt a view closer to what is historical called "Epicureanism" and see pleasure as naturally good and thus pursue it. Cynics really want to go back to nature and argue that we ought to behave more like animals and divorce ourselves from civilized mores. The Pyrrhonists, being skeptics, don't have any sort of theory about how to live at all, but when asked how in fact they do get on with life they report that they follow nature and their natural impressions as to what to do and what they have been trained to do.

There is much more variety within each of these views but this isn't the place to set them out or attempt to adjudicate them. Rather we should note that they can all generally agree that we ought to live according to nature. This is an easy way for them to talk and they think that substantive norms do in fact follow from this—there is by nature a way one ought to live. Their debates are really over what exactly is the natural way to live.

Modernity has brought a mechanical conception of nature. This has been good in the sense that our theories have become more fruitful and enabled great technological advances. But it has been troubling because we put ourselves in nature and come to see ourselves as machines and thereby lose our essence as autonomous self-conscious rational beings. This leads us into an unacceptable dilemma: we can re-assert the ancient picture with full force and reject the modern conception of nature or we can reject any robust conception of normativity as incompatible with the modern conception of nature. The former is done predominately with a theological move in which science is either rejected as false because it is incompatible with the revealed truth or is accepted with the caveat that in the end the theological is the ultimate grounding and explanation. This may involve a whole-hearted return to long-standing religions or new fangled spiritualist or mystic moves that differ in content but make the same sort of theological appeal.[1]

The latter forces us to unmask our moral lives and seems to lead to a formless relativism in which anything goes and thus in reality nothing goes at all. Nietzsche saw this most clearly and his prophetic works articulate the landscape after God is dead, or telos is banished from the world. Both responses are nearly impossible to swallow because we *do* have a modern conception of nature and it works quite well and we also *do* live a life that is manifestly full of normative import.

This book, in part, is an attempt to sketch a way out of this dilemma by arguing that if we start where we are rather than with some ultimate theory we can accept both the correctness of the modern conception of nature as it studies the phenomena of the physical world and the reality of moral space as phenomena of being autonomous self-conscious rational beings. If we stop being obsessed with ontology and start by simply understanding the world and our lives from the perspective of what we have we don't have to make grand pronouncements that lead us to the forced choice between unacceptable alternatives. We must remember that we are men, not gods.

Hence I accept, in part at least, the ancient teleological conception of nature and believe with them that it is good to talk about ethics in terms of fulfilling ones nature. To do so, however, we must be clear that we are using variant concepts of nature when engaged in different sorts of intellectual activity. "Nature," then, is a generalized term referring back to the domain of the phenomena being inquired into. The difference between ancient use of nature and my use of nature is essentially that I cannot and do not see a continuity of nature in one grand scheme that encompasses a theory of

---

1 The felt need for the religious infusion of life combined with the stress on authenticity drives many to declare themselves to be "spiritual" which often seems to mean that they are religious but not in the bad old way.

everything because essential features of the space we look into in various inquires are not the same. I haven't made any assertions about what is "real," whatever that means in the end. My approach refuses to engage in prior ontology that serves to limit the fields of inquiry because things we seek an account of are no longer deemed real.

The use of different conceptions of nature is the most obvious and general difference between ancient ethics and the approach I encourage. Put another way, in the current inquiry we cannot see a clear continuity between ethical inquiry and other "scientific" inquiry whereas for ancient ethics there is no difficulty seeing ethics right alongside other forms of inquiry.

There are also more specific differences that will clarify the general conception of identity and roles articulated above. A good place to begin is the passage quoted in the first chapter from Cicero: "Above all we must decide who and what sort of people we want to be, and what kind of life we want to lead; and this is the most difficult question of all."[1] I agree: the most difficult and important questions in ethics boil to who we are and who we ought to be and what kind of life we want to lead. We must figure out based on the roles and circumstances that define us what to do with our lives.

In answering this question I, like Cicero, focus on roles. In sketching the general Stoic approach Cicero points out four sorts of roles that determine duties: the universal, the individual, the chanced, and the chosen. Cicero's universal role is based on our faculty of reason that raises us above the beasts. We all possess reason and based on this feature we all have universal duties as rational animals as to our proper functions. Individual roles are based on the natural difference between people. We share a universal nature for reason but out natures are also individualized based on our peculiar talents. These roles must be understood and create individualized duties for people. For example, those who are naturally mentally gifted at government have duties to govern. In the same way we might argue, with Aristotle notoriously (and certainly Cicero as well), that if by nature we possess the disposition of a slave, we ought to be a slave (and that these natural slaves are better off being enslaved).[2] Both are fulfilling their natures by living according to the individual roles that nature has created.

Roles of chance are those that in the course of life are thrust upon us. For example, being of noble birth or finding oneself with public office are matters of chance. We happen into these roles not by nature but as a matter of our circumstances in the world. Still they are important roles that create duties. The last sort of role is that which is chosen by an individual. Cicero here has in mind predominately professional roles in that we choose to become a

---

1 *On Duties* I.117.
2 Aristotle. *Politics*.

philosopher or a politician or a lawyer, etc. and that when we choose these roles we shape who we are and the duties that bind us.

In these passages Cicero is articulating his conception of duties from a Stoic perspective.[1] Most of the work is done tracing out the duties required of nature rather than analyzing various roles. This is one way what is offered here departs. In my view tracing duties drifts too far towards the moralist, and indeed *On Duties* reads this way: Cicero is ostensibly telling his son all of the duties that he has and urging him to follow them.[2] My aim is different: I want to understand why ethics is so difficult and confounding and hence I am not so much concerned with the exact content of duties but how they come about. For the Stoics this is nature, individual and general and then several other roles are added on. Here I have suggested that things are more complex in that roles create duties and come to be in many different ways, not just by reference to nature.

Still, I agree that there are generalized roles that all humans share and that do create some duties. But I don't extend them as broadly. For example, familial and community roles are for many ancients natural and follow from mans nature. Man is a social animal and as a social animal has duties to his community and friends. There is nothing wrong with this, but I would refer to see it as we in coming to be within a community have a role within that community and duties attendant to it. There is no real difference except that we can get rid of the reference to nature as a rich source of particular duties.

Additionally, I am not prepared to make the clear distinction between individual roles and roles of chance that Cicero is here. For him individual roles are not a matter of chance but rather are one's personal nature requiring that one live up to it. This sort of move leads to the historically popular view that some are by nature powerful, or rich, or slaves, etc. Yet many of these features are more matters of chance than nature's plan. They are natural conditions, in a sense, but they are not part of a grand natural plan for who one ought to be. One's gifts certainly have moral relevance, but they are not so designed to give one some nature that requires one to take on a particular role or would justify the subjugation and denigration of another human because his nature is deficient.

Similarly, the categories I explicated above are more particular and

---

1 Though Cicero identifies most as a member of the new, fallabilistic/ skeptical academy in *On Duties* he explicitly adopts a Stoic approach because it serves him well in his aims. He follows Panaetius, but seems clear that he isn't asserting anything with absolute certainty.

2 Indeed Book I of *On Duties* can be a bit trying to read because it is so moralistically preachy. The style, however, reflects his purpose and a common way of talking ethics through most of history. And of course Cicero was multitalented, including being perhaps the most skilled Roman rhetorician of the day (and perhaps ever). His writing often reflects his rhetorical prowess.

numerous than those identified by Cicero. The key difference is that Cicero is looking at the source of the roles and duties that follow while I am looking at the type of role and duties that follow—the domain of its application. The reason for this difference is that I do not think we can clearly separate the categories by source because roles have their origin and evolution in many different sources: nature, chance externalities, choice, other roles, etc. It is more helpful to think of roles in terms of when they apply and how strongly they do in various contexts and who or what they apply to. This will allow a richer understanding of moral problems and contradictions.

Finally, the Stoics are manifestly offering a theory based on what nature requires while I am just trying to understand our ethical condition by conceptualizing it in terms of roles. So the older Stoics talk of a perfect wise man who we should attempt to emulate (and some go so far as to declare that everyone who is not the wise man is wicked, problematic because the wise man is extremely rare). And Cicero spends lots of time talking about duties we have. The difference is one of focus. I am trying to make sense of the possibility of duty and how to think about situations in which we are ethically torn, not tell everyone that they ought to live according to nature and then tell them what that means.

In my view nature and identity refers to no extrinsic theory but the self-consciousness that emerges in a life in which we have autonomy and rationality and a myriad of roles given only in the sense that that is where we are when ethical inquiry begins. Hence there is no foundation in the sense sought by ancient stoics and uttering "nature" doesn't solve a problem (if anything it exacerbates it). Rather it is a process of understanding what and where we are and clashing out the norms and roles that constitute who we are.

Conclusion: Identity Again

This chapter has made a number of points about roles and how they function to constitute identity. Before moving on it will be helpful to summarize the understanding given of identity so far.

We take on roles in all of aspects of our lives and together they constitute our identity. The sorts of roles that constitute who one is have been incompletely sketched in the previous chapter. No person is made up of just one role but rather a complex system of many. It is not the case that each role forms a sort of separate personality. This would imply that we are to understand identity in terms of a lot of little people making up a large one. Clearly this gets us nowhere for our understanding of how the little people function depends on prior grasp on an individual identity and this is just what we are trying to explain! Moreover in such a picture the very idea of an integrated identity is lost. We must rather think of roles as just that, simple roles that bring with them certain preconditions, dispositions, obligations, and thoughts.

Identity is made up of various roles that stand in various relationships to others. Some are more important than others. In many cases various roles will interact in ways that set the proper action or disposition. Roles can be thought of as rules, or sets of rules. One is a parent and so one behaves as follows. There is no conflict. Conflict arises as roles interact and produce the chaos that is our sense of self and identity. Our lives are rich because we are so many different sorts of things all at the same time and continual mold them to form our unique selves.

The new thought here is not to stress how important roles are. Many people do this. But when we ordinarily talk about roles we think of a separate self that takes various roles on. My claim is more radical and basic— roles are not things that a separate self takes on but rather roles *constitute* the self within the realm of moral understanding. There is no ethereal nameless formless shapeless self that takes on roles. There is a constant temptation when thinking about identity to picture some abstract entity with no form whatsoever. When thinking about roles then we attach roles to this identity. Such a view is a species of what I would term the "name-tag" theory of identity wherein we focus on a label attached to a person and mistakenly reify this.[1] In my view the name tags we attach to people are immaterial— it is the roles and the relation they have to one another that constitute an individual identity.[2] The ethereal self that stands behind anything that can be understood or analyzed is a wheel that does not turn and should be abandoned.

There are three major differences between my discussion of identity and others. First I reject the myth of the ethereal or abstract self that exists separate from any identity and somehow chooses identities. The posit of the ethereal self that is formless and not of this world is a dangerous confusion. Second, most discussions of identity focus on how we differ from one another and operate within cultural, religious, or national types. I am interested in these but am perhaps more interested in the roles we all share as human beings and as members of various communities. Third, often discussions

---

1 The term is taken from Quine's critique of many theories of meaning.
2 Put alternatively: I am an individual Michael S. Perry who has various roles. An attractive mistake is to think that the important piece is that I am "Michael S. Perry" and that this picks out some abstract substance and identity that in turn takes on various roles. I am urging that the important piece for identity is the roles, not the label. Who I am is the roles I occupy even though some of these will change over time. What I am called is "Michael S. Perry." Being so called doesn't magically pick out a formless ethereal self that magically stands behind all of the roles that I live with. Note that this point is entirely separate from how we use proper names as rigid designators.

of identity are compartmentalized into a particular role type and tend to think of one as an *x* or a *y* or etc. In these discussions, that particular type then becomes all important and essential and the expense of the others. This is a mistake, in my view, and this mistake has led to the shape of inquiry into identity. Rather we must think of identity in terms of conjunctions, not disjunctions. I am an *x* and a *y* and etc., and it is in the confluence and relation of these roles that identity is to be found.

We must also distinguish between acting against identity and changing identity. For example, if I betray a friend I do not necessarily end that friendship, though I have acted against that role in so doing. If the betrayal is deep enough or it constitutes a habit or if vacating the friendship is my goal I may end up changing roles by that act. Some roles are more difficult to vacate than others. For example shedding the role of being a member of the PTA is rather easy, shedding the role of a parent is incredibly difficult. I may act so as to compromise both in some way, but in the latter case I will be acting against identity, not changing identity. The distinction between the two is not clear cut—it is one of degree, not kind. Roughly it is when an action leads to consequences that are unsustainable for one given such a role and either no remedial action is possible or if possible undertaken that a role is abandoned and not merely acted against. This distinction emerges in how we judge actions legally and ethically. Given a certain criminal act we show more leniency to one who is acting out of character than to one is acting upon criminal character. The act may be the same, but because in the former case it emerges as an uncharacteristic exception we punish lightly. When someone makes a habit of such behavior or becomes a criminal person then we punish more harshly. The same holds of moral judgment—we are forgiving of wrongs that are done out of and against character while we are not for wrong that emerge from vicious character.

Some roles are more essential to our identity than others. This may by simply by nature, in virtue of facts about our context, or in virtue of choices we have made in the past. We can change roles—sometimes in radical ways— but can do so only by keeping most other roles in place. Natural roles and familial roles are generally more central than professional and communal roles. Being a member of the PTA is part of who I am but not a big part. It can be easily shed without much loss. It may even be the case that it is beneficial to do so because it brings balance to myself—I may occupy other roles in some tension with that particular role.

Usually when we think of roles as something we take on rather than something that make us up we think of roles that are peripheral to our identity. Since these are easily shed with little change it is easy to see them in this way. But if we try to imagine shedding all of our roles or even shedding the most important roles we inhabit we quickly lose ourselves. For any parent it may be almost impossible to imagine oneself as not a parent. It would make one a different person. Religious believers often feel the same way. We might be able to imagine people who are different and even sketch what life would look like if we were that way, but because what we are changing is so important what we see is no longer ourselves.

Further, imagine that one changed every role one occupies. Is one the same person? Surely not—everything about one has changed in a drastic way and there is no continuity. In a mental sense such a change would be akin to death. The ethereal self is a myth. If there were such a self we should be able to make sense of changing every role and yet remaining the same person. Yet this is difficult. The only way I can imagine this is if there were some traumatic event that caused a radical mental break. But here we would say that I had become a different person and was deeply sick. Though we can make sense of persisting through some change in role the thought of radical change in all roles is absurd and hence we must accept that we are the roles we inhabit.

Change in roles occurs by holding many other roles in place. Often when faced with a crisis that requires me to reconcile competing roles or to change one I will rely more heavily on other roles that are not up for grabs. This is especially the case with quite important roles. Think of an important friendship that for one reason or another one is repudiating. In this process it is natural to turn to other roles as the basis on which to define oneself anew without this friendship. By doing so we can maintain a real continuity of the self through change in the self. Important parts or aspects can change but only because most do not. No one role need be privileged in this process—it may be the case that all roles can be open to question—but the condition of the continuity of identity is that through any change most roles remain the same—it may not be the case all roles can be open to question at the same time. This process of both conscious and unconscious self-evolution and development makes clear how we are the same person over time but also come to see that who we are has changed over the course of life. Both senses of the self are worthy of preserving. Of course over time we are the same person but we also recognize that who we are changes. Taking on board an analysis of identity in terms of a web of a plurality of roles allows us to understand both the sense in which we remain the same person throughout our lives while also changing who we are in important ways.

No doubt it is tempting to be left with the nagging feeling that there is something left out here, some ethereal self that is formless and stands behind all roles. This must be resisted if we are ever to understand identity. No matter how identity is analyzed a similar urge will remain. This is so because we are self-conscious, we reflect as ourselves on ourselves and thus are led to see the reflector and reflected as somehow different and picture the self-conscious reflector as some undefined being occupying the view from nowhere and dispassionately bracketing the first-order self that lives in the real world.

The only way to countenance the ethereal self as fundamentally different is to posit something as "analysis" that is entirely unclear, e.g., the soul, and then not analyze this. I have nothing against the idea of the soul—indeed I think it is a good one, though unfortunately laden with too much dogmatic theology.[1] What I am resisting is the thought that we can define our identities by reference to a soul and then say nothing more about what the soul is while pretending to arrived at something profound and enlightening. Such a move would rescue the ethereal self but at the cost of eliminating any understanding. If we seek understanding and then attempt to analyze what the soul is we will be right back to the original project. I will claim that the soul is the network of roles one inhabits and again we will feel as if we have lost the ethereal self. The temptation must be resisted by focusing on roles we cannot shed. By doing so we can accept that we are the roles we inhabit. Identity is complex and fluid system of many roles and though it may change with a change in roles—something we should hope for in any theory—it is constitutionally dependent upon the roles we inhabit.

---

1 The use of "soul" in ancient philosophy is much less theory-laden. Used as that which makes humans essentially different from non-humans "soul" is a nice term. But over the history of thought so many different conceptions of what that exactly is have been built into the term that it is too confusing to be worth relying on.

Chapter Nine: The Identity Approach in Practice

In the last few chapters I have sketched an approach to grounding norms that focuses on identity and then understands identity as a systematic, dynamic web of roles. To add to this picture it is helpful to consider some examples of how various roles shift in different areas and lead to ethical confusion and conflict. This will pave the way for understanding moral dilemmas. Below I offer an extended discussion of legal ethics. By focusing on roles we can understand the conflicts and tensions lawyers face and how they might deal with them. Next I offer a few other examples designed to show how we can understand ethical problems and intuitions that are common, in particular business ethics and how to think about the varying ethical obligations of those in leadership positions or acting as state agents. I then turn to how we can understand and accept both solidarity and cosmopolitanism by looking to roles as constituting identity and thus as the basis for various sorts of normative commitments. The chapter concludes with a sketch of how we can understand the common phenomenon of addiction and recovery in terms of the self as defined by roles. The addict's roles have been severely compromised by the addiction and the unwanted but acquired role of being an addict. Though the issue is immensely complicated, my explication of identity can be better understood by using addiction and recovery as an example. My aim here is to provide discussions of concrete topics in terms of identity and roles. The discussions both explicate how the identity approach works and, hopefully, provide enlightening comments on the topics discussed.

Lawyers and Legal Ethics

Lawyers are often, sometimes rightly, derided as morally depraved individuals driven only to make money by subverting justice.[1] They are accused of stirring up disputes when the two parties could easily resolve the problem without resorting to the legal system. They are viewed as amoral beings who use technicalities and confusing arguments to thwart justice. They are charged with both shopping for plaintiffs in order to make a quick buck and of protecting corporations and the rich through prolonged legal maneuvering. They prevent the wronged from getting their due and keep evil-doers from being held accountable.

Many lawyers, however, view these criticisms as misplaced and based on a misunderstanding of our legal system and the duties incumbent upon lawyers. Indeed, lawyers are taught and are, at least in theory, accountable to an ethical code. Law schools require some course in legal ethics. To be admitted to the bar they must pass a legal ethics test and if they deviate from their duties as a lawyer they can be sanctioned. So from one perspective lawyers appear to be devoid of ethics altogether, while from another they are tightly bound by duty based on their profession. How can we make sense of this?

Actually it is quite easy, at least to begin with. There is a disconnect between the duties that follow from being part of the legal profession and the ordinary duties that one has as an individual in daily life. This in and of itself is not extraordinary because lots of professions have ethical codes that govern conduct as a member of that profession. Lawyers are particularly interesting, however, because their code produces situations in which conduct appears decidedly at odds with what appears to be required for non-lawyers. Thus for those outside of the profession lawyers appear evil precisely because as lawyers they are responding to a different set of norms that those on the outside do not know and do not understand. Lawyers become frustrated with the criticism because they believe that in their ordinary lives outside of their profession they are morally upright human beings and that as lawyers they are morally upright because they follow the norms that guide their conduct as lawyers.

The key ethical norm that creates the confusion—and problem—is that lawyers are duty-bound to serve their clients and further the interests of their client.[2] There are limitations. Lawyers also have duties to the court as

---

1 By no means is this a new phenomenon: in Aristophanes' *Clouds* on of the foremost indictments of Socrates as a representative of the sophists is that he teaches people how succeed in court through tricks that make the unjust argument stronger.
2 The ABA model rules set out a duty of representation, divide authority for decisions between lawyer and client, and specify limits to representation,

officers of the court. They cannot knowingly suborn perjury by their client or witnesses, cannot disobey court orders, cannot hide documents and other evidence that their adversary has a right to, cannot mislead the court about the relevant law, cannot knowingly bring exceedingly frivolous suits, etc. But the key point is that the primary duty of a lawyer, and the one that causes the most ethical problems, is to best serve the client, not to see that in the end justice is done. It is a duty of the justice system, both criminal and civil, to see that justice is done and disputes are resolved in a fair and proper way. But lawyers are part of that system, not the system itself. Their job in our adversarial system is to do the best for their client within the rules.

I am not concerned with the caricature of the immoral lawyer who bends and breaks all of the rules. Actions disapproved of by many, like ambulance chasing, are against legal codes of ethics. The interesting problem is lawyers who are duty-bound to act in a certain way as lawyers but who nonetheless are often viewed as immoral because of those actions. Some examples will help explain what is going on and provide a better understanding of how shifting roles causes potential problems.

Civil: Plaintiffs' Attorneys

Plaintiff's attorneys are derided for bringing frivolous claims on behalf of clients and demanding exurbanite damages. They are motivated only by money and sue corporations and people with deep pockets in order to, in effect, coerce them into a settlement that is undeserved. Attorneys cost a lot of money and lawsuits bring bad press and so even when a claim is without merit a defendant's best choice is often to simply reach a quick settlement without admitting fault if initial motions to dismiss and (maybe) motions for summary judgment fail. So long as the plaintiff can plead a case that alleges conduct that by law is actionable motions to dismiss will fail. And so long as there is some factual basis for these allegations motions for summary judgment will fail. Hence even when a defendant believes that they are not at fault they may be forced to pay a settlement that proves a windfall for a meritless defendant and, of course, the attorney as well.

A popular and well-known example of this sort of case is the woman who sued McDonalds because its coffee was too hot. The woman in question ordered coffee at a McDonald's drive-through. At the time, the cups themselves did not contain warnings that the coffee was hot. Of course, coffee is generally hot unless ordered cold, and so this should have been obvious. But, plaintiff alleged, McDonald's coffee was *really* hot. She drove

---

such as engaging in crime or fraud on behalf of or with the client. The goals of representation are given to the client, not the lawyer. The lawyer is primarily responsible for determining the strategy to be used, within specified bounds, to achieve those goals.

off with the coffee, proceeded to spill it on herself, and suffered very painful burns. She sued McDonalds to recover damages.

Most people believe this to be a frivolous and altogether silly suit. Coffee is hot and she spilled it on herself. That is her fault, not McDonalds'. We are sorry that she suffered the injuries she did, and indeed they were quite serious, but we do not think that McDonalds should bear the responsibility for those injuries. A reasonable jury would likely find for McDonalds in the case, since it would hold that any reasonable person would know that coffee is hot and can burn you, if you spill it on yourself. But that is not what happened. The jury found for the plaintiff and awarded damages. This was appealed, but the parties then settled without McDonalds admitting fault. Plaintiff and her attorney received a sizable sum of money. And McDonalds now warns us in several places that coffee is, indeed, quite hot. Most of us find these (and the multitude of other warnings of obvious dangers placed on consumer products) silly, but they are there because they help foreclose the possibility of being sued by someone ignorant of obvious dangers.[1]

Such cases make people dislike lawyers and decry them as money-driven plagues on society. They look at the case and believe that the correct outcome is that McDonalds wins and the plaintiff and lawyer are given a sound scolding by the judge. Instead, the lawyer was able to drum up sympathy for an injured victim against a giant faceless corporation (we can easily imagine a juror thinking, "it would be nice for that poor women to get some help with her terrible injuries and pain, and McDonalds can surely afford it") and in the end exact ransom from the company to make the case go away. The plaintiff and lawyer recovered because McDonalds judged it better for its reputation and bottom line to end the litigation than to keep litigating what it thought was a winning appeal.

From a lawyer's perspective, however, the situation is quite different. When someone is injured and seeks to recover by the party he or she believes to be at fault the lawyer evaluates the case to see if it is plausible. If the lawyer believes that there is a case for the injured party then he or she may take the party on as a client. At this point the ethical situation changes

---

1 This happens because in the eyes of the law everyone is generally informed about dangers mentioned on labels, even if they did not read them or indeed if no reasonable person reads them but if there are no labels is only thought to be informed of what the jury thinks a reasonable person would expect. This incentivizes warnings for any possible dangers because what a reasonable person is informed of is up to the jury and given serious injuries big companies do not get a lot of sympathy and because even if it is an obvious danger getting a jury to say that means going through a trial and that costs money. The result: ridiculous numbers of warnings of obvious dangers. This isn't because lawyers are stupid—it is because they are smart and doing the best they can for the company they are working for given the way these cases work.

dramatically. The lawyer is now acting towards the client in the role of the lawyer and the professional norms that define that relationship govern his or her ethical duties within that role. That means that the lawyer must do the best possible for the client within the bounds set by the court and other norms of professional conduct. The duty is not to reach what the lawyer, standing outside the role of lawyer *for that client* believes all things considered to be the correct outcome, but to operate within the role of the lawyer to serve the client's interests.

So in the McDonalds case the lawyer believed that there was a case to be made and that it was not frivolous, if we assume a lawyer operating within the rules of professional conduct. Some lawyers, of course, do not do so and are really just extorting parties with deep pockets. This may well be a case in which there was such a lawyer. I don't know. But there are many cases that are questionable that nonetheless are viable and not frivolous. In these the duty of the lawyer is to best serve the client and that is what is being done. It is the job of the civil justice system as a whole to ensure that the just outcome is achieved as often as possible. Perhaps it fails to do this and reforms are needed. But then the objection is to the rules of the system, not the operation of the lawyer who is following the norms that bind one in the role of a lawyer.

Civil: Defendants' Attorneys

Plaintiffs' attorneys in civil cases are not alone in being subject to moral scorn by many people—defendants' attorneys are also viewed as morally bankrupt villains seeking only money. Whereas plaintiffs' attorneys generally bill on a contingency basis—they only get paid if their client recovers something—defendants' attorneys generally bill by the hour. Most large law firms represent clients with deep pockets, usually corporations and other business interests. Their motivation is to frustrate plaintiffs even if the aggrieved party has a legitimate claim. Their clients have money and may often be willing to pay lawyers exorbitant fees to make cases go away, especially if they may be forced to admit fault or a settlement may lead to numerous other cases that could cost them in the long run.

These lawyers are derided for selling out justice and defending the powerful bad actors to get rich. They use every possible mean to delay trials and prevent lawsuits. They produce massive amounts of paper designed to overwhelm wronged plaintiffs and use obscure rules to prevent justice from being served.

As above this can cross the line within legal ethics. Motions that are made must have some basis in law. Yet within reasonable bounds such lawyers are acting ethically proper within their role as lawyers. They too are cogs in the system and their clients have enrolled them to seek the best possible outcome. Thus they explore every way possible to secure a favorable outcome and work hard at doing it because their clients are paying them to do just that. Their ethical duty is not to the plaintiff and it is the job of the system to produce proper outcomes, not the attorney for one party. As lawyers, they are doing what they are duty bound to do, even though evaluated within the broader scheme of things their conduct can appear morally deficient.

Criminal: Representing the Guilty

Another criticism of lawyers is that they are willing to represent evil people they know to be guilty and work to ensure that justice is not done, the opposite of what the criminal justice system is supposed to do. This criticism relates to all defense attorneys to some degree but is especially targeted at lawyers for rich clients and lawyers for clients who are notorious and whose cases are prominent in the media. Paradigm cases of the first are mob bosses and celebrities who have committed awful crimes. Think, for example, about the O.J. Simpson case. Some people were disgusted with the defense lawyers because they did everything possible to obscure what was believed to be clear evidence and were able, by expending extraordinary resources, to free a (supposed) killer. Why would they do this? The evidence was clear and yet they seemed more interested in freeing a guilty man and pocketing lots of money than seeing that justice was done for the victims.

The second sort of case is exemplified by lawyers who defend terrorists. Indeed many lawyers *rush* to defend notorious terrorists whose trials are of great public interest. Or, when there is no trial, they file briefs on their behalf, even though they do not know them, and try to make it hard for the government to conduct the war on terror. Many in the public see these people as perpetrators of evil attacks on innocent civilians and continuing threats to our national security. Yet lawyers line up to defend them and try to secure their release. The lawyer becomes famous and gets to bask in the limelight. But if the lawyer is successful a terrorist may do more damage in the future and cost American lives. How could one do such a thing?

The lawyer's answer should be clear from above: in our system the lawyer in his role as a lawyer has a primary ethical duty to the client, not some abstract notion of ultimate justice (or more accurately, it is to justice but his part in achieving justice is to advocate for a client). In his roles outside of the profession he may have ethical duties to support national security or see the clearly guilty punished, but within his role as a lawyer a different sort of ethical norms are in force and these compel actions that the public may find ethically deficient.

Criminal: Constitutional Violations and Technicalities

The same holds for another criticism often made of lawyers: that they fish for constitutional violations that are really good faith mistakes in order to get criminals off on a technicality. The evidence is clear and the person in question is guilty. But somewhere a mistake was made and that undermines the case. Justice is not served and the bad actor is set free to continue in his nefarious ways.

A lawyer responds by pointing out that his duty is to do the best for his client and that our legal system is structured to enforce constitutional protections for the accused. If it was not, police and prosecutors would have no real deterrent against violating the constitutional rights we enjoy. Those who find it ethically abhorrent that the guilty go free on constitutional technicalities should direct their ire at the rules that are part of our system or, more appropriately, at the police and prosecutors who committed the constitutional violation in the first place. The lawyer's duty is to do the best for the client, and that is exactly what is being done. Indeed, a defense lawyer in his role as lawyer representing a defendant could fulfill his ethical obligations as a lawyer by exploiting inadvertent constitutional violations to free his client while at the same time believing in his role as citizen or legal/constitutional thinker believe that it is his duty to advocate changing the rules so that these violations do not undermine the evidence in question. This can be consistent because the roles that govern the duties in play change in significant ways.

Criminal: Plea Bargaining

Both prosecutors and lawyers for defendants are derided based on the practice of plea bargaining. Plea bargaining is ubiquitous in the criminal justice system, just as negotiated settlements are prevalent in the civil system. The vast majority of cases are resolved through plea bargains to lesser charges or on the condition of a recommended lesser sentence. Our criminal justice system could not function without it—quickly it would be so overburdened that it would cease to operate. Yet the practice is questionable. Often criminals are convicted of charges that are vastly less serious than their actual conduct and receive slap on the wrist sentences for serious malfeasance. On the other hand, we worry that the innocent are coerced into pleading guilty to offenses they did not commit because if they go to trial they risk a long sentence in prison. The accused is deprived of the constitutional right to trial through coercion. Of course the accused has the choice to go to trial, but it is a forced choice because of the leverage the prosecution has.

The prosecutor is sometimes viewed as ethically deficient for both of these reasons. First, part of the goal of punishment is to give the criminal what he deserves based on his actual conduct. Plea bargaining leads to convictions for lesser crimes. Though sentencing regimes sometimes work to counteract this, they cannot achieve the desired end. Prosecutors can choose charges that carry maximum sentences below what would be given if the criminal was convicted of the actual conduct. Additionally, prosecutors have a great deal of control over recommended sentences and the facts that are presented in the sentencing phase. The accusation against them is that they are forsaking their duties to society in order to make their jobs easier and avoid trials that might be difficult.

On the other side, they can be accused of failing in their ethical duties because they coerce defendants into pleading guilty when they really want a trial. They can threaten so much possible harm and exact conditions that the accused has an anathema to. We value a criminal justice system that protects the constitutional rights embodied in a trial and uses juries and rules of evidence to ensure that the innocent go free. Prosecutors can make the risk of trial so great that defendant's are compelled to forfeit rights and even plead guilty to crimes they are innocent of committing.

But from the perspective of the prosecutor plea bargaining practices are in many ways ethically compelled within the role of a lawyer and specifically a prosecutor. Trials are expensive and there are simply too many criminal cases for the system to handle if most went to trial. In order to keep the system working we need plea bargaining. Prosecutors exercise discretion as to what is appropriate in each case to best serve the needs of its client, society as a whole. In response to the other accusation the prosecutor can point out that he is working within a system and is not denying any rights. His duty is to punish those who have committed criminal acts and part of the way this is achieved is by offering deals that benefit both parties. Of course lines can be crossed, but within his role as a prosecutor he isn't subverting the constitution. He is doing his job. If we are troubled with this aspect of plea bargaining then we should change the way the system works, not direct our ire at prosecutors doing their jobs.

Defendant's lawyers are also sometimes accused of ethical failings in the plea bargaining process because they use the fact that the judicial system is strained and needs to avoid most trials to get better deals than their clients deserve. On this accusation the same point made above applies: as a lawyer the duty is to the client and simply playing by the rules of the game shows no ethical failing as a lawyer. If we don't like the practice, we should invest more to eliminate this leverage defendant's lawyers have.

It does, however, get more complicated. Imagine the following example, inspired by an actual case from New York in the 1970s.[1] A child has disappeared and a man has been arrested. The evidence against him is solid. Witnesses saw him take the child, the child's blood has been found on his clothes, a murder weapon has been found, another witness saw him attack the child at another location, he has a long criminal history, he has confessed to police, though he now wishes to retract the confession, etc. But after a week of searching the body cannot be found. The man is very familiar with the large woods in the area and it is believed that he hid the body in a place that authorities have had no luck finding. He will not divulge the location of the body and the parents of the child are distraught for both personal and religious reasons. They want to give their child a decent burial but cannot do so.

The case has gained lots of media attention and the public has called for the prosecutor to seek the death penalty. She has indicated in no uncertain terms that she will. The defendant retains counsel and indicates that he will plead guilty and accept life in prison without the possibility of parole if the death penalty is taken off of the table. Counsel presents this to the prosecutor but it is roundly rejected. The only information that the defendant has that is wanted is the location of the body. The defendant tells his lawyer where it can be found. The lawyer, knowing better than to blindly trust the defendant, verifies the location of the body.

Now the lawyer goes to the prosecutor and says that if the death penalty is off of the table, the defendant will plead guilty to the crime and reveal the location of the body. The prosecutor rejects this and demands to know the location of the body. The parents appeal to the lawyer personally to just tell them where the body is so that they can give the child a decent burial. The lawyer refuses, saying that he cannot do this because it is protected privileged information and his client has directed that it be used only to secure a better deal.

It doesn't matter what happens next in the story—the moral dilemma should be evident. As a human being most if not all would agree that the lawyer has a duty to tell the parents where the body is. Indeed by not doing so the lawyer becomes complicit in inflicting further injury on the family and a greater loss of dignity for the child. But as a lawyer the duty is to his client and his client's sole wish is to avoid the death penalty. The only way to do this is to withhold the location of the body as leverage in the negotiations. In a way, the lawyer's actions are an exemplar of professional ethics because of how difficult the situation is. We can understand the ethical norms in play much better once we look at the various roles in play. Lawyers, of course,

---

1 *See* Alibrandi, Tom and Armani, Frank *Privileged Information*. The case is a standard example in legal ethics. It is used mainly as a way to think about attorney-client privilege.

are often quite unethical, but the easy accusations of them miss the mark precisely because they evaluate the conduct that is undertaken by someone in one role from the perspective of an entirely different role.

The Problem Transformed

The above analysis does not and is not meant to demonstrate that all lawyers are ethical or that lawyers who are generally ethical face no ethical problem. There are morally deficient lawyers who are in it for fame or money and are willing to behave wrongly to achieve their goals. But these lawyers are failing to fulfill their duties as lawyers—in terms of their duties within the role of the lawyer they have gone astray. Even if they strictly follow the rules of conduct they may engage in unethical behavior based on other roles that their roles as a lawyer does not compel. For example, someone might represent a client adequately but do so for devious reasons that contradict duties of other sorts (e.g., imagine a lawyer who represents a party well but chooses that client based on unfounded and spiteful animosity to the adversary or the lawyer/law firm that represents the adversary). These duties are not abrogated on account of one acting within one's role as a lawyer because the norms that define that role have no bearing on those issues and decisions.

Neither have I shown or attempted to show that all lawyers do not face an ethical problem. They do. Indeed they face a general moral dilemma in that their duties that follow professional role as a lawyer may, and likely will, come to conflict with other duties that follow from other roles, such as the role of a citizen, a member of a community, a member of a religious group, an adherent of a philosophy, a member of a political or social movement, or simply being an autonomous self-conscious rational being. What I have attempted to show is that the common ethical derision of lawyers confuses the real problem. To understand the ethical situation lawyer's face we must transform the problem from criticism from the outside to an analysis of how a lawyer can and should balance roles with sometimes conflicting ethical norms. By doing so we can better understand the ethical situation and hopefully the way various roles that form who we are create the moral dilemmas we confront in our lives.

Possible Solutions

There are several ways to resolve or deal with the problem, or tension, explicated above. I will survey four. The first solution is quite easy: don't be a lawyer. The same holds for many other professions and, indeed, for all sorts of roles. If you want to be able to be subject to consistent and relatively tension-free sets of norms throughout your life, then you must not take on roles that would upset the moral harmony you think you have. And when you are faced with a real tension one or more roles must be abandoned. For a lawyer who comes to believe that he cannot reconcile defending evil corporations or known criminals, etc. with his other roles in life and that his profession is causing him to live in bad faith, this solution is the way out. Find a different profession. This, of course, is easier said than done for financial and other reasons. But it does solve the problem.

Second, a lawyer can engage in a radical sort of insulation of roles and thereby erase the tension. This way of solving the problem means a whole-hearted embrace of the profession. The lawyer is governed by one set of norms in ordinary life (though these will shift from context to context as roles change and interact) and an entirely different set of norms as a lawyer, within the profession. Importantly, the norms that follow from being a lawyer have *no* bearing on the norms that govern other roles and the norms that govern other roles have *no* bearing on one's activities as a lawyer. This is why the solution is one that looks to *radical* insulation. It is not that the shape the norms take change as the roles in play change, it is that when the lawyer is engaged in professional life the norms that define the role of a lawyer are the *only* norms in play.

This solves the problem because now there need not be any worry about contradictions. Since the insulation erases the bearing of one set of norms on all other sets of norms there will never be an actual contradiction or even tension in life. For there to be such a problem there would need to be some stance the person could take in which all of the norms are in play at once, but this is exactly what is being rejected. This solves the problem in its way, but at the same time it creates a new one. The deep issue this person confronts is that we *want* to have a stance or perspective that we can take such that we can understand our life and roles in a unified way and are not split into radically separate selves. We are rational, autonomous, self-conscious beings and this person is losing something by splitting her identity so cleanly. There is a trace of Dr. Jekyll and Mr. Hyde in play here—two identities in one person that are different and do not interact. There is something deficient in a life and identity that cannot be unified.

The third way out of the problem is for the lawyer to develop an over-arching narrative or theory that places him and his particular duties as a lawyer within a larger system that fulfills, or at least aims to fulfill, duties that are in harmony with the other ethical obligations we have. This is both an optimistic and humble response. Above the thread that connected that various indictments of the lawyer was that in some way their practice perverted justice. This is troubling to a lawyer who is unwilling to embrace a radical isolation. But the lawyer can develop the following line of reasoning.

I am part of a legal system and my actions are guided by rules of professional conduct. Our legal system is based on adversarial representation and hearing of disputes. The goal of the legal system as a whole is to arrive at the just resolution of disputes and cases. This end is consistent with other ethical duties. My particular actions may not be consistent when viewed individually, but this is the wrong perspective to take. The lawyer is one gear in a massive legal system and must be understood, ethically, in the context of the system as a whole. Hence by taking actions that viewed individually are morally in tension or even contradiction with other duties the system is best served and the system itself does serve ends that are in harmony with the norms that govern one in other roles and as a human being.

What are we to make of this? Well it is humble in that the lawyer does and must claim that he alone is not in the business of seeking justice. He plays a particular role in a larger whole that seeks justice. It is also optimistic in that such a lawyer places blind faith in a legal system believing that it does in fact achieve justice even though he may work at times to thwart it. The moral resolution of the problem thus is wholly contingent upon the virtue of the legal system. And it is here that we run into trouble. Our legal system is good, but there is plenty of room for improvement. Money matters. Race matters. The ability to drown the other side in paper is powerful. Sometimes criminal verdicts go wrong.

This is not an essay directed at legal reform. The only point I wish to make and need is that for a person who hinges the resolution between the lawyer-role and other roles on the legal system as a whole there is still a great deal of uneasiness. For example, take an attorney at a large corporate law firm who is representing a client that has caused a lot of damage through reckless environmental practices. He knows this. He knows the harm that has been caused, but nonetheless it is his duty as a lawyer to do whatever possible to limit liability as much as possible and make cases go away. He also knows that the victims of the damage have almost no resources to get adequate help. Now imagine this person also believes he has a duty, as a person and citizen and parent, to work to protect the environment. His professional work is anathema to this duty, but he tries to solve the problem by reference to the system as a whole. Such a person would have to be naïve or willfully ignorant to think that in the end his real values are served by a system when he knows that he will likely prevail and thwart the values he seeks in his life as a whole. Reference to the system does help resolve the tension I have been pointing to, but it cannot be the last word.

The final possible response I will consider is that the lawyer should design her practice such that she is not put into situations in which her professional duties are in deep tension with the duties she has taken on based on other roles she plays. To continue the example above, the resolution for a lawyer who is deeply committed to the environment would be to not work for a big firm that represents companies that pollute the environment. She need not engage in a practice that helps the environment (though of course she could). She could instead work in an area in which those kinds of cases do not come up. If one cannot reconcile defending the guilty or notorious bad actors, then one should not be a criminal defense attorney (unless, of course, one is willing and able to be very picky). Rather pursue a different area of law. These sorts of moves do not erase the tensions since the role of a lawyer changes the normative landscape in important ways. But hopefully deep conflicts between roles can be avoided and one can learn to live with the tension in other ways.

The problem with this approach is two-fold. First, it is overly optimistic in thinking that conflicts will in fact be limited by restricting one's practice. It is unrealistic to think that there is simply one situation a lawyer will find herself in that will be ethically troubling based on other roles and their norms. Once we move from a one-dimensional analysis to an actual human life, moral dilemmas will emerge and be very challenging, especially given that a lawyer cannot control all of the situations she is put in. Second, there are practical questions that bear on defining one's practice. For example, it is hard for most lawyers to make a living and also exercise the requisite control over their practice. Law is a profession and lawyers need work to survive. Radically limiting one's practice to clients and issues one is ethically at one with in other respects will likely prevent a successful career.

There is a fifth "solution" worth mentioning, though I put it in scare quotes because in the end I don't think it is any solution at all. Above the first way out was to not be a lawyer. Conversely, one might think that a lawyer could abandon all of the roles that come into conflict with the norms that follow from the lawyer-role. We can imagine here someone who cares only for the duties of the profession and nothing else. It should be clear why this isn't really a solution. Certainly this can be done sometimes in that we can shed some roles. But some roles follow by nature in that we enter normative space by becoming autonomous self-conscious rational beings and that role, as well as others that follow from it or are related to it, are one's we can deny but not shed. If this were not so we would be forced to conclude that a mass murderer could be an ethically fit person if he discarded any roles that conflicted with his role as a mass murderer. Normative tension among roles defines who we are and cannot be escaped. Some roles, like professional roles, we can abandon to relieve this tension. But we cannot abandon all roles in favor of one and eliminate the tension altogether. To attempt to do so is to live in bad faith because one attempts to abandon roles that cannot be divested from oneself.

Business Ethics

I have focused on legal ethics because I am familiar with it and because it nicely illustrates the way roles function. Lawyers comprise a profession with an ethical code that is more or less explicit and conflicts in some clear ways with ordinary views. Professional roles will often have explicit codes, though of course this depends on the profession. Likewise, the codes that bind various professions will differ in how much tension they create with intuitive views about what is morally correct. The above analysis could fairly easily be imported, for instance, into medicine, though the contours of the conflicts and how they play out would vary.

Once we have this sort of analysis clear it can be easily expanded to other issues that are less defined but quite problematic. For example, consider business ethics. Generally it is the subject of what norms businesses and those running them ought to follow. Some people outright deny there is such a thing. But interestingly they do so for different reasons. Some argue that there is no such thing as business ethics because they same norms that govern a person in daily life govern that person in business.[1] From this perspective business ethics is a fallacious way to try to lessen or change ordinary moral norms and should be resisted. On the other hand there are those who claim that there is no such thing as business ethics because in the role of a businessman or woman one has a duty solely to do what is best for the company, to make money. Business ethics is wrongheaded because it tries to import ordinary moral norms into a practice that has no place for them. Business is business, and the only reason to do good or play fair, etc., is the benefit of the company.

Both views are misguided. I agree with them that it is wrong to see business ethics as a separate field, but at the same time I think that the moral landscape changes for people when they are playing a role within a business. Profit is important of course and one's job is to make money. That changes how one ought to act. But at the same time I reject the view that all norms get wiped away when one goes to work. This sort of insulation is wrong, in my view, because it leads to a sort of bad faith wherein one has to attempt to be two different people in conflict with one another. Our roles shift and norms change in different roles, but we are still one unified person who needs to make sense out of who we are and want to be.

Moreover, I reject the view that businesses are individuals and react to

---

1 In *There's No Such Things as "Business" Ethics*, John C. Maxwell takes this approach, moralistically averring (so much so that each chapter comes complete with study questions and blank lines for the reader to write in answers) that the golden rule is applicable in all areas of life and decrying situational ethics, though he does not realize that what the golden rule actually means may be dependent on context.

norms in the same way as individuals do. And I reject the view that they are not bound by any norms beyond self-interest. Of course businesses are different, but at the same time the role they play in society is not simply as a money making enterprise.[1] We are led to such a view because of a fallacious and overly-simple picture of the nature of society in which businesses and individuals come to be out of nowhere and by their existence owe nothing to anybody. Things are more complicated.

Sketching the content of business ethics as another topic altogether—I only point out that approaching ethics through identity understood as a web of roles we can understand the topic, reject extreme positions, and hopefully find a way to more fruitfully explore the subject.

Political and Other Leadership

Another example to consider is the situations that leaders of societies or institutions often face. Consider the President of the United States. He is forced to make decisions that may lead to the loss of life, even innocent life. He may endanger soldiers. As an individual, these acts would be wrong. But as President he has taken on a role that requires him to act in the best interests of the country as a whole, and that means that bad things will happen. He behaves much like a utilitarian, but one who gives much greater weight to the members of the country he leads. Of course it is more complex but the point should be clear—there are different norms in play for the President than for an ordinary citizen because of the important role he is playing.

A role based approach to understanding norms makes clear sense of this. Being a leader of an institution is a role that requires one to act in the best interests of the institution, or to follow the norms that govern the institution. These may well conflict with norms that hold sway in other parts of life. This does not solve the normative problem—as above it helps us understand it. Taking on more roles, especially roles with sorts of responsibilities quite different from those an individual ordinary bears, creates ethical tension. Potential leaders must seriously reflect on the obligations that come with a leadership role and what that will mean for their lives not just practical but in terms of preserving a unified personal integrity. This can often be done

---

1 The point generally is that business plays the role of serving a societal need and makes money doing so. Businesses that do only harm are either illegal or heavily regulated as a social evil. Historical evidence for this point can be found in corporations: these were first chartered by legislatures to achieve public goals. The profit they gained thereby was reward for serving this need. Corporate law has greatly liberalized and we certainly don't need a legislature to approve our corporate purpose, but this has followed our economic views on how to best create a vibrant economy, not a standalone view that corporations should only make money.

by shaping the type of leader one will be and engaging in some insulation. It may well be the case with some people sometimes that the only true solution is to not be a leader. Power is often the road to perdition and the price of eternal glory may be eternal guilt.

Unjust or Immoral Laws and Orders

We can also now better understand another problem that often bothers students of ethics and law: how should one behave if the law is unjust or immoral? For example, how should a citizen in Nazi Germany behave? On the one hand there seems to be a clear moral duty not to aid in any way the regime that is doing evil. On the other there is a duty to follow the law because one is a citizen and member of the country. To make the case more particular imagine there is a law requiring reporting any hidden Jews to the authorities. A citizen knows the location of a hidden Jew. Must she report it? Must she not?

Here my intuitions clearly say she does not. Yours may vary. But if I am right is there no obligation not to break the law since here I reject that? There is such an obligation based on one's role as a citizen but that obligation is *defeasible*. Here my basic role as a human being demands that I not send an innocent person to death. That overcomes my role as a citizen, and so when I break the law, I compromise that role in some way. But this is not tragic, since because of the regime that role is not one I wish to live up to.

What about the Nazi judge? Ought he to apply the law? Well, as a judge he has a duty to apply the law regardless of his personal views about it. But as a human being, he ought to avoid being part of a legal process that is so unethical. This is a contrast between two roles and figuring out how to hold onto both at once. One option is to twist the law in various ways to avoid evil rulings. This might be justified by viewing the regime, or at least aspects of it, as itself operating illegally. Another solution is to simply not be a judge. If one decides that in good conscience the role of a judge cannot be fulfilled that role should be discarded. And that is the most sensible response to this question: don't be a judge in a Nazi regime.

Things obviously can get more difficult. Imagine that someone is forced into the army and to be a guard at a concentration camp. He now occupies a role that requires that he aide in a death machine he knows to be immoral. What should he do? Abstractly we say he must resist and refuse. But we also know what follows: he dies quickly and nothing changes. Whatever he does, a role is comprised. But he can't just go along and feel guilt-free because in doing so he is operating in bad faith by acting against his role as a human being. It would be best if he could simply not be a guard, but that isn't an option. Here he has been forced into a role he wants out of, but cannot get out of because it is beyond his power. The best answer, I think, is that he ought to do what he can to undermine that role without comprising his life or the other duties he wishes to hold onto. What this means will depend on the circumstances. Even if he stays we will almost certainly not attach guilt—and indeed this is what we have generally done legally in cases involving individuals who were neither cruel nor zealous in playing the role assigned to them.

I am not advocating lawlessness whenever one has moral qualms against a law or believes that following a law compromises an important role. Rather I am saying this is an option, but I am resisting the view that when a law is immoral one has no duty at all to follow it and has not violated a role when one breaks it. This view has the moral erase the legal (though on a deeper analysis I think that legal norms are a special sort of moral norms, different importantly here in that the content of legal norms are not a matter of choice and can push one into tension between roles) while I urge that it defeats it but does not erase the fact that one has violated a duty and acted against a role. One should have done so in that situation, but in order to recognize the difficulty of the situation and not blithely license lawlessness we should hold onto the legal duty even when defeated.

To put the point in a different way: I support civil disobedience when someone believes the law in question is wrong and thinks that his or her action will aid in changing it. But I also hold that part of civil disobedience is willingly accepting the legal sanction. That is what makes it powerful. I do not understand those who claim to practice civil disobedience but then protest when they are arrested.[1] Part of the point is to get arrested! A reflective approach to the situation would require an understanding that this is important enough to violate a duty and compromise a role and suffer the results of doing so. The hope, of course, is that faced with the protest the law will be altered or the authorities will refuse to enforce it, but nonetheless one is disobeying a legal norm and role and is liable for consequences that may follow.

Solidarity

In the previous chapter I pointed out that roles are essentially particularized—referring to a particular class of things within which the role has application and meaning. Abstractly this point isn't shocking, but it is worth explicitly noting because it helps to make sense out of an issue that has puzzled modern ethics. Intuitively we think we owe more moral

---

1 In the same way it seems incorrect to term Edward Snowden's actions civil disobedience: in disagreement with a policy he stole a number of documents and fled to China and then Russia rather than going public at home.

duty to those close to us, whether family, friends, or fellow members of community or country, than to those who are far away. But why is this so? Is not the suffering of the starving boy thousands of miles away just as morally demanding as the suffering of my brother here? We might say that it is, but there are practical limitations that define the scope of the duty. However, in an age where charities can be funded to help those in the distance and to whom we bear no deep relation, this answer loses force. We seem to be left with an appeal to emotion and what not, but this isn't satisfying because now it appears there is something wrong and irrational about our being more obligated to those we have relationships with.

One possible answer is that we have a sort of solidarity with those we have relationships with and this is why we have more duties to them. Solidarity reflects the sorts of greater obligations we have to those who are close to us, part of some group community or project. I think this is right way to think about the differing scope of duties and that it is right because duties follow from norms and norms come from roles we inhabit and as a matter of fact we have more roles in relation to those close to us. That isn't something to bemoan as irrational. We are local beings who are part of families and communities and being in those means playing roles particularized to them. Hence we do have more extensive duties to those we share relationships with. Of course this doesn't mean we don't have duties to humanity as a whole, just that we can understand, without embarrassment, why we have more and different sorts of duties to those who are closer to our lives.

We need not be ashamed that we feel more duties to those around us and those in our country than to the world as a whole. We have many roles, and many of the important ones are defined by local relations. Hence we have more extensive or different duties to them than we do to the world at large. Our sense of solidarity is not irrational affinity but a product of the way in which we are defined as individuals in terms of our place in society. In earlier periods of human history localized communal roles were much more central than they are at present. Our concept of the other allowed inhuman treatment of those placed on the outside of our most important moral sphere, be it the free-born, citizens, members of a particular race or ethnicity, or religious group. When these localized roles dominate a sense of our role as an autonomous self-conscious rational being (or put another way, citizen of the world) solidarity with our fellows, and a dearth of duties beyond them, is much clearer than it is now. Presently we locate the moral sphere as encompassing duties to all of humanity, and for some people all of existence. This should not be lost in a return to "pure" solidarity. What I am arguing is that when we look to identity to ground norms and roles to explicate identity we can make sense of solidarity with local communities and groups in our present ethical thought that encompasses all of humanity because narrower roles are still present and important and ground more local duties that account for our proper sense of solidarity.

Cosmopolitanism

Diogenes the Cynic coined the term "cosmopolitan" as a way to express his sense that he was not a citizen of this or the other city-state but a citizen of the cosmos, of the world. Ethical thought, especially among the educated, stresses cosmopolitanism. Thinking ethically means seeing oneself as a citizen of the world at large, not stuck identifying with local fads and fashions that lead to irrational affinities. And indeed ethical progress, if there has been such progress on the whole, can be seen in expanding the scope of the "we" to whom we take ourselves to have duties. It is no longer sensible for most of us to define groups of human beings as the other we can have no duties towards. But throughout history the opposite has been true. Our cosmopolitanism and development of the idea of *human* rights seems to be threatened if in fact solidarity is important and we have more duties to those close to us.

In a sense it is, but only in the sense that the cosmopolitanism would vanquish the local. And this I think is a mistake. We are citizens of the world. But we are citizens of a country, a society, a city, a family, a social group as well. We have duties to all human beings because of our roles as human beings, but that does not mean that we don't also have localized duties as well. We can accept solidarity and cosmopolitanism as both being very important in terms of norms and defining who we are. The only reason there seems to be a conflict here is the assumption that there must be one moral source and if it is local it cannot be global and vice-versa. But this assumption is precisely what I have denied here: the moral source is identity and identity is pluralistic containing roles that vary on a broad spectrum between local and global.

We easily become puzzled at what seem to be deep conflicts between our senses of cosmopolitanism and solidarity and the duties associated with each. If we stress solidarity, we seem to return to a cruel past in which vast swathes of humanity could be placed at a much lower level of moral value or outside of moral space altogether. But if we stress cosmopolitanism, we lose our sense of closeness to those local to us and our sense of greater duties to them. A role-based explication of identity offers a way to hold onto both. We have both sets of duties. Those local to us are of more moral import in our lives because of the roles we play within those localities. But this does not undermine the moral value or humanity of all others because this is understood in terms of our roles as autonomous self-conscious rational beings. There will, of course, be conflict in some cases. But conflict is inevitable for complex beings whose identity is fixed through a system of multiple roles, sometimes in tension and conflict with each other. We need not choose between solidarity and cosmopolitanism or cash one out in terms of the other. Both are important because they capture central feature of roles that define us.[1]

Addiction and Recovery

Addiction and recovery touch, in some capacity, most people in our society. The addict has, in a way, been hijacked by a compulsion to use a certain substance or engage in an activity that overrides desires not to do so and any will power of the addict. The topic is immense, and I have no pretense of offering a real analysis of it. I do, however, wish to sketch how we can understand addiction and recovery in terms of roles, because I believe such an understanding is revealing and explicatory of roles. Thus it will be helpful in explaining the picture of identity I have been offering, partly because many people have experience as an addict or being close to an addict.

Addiction and our responses to it offer a way to probe how we come to take on roles against our will, create profound personal identity crises that can lead to tragedy, and also can work to take ownership of roles, and reform them and ourselves so as to work within our thrown position to build a coherent and exemplary identity out of tragedy.

The addict is ill. The illness is both mental and physical. Mentally, the addict has become obsessed with his drug of choice. It is his answer for everything—happiness and sadness, success and failure, stress and leisure, social interaction and coping alone. Physically, once exposed to the drug of choice, craving takes over and having more becomes the most important thing to him. No matter what the consequences, the addict will continue to use when under the influence. The obsession leads the addict back to the drug of choice and no matter how much the addict has planned, how strong his or her will is, and how many sincere promises he or she has made to do it differently this time, once use starts the physical craving will take over and lead to oblivion or perhaps even death.

Consider the alcoholic. The alcoholic has an allergy to alcohol—his reaction is abnormal and harmful. Most people have a few drinks and then

---

1 See Kwame Anthony Appiah's *Cosmopolitanism* for a insightful discussion of cosmopolitanism generally. His project differs from mine in that he is interested in making sense of cosmopolitanism and our current moral terrain while still holding onto objective values whereas I am more interested in figuring ought how we should engage in moral reflection generally in a way that makes sense of cosmopolitanism and solidarity, objective value and tolerance.

no longer desire more. Sometimes they over-indulge and there are bad consequences. Noting this they do not drink as much. If the stakes are high, the normal person has no trouble refraining from use. Alcohol is a poison of sorts, though quite pleasurable in moderate amounts. Normal people generally conform their behavior to this truth—after a few drinks they desire no more and stop.

The alcoholic does not share this reaction. For him, the reaction to alcohol is a physical craving for me. In some this develops over time. Other alcoholics say that they were alcoholic from birth or from their first drink. Whatever the particular case, alcoholics, when physically influenced by alcohol, seek more and will keep on doing so until it is not possible for some reason. Most alcoholics are able to maintain control in most cases for a period of time. By help from others and exercise of will they force themselves to stop, though there is the physical craving for more. But it is a progressive disease, and eventually once alcohol is in the body they are off to the races no matter what the stakes and the consequences. In the presence of their drug of choice the only thing that matters in the world is getting more alcohol. That is it. They come to not even enjoy being drunk. They may blackout easily and wake up days later. They may drink alone, not eating or doing anything but drinking. They will drink until they run out, pass out, or are thrown out. And yet their minds will constantly return them to the first drink because it has become their answer to everything.

There is much more to be said, of course, but my interest in how to understand addiction in terms of roles, and how roles can be better understood through the phenomenon of addiction and recovery. Clearly, becoming an addict and behaving as such reeks havoc on one's other roles and one's identity. Everything becomes compromised. Imagine an alcoholic who is married, has two children, has lost several jobs, has been arrested for alcohol related offenses, owes money to the government, family, and others, and can only count as "friends" those he drinks with. He is an addict and others treat him as such whether or not he self-attributes this condition and role to himself. As far as unravelings go, such a general picture is not out of the ordinary and certainly not nearly the most tragic or desperate.

We can understand the pathetic state of affairs such a person finds himself in by reference to roles. His relationship with his partner is likely tense and deteriorating. They may still have a future, but this is uncertain. He has failed to be a proper husband because of the addiction. He is also likely a bad father. His children may be afraid of him and embarrassed by him. He is not present for them and does not operate as a parent, or when he does he does so inconsistently and irrationally. His professional roles have largely disappeared. He is unemployable and moves from one job to the next. He is not a good worker because he cannot be counted on to show up and show up sober. If he belonged to a formal profession (e.g., law, medicine, aviation) he is likely barred, at least temporarily from his chosen line of work. Even if not, no professional role can give him any real content or satisfaction—they are too fleeting and he can meet the normative requirements of none. As a citizen he is compromised, he breaks the law and has been caught. He faces legal consequences, but following the addiction and the addicted self he continues to break the law. He is drowning in debt, ruining friendships and family relationships. He is behind on taxes and thus failing to be a proper citizen in another way. He likely has few real friends, rather just a group of drinking buddies who know him little. Indeed he knows himself little, his spiritual condition has been undermined wholly and there are no real religious or philosophical roles of any import. The addiction consumes him and he oscillates between periods of doing the necessary to keep afloat and periods of oblivion in which he is primarily playing the role of the addict.

One way to see the crisis the addict finds himself in is by understanding him as having unwittingly taken on a role, being an addict with its physical craving and mental obsession, that he cannot shed and which operates while in active addiction to take over all other roles, trumping them and leading to a state of affairs where the addict has failed to live up to the basic normative requirements of other roles, losing many of them (e.g., professional, social) and severely undermining others (e.g., familial, natural). Consumed by the addiction he does not operate as a fully autonomous, self-conscious, rational being. He is slave to the addiction and fails to live autonomously. His actions and thoughts are rarely engaged in self-consciously and reflection has little bearing on the course of his life. And his life is a form of insanity, not rationality—despite the fact that the addiction has destroyed his life and identity by thwarting other roles he continues to feed it, either consumed by the irrational thought that this time will be different or not thinking at all.

The addict will often deny the addiction, but others will be able to attribute the role to him. There are objective conditions to it, even though it is also in some ways a socially constructed role. This may appear puzzling, but it is important to understand how roles take on both objective and socially constructed aspects. The addict has an illness, the addiction. This is what makes him an addict. But being an addict comes with various commitments and entitlements that depend, to some degree, on the community in which the natural condition, the addiction, is shaped into the role of an addict. We tend to believe that an addict ought to get treatment and is entitled to some understanding of the addiction. We think he ought to stop. If he is sent to prison as punishment for his actions, we also often include treatment as part of the sentence. The addict loses entitlements socially and legally and even within the family.

Now this is all pretty basic. The point I'm getting at can be best explicated by considering other ways we might treat someone who has becoming physically and mentally dependent on a substance. We may come to revere such a person, thinking that in the throes of his addiction he is communing with the divine or living a deeply poetic, if tragic, life. Or, more likely, we may come to believe that he is possessed by a demon. This is how mental illnesses have often been treated in human history. When such similar objective conditions are met but the "addict" concept isn't used (it may not exist in any developed form or may exist but be dismissed as a bad concept) and the "possessed" concept is deployed instead. The way we approach such a person and indeed the norms that he becomes bound by are strikingly different. He needs exorcism, not treatment. He is perhaps cursed by a god (or God). He ought to be shunned and he should remove himself from society as he is unclean. The role of addict and of demon-possessed share some features, but differ importantly. In coming to reject the demon-possessed (or for that matter the addict) role and use the addict (or demon-possessed) role for such people we reject the former because we think it is a bad concept for a role. What we have is physical and mental conditions that are shaped by social attitudes and beliefs resulting in various roles one can take on depending on those attitudes and beliefs. We seek to better understand the malady the addict presents, and in our society this has come to mean a deeper construction and application of the addict role and the rejection, in most quarters, of the demon-possessed role (with its attendant beliefs considered false and normative commitments and entitlements considered barbaric) as one that has any application in this case.

The addict will likely deny the role even though the addiction is present and others attribute that role to him. The addict does not wish to be an addict and has never chosen it, so the acknowledgement of the role is difficult, for some impossible. But as the illness progresses the addict's situation becomes dire. He has become consumed by a role he cannot abandon and that has destroyed or undermined most of his other roles, leaving a ruined identity knowing only moral degradation and desperation. In Twelve Step recovery programs the first step is admitting the role of an addict: admitting that one is powerless over the drug and that life has become unmanageable. To someone with little knowledge of addiction and addicts, this may seem a small, insignificant step. It is clear such people are addicted and stating the obvious accomplishes little. For the addict, however, such a step is a sea change. Active addiction thrives on denial, of denying the role of the addict because it is not a role that one wants to be part of oneself. Admitting defeat and taking on that role opens the door to reconstructing one's life and identity. Running from the problem through denial always boomeranged, since once addicted the addict cannot as a matter of free choice choose not to be addicted. The addiction must be dealt with another way if it is to be dealt with at all. And admitting one's addiction and thereby self-attributing the role is a foundation for reconciling that role, what cannot be changed, with a reconstructed life and identity.

Recovery is many things, but from the understanding offered in this work, it can be viewed as the process of accepting the role of addict in its positive sense as a *recovering* addict and working to rebuild and remodel one's life and one's roles to make oneself a whole, coherent, vibrant identity once again (or, for some, for the first time). Addicts rely on a higher power, however they wish to define this, in this process. The point is simple—they are not the solution; they must place faith or trust in something else, even if they do not understand it, because they alone are consumed by addiction.

On this basis a recovery program can be built. It begins with a moral inventory that takes account of all of the aspects of one's life. This is a process of coming to recognize where and who one is as well as the resentments, fears, etc., that have driven the addict to this state of affairs and consume him. From this the addict works to become free of shortcomings and to make amends, to repair roles that have been compromised. This may mean abandoning roles. A marriage may be ended because it cannot or should not be saved. Family members may want nothing to do with the recovering addicts. Careers may now be barred and friendships may be lost. But it usually means repairing roles by admitting the past and being accountable for the future. By working to behave as a husband, father, worker, friend, citizen ought to addict works at becoming whole while also acknowledging, as he must, the fact of addiction and the role of addict. But now it is the role of a recovering addict, building a fuller identity.

To some being a proper husband, father, worker, friend, citizen, etc., may seem small, something to be taken for granted as the basis of who they are. But the addict has lost his good faith standing in these roles and it is hard, admirable work to regain such standing through making amends and living a life free of active addiction and in accordance with the normative aspects of those roles. He becomes whole again, and whole in a different way. Indeed some recovering addicts are quite thankful for their addiction and would have it no other way—for them the addiction led to recovery and their program of recovery has led to a life and identity that is richer than anything they could have imagined.

Conclusion: Complex Identity and the Integration of the Self

This chapter has explicated the identity approach through application. Once we focus on roles and how they can shift we can understand other issues as well: for instance the obligations of soldiers, teachers, athletes, etc., or the sorts of personal crises and transformations individuals must go through when a role (e.g., parenthood) is thrust upon them.[1] We take on varying roles in life and these roles lead us into norms that we need to pay heed to. The problem then becomes how to understand oneself as a morally unified being in various roles. Instead of fruitlessly searching for the one true theory or ethical Holy Grail that will solve all problems we should recognize that we are thinking about the problem wrong. Norms are grounded in who we are and the deep ethical task of life is discovering and developing oneself in a coherent and value-laden way. We occupy and take on many roles and our duties shift form and existence with them. But we are also a unified identity. The deep ethical problem we face is having both a complex and unified identity. This creates enormous possibilities, but it is also fraught with danger because we can easily be led into moral dilemmas or tensions or bad faith or be forced to abandon roles.

We can be constituted by roles, like the professional and political roles discussed above, that create conflicts with other roles. Roles of different scopes, referencing solidarity and cosmopolitanism, can pull us in different directions. And, as in the case of the addict, we may unwillingly take on roles that tear apart our identities and undermine other roles in our lives, requiring a process of recovery and rebuilding and remodeling of the self.

The above discussion hasn't offered any end solution to the moral tension and problems at issue. Rather I hope to have shown that approaching ethical issues through the perspective of an identity-based ethic in which norms follow from various roles that define who we are as individuals transforms the problem a lawyer, or any professional, faces and that this transformation clarifies the problem and helps us think about it in a different way. The solutions sketched and the way to understand problems like addiction

---

1 Tolstoy's argument in *The Kingdom of God is Within You* is relevant to this point. His baseline view is that Christianity requires non-violence, full stop. Hence he rails against those who inhabit roles, like soldiers, who require violence targeted at foreign enemies and domestic discontents and those who inhabit roles, like elites, in which they benefit from and tacitly engage in violence through others. From my perspective his view is that they live in a sort of bad faith because they have not understood and integrated their role as Christians and as human beings. Resolution requires transforming or rejecting the roles that are party to violence. His argument uses a totalizing role that trumps all others as to any violent conduct. I do not endorse that here—I just note its possibility and understandability in terms of the approach I am advocating. Other resolutions are possible.

and solidarity vs. cosmopolitanism are meant as possible approaches that can be taken in order to deal with the tension that is implicit in occupying various roles. There is no clean way out of these problems and tensions—no axiomatic theory that gives us the right answer and defines the good life. But I hope making the problem and ways to approach it explicit we can come to think about these ethical issues that reach beyond conduct to who and how one is and ought to be in a more enlightened way.

To return to the first discussion, in actual practice a lawyer is likely to deal with the tension by using a variety of approaches to various degrees, for example restricting one's practice to some degree to avoid the deepest problems, insulating one's professional role in a non-radical way, and placing some trust in the system as a whole while also working to reform it in various ways to make it better. And of course different people will take different approaches.

The ethical problems remain but we do have tools with which to understand and cope with the problem. We must deal with the tension and forge a coherent, rich, and unified self.

Introduction

Moral dilemmas are generally viewed as problems for ethical theories. They present contradictions that need to be ignored or overcome. They are thought to refute theories or even undermine the possibility of a grounded ethics as a whole. Insofar as theorists take them seriously, they attempt to solve them in a way that makes clear why we are prone to dilemma and helps us think about how to deal with these situations. On the approach I am offering, however, moral dilemmas are a key piece of *evidence* for a better understanding of our moral condition, not an annoying or grievous problem for ethics as a whole. Rather than trying to solve moral dilemmas, we ought to attempt to understand them in some way and thereby understand the ethical challenges we face as human beings.

Viewing complex, pluralistic identity as the grounding of norms allows us to do this. Because identity is constituted by a plurality of roles it is entirely probable that we will face constant tension and occasional dilemma when differing roles call for differing actions. Hence the presence of moral dilemmas is good reason to believe that the identity approach is proper. Indeed, from the perspective favored here moral dilemmas are really just quite explicit and extreme examples of the moral tension that is part of what it means to be human. We constantly must weigh various aspects of our identity and forge who we are in the light of who we ought to be. Moral dilemmas are cases where these choices become manifest in a single action. They are a natural result of tensions inevitable for a complex normative being.

On my approach the general treatment of each variety of dilemma is the same.

In each case we are faced with a decision that is difficult because a role we occupy speaks in favor of each incompatible action. At base, moral dilemmas are conflicts between roles we take ourselves to occupy and hence force us to choose between them. Since both roles are part of who we are such decisions are difficult. The degree of difficulty or the starkness of the dilemma will depend on the specific case. There is nothing that is necessarily wrong about occupying roles that are in tension with one another—this is part of what it means to be human (and life would be both boring and foreign otherwise). Moral dilemmas, then, are an unfortunate consequence of being the sort of beings that we are. In order to deal with them we must understand the roles that are leading us into dilemma, discern what is at stake in the dilemma, and then make a decision as to the sort of person we wish to become. Such decisions involve tradeoffs and sacrifices, but again are a necessary part of being who we are, beings with pluralistic identities harmonized in various ways. These general thoughts can be made more concrete by reconsidering each sort of moral dilemma in turn.

Pedestrian Dilemmas

Pedestrian dilemmas are the most common and the most ignored. This is unfortunate. The thought is that while they are disconcerting, they are neither important enough nor stark enough to merit attention. Yet they pervade life. Pedestrian dilemmas are very important from the perspective I have developed above. My underlying thought has been that we ground norms in identity and explain identity in terms of a plurality of roles one occupies. Once this is done pedestrian dilemmas are easily explained. In fact, the ubiquity of pedestrian dilemmas is a very strong reason to adopt a role-based understanding of ethics.

In pedestrian dilemmas we find ourselves pulled between two or more roles, each demanding an opposite action. We must discern which role is most important or find some way to split the difference. There is no abstract solution to these dilemmas as a kind—rather the individual characteristics of the dilemma and the person in it are essential to discerning the correct action, though these features are objective but not abstract so the rejection of a generalized solution is not a descent into formless relativism. Insofar as there is something general to say about a solution to these dilemmas, it is simply an injunction to avoid them as best one can. A pedestrian dilemma emerges because of the plurality of roles that make up our identity. Because we are so complex it is bound to be the case that sometimes we will find ourselves in tension with ourselves. Often this is forgivable and a simple part of life. Sometimes it is not. We ought to work to avoid roles that conflict with each other and avoid situations that require us to favor one role over another. Even so we should recognize that we do not control the world and sometimes out of bad luck or just in the course of normal life we will be forced into a pedestrian dilemma and have to choose. Some examples will make this clearer.

Recall the case wherein we have made a promise to a friend to meet after work but now find that important work cannot be finished in time and we feel obligated to stay. This is a pedestrian moral dilemma. Our duty to our friend and our duty to our employer demand incompatible actions. The best way to deal with such a dilemma is to phone the friend and reschedule. This sort of thing is usually disappointing but easily understood. Still, one must make a choice, and this choice is even more difficult if one cannot contact the friend or if the meeting is quite important. Here one's role as a friend and role as an employee are in conflict. This is a case of tension between a social role and a professional role. The conflict doesn't refute any ethical theory or lead to a crisis because we must understand the plurality of norms in play. Reflection on the various roles and their importance ought to be able to lead us to the best, though still regrettable, resolution.

Most cases like this involve no real moral failure because the conflict was unexpected and not of one's doing. There are, however, cases in which the pedestrian dilemma does reflect poorly on a person. For example, if one knew that work would likely require one to stay late, or one goofed off all day without getting the work done, or one made the promise knowing it couldn't be fulfilled, then one bears responsibility for the dilemma and has acted poorly. We ought to manage our lives to avoid dilemmas by not taking on roles that we should know will lead to them and by not acting in ways that we should know will create them.

Additionally, if one continually gets oneself into such dilemmas, even unknowingly, one is failing in fulfilling one or more of the roles. It is our duty to do our best to avoid pedestrian dilemmas and this requires not just that we avoid knowingly making incompatible commitments but that we are vigilant in understanding our obligations such that we can anticipate possible dilemmas. If we fail in this we are responsible for the dilemma we find ourselves in to a large degree—even though there is no pure solution and hence we are not wholly blameworthy for the exact wrong done. The situation should have been avoided and hence we are at fault for the dilemma. Complaining about a seemingly impossible dilemma is morally immature if our being is such a situation is our fault.

Some people make bad habits out of encountering pedestrian dilemmas because they make too many commitments or take on too many roles that end up in tension with one another. This can be avoided. It is our duty to manage our lives so that the roles we take on can be in harmony with one another. Failing to do so leads to constant bad faith and chaos in one's identity. Tensions are not resolved and one's identity is in continual flux. For those who engage in self-reflection, this is a very disconcerting state to be in. Sometimes we will fail to avoid conflict despite our best efforts, but our best efforts can do a great deal to keep us out of pedestrian dilemmas in the first place. Hence the general rule here is simply to avoid pedestrian dilemmas. Be clear about which roles are the most important, harmonize them with each other, avoid making tenuous commitments, and live in such a way that dilemmas are avoided. These moral rules may seem obvious and trite, but there is a great deal of wisdom contained in them that many of us do not heed in our lives.

The other cases given as examples above can be analyzed in similar ways. One is torn between caring for an aging mother and spending time at a charity. Ideally a compromise is reached. But the dilemma is between one's filial role and one's social role. Given the situation both cannot be wholly fulfilled and thus there is an internal tension. In the case wherein one is told something in confidence by a friend and later faces a legal obligation to reveal the truth there is tension between the social role of friendship and a legal role as a citizen or person subject to the law. In such cases how one ought to act will depend on the closeness of the friend, the seriousness of the crime, and how one sees oneself. Usually in mere friendships legal roles will win out. Such is not the case regarding familial roles. For example, we do not (generally) require spouses to testify against each other, recognizing that the role as a spouse trumps the legal role in these cases. Further, we understand when parents or children hide the truth about a loved one out of respect for the familial role they inhabit. Though they may face legal repercussions, in many cases prosecution is not pursued. Moreover, we generally don't find such people to be at fault morally.

What about the case of the white lie? Here, one is asked the truth but knows that the truth will be quite harmful while serving no good end beyond the truth itself. The conflict in roles here is between one's role as an honest person and any role that leads one to seek the best outcome. For example, the social role of friendship generates an obligation to seek benefit for one's friend. Thus there is a temptation to tell the white lie. This temptation is not necessarily evil or bad in any sense. Rather, it can be quite good—it is proper to seek to benefit one's friend, and sometimes it is the case that the truth causes unnecessary harm. What exactly one ought to do will depend on the specific case and what one values more.

Pedestrian dilemmas make a great deal of sense on the approach I have adopted and the fact that they are so prevalent speaks strongly in favor of my analysis. In such cases two or more roles are in tension with one another and thus there is an internal conflict in our identity. Specifics of the case as well as what we chose to value more about ourselves determine how we ought to act. In solving pedestrian dilemmas we must adopt a pragmatic approach. We might offer some rules of thumb for deciding cases but cannot posit absolute rules. Rather, we must approach each case individually by understanding both sides and then discerning which role is more important in this case. Grounding ethics in a web of roles helps us in this process. Pedestrian dilemmas are not trouble for ethics when thought about the right way but the inevitable consequence of being complex beings with multifaceted identities.

In pedestrian dilemmas duties grounded in two roles we inhabit conflict. But, importantly, acting against one of the duties does not mean that we have forfeited the role associated with it. This is a key difference between pedestrian dilemmas and critical dilemmas. If I stay late at work and break a promise to a friend, I have done wrong by my friend and acted against my role as a friend. But I have not forfeited this role altogether. Rather I have only damaged my standing as a good friend. Hence, in dealing with pedestrian dilemmas we must weigh not only the importance of each role but also the damage done to that role by acting against it in this case. If my role as a friend to this person is much more important than my role as an employee but I realize that I will cause a great deal more damage to my role as an employee if I act against it I may be justified in staying at work.

There are, then, multiple dimensions that must be considered in dealing with pedestrian dilemmas: the importance of the roles in conflict, the nature of the duties relative to each role, the damage done to each role by failing to fulfill the duty in question, etc. At best these general considerations are rules of thumb; actually resolving pedestrian dilemmas is highly dependent on specific considerations of the case in question, not abstract rules that apply in the same way to all cases.

The tension that becomes explicit in pedestrian dilemmas is commonplace and mundane. We are pluralistic beings and must decide which roles take precedence over others. We need not abandon a role in most cases because we can still fulfill it in a subordinate role. Yet difficult decisions of identity must be made in discerning what is most important. Is one first and foremost a good employee or a good friend? Such questions of identity are usually not made entirely explicit but rather occur over the course a multitude of mundane situations. In the course of our lives the answer emerges. There is tension between roles but usually not contradiction—we can manage our lives such that we can be a great number of roles, some more important than others. Pedestrian dilemmas are cases where this natural tension becomes explicit in a single situation: a single choice must be made as to what to do on this occasion and each choice pits one role against another. As such in one decision we must decide which role is more important. It is a dilemma because we seek to avoid such explicit and stark choices. But though we may often avoid pedestrian dilemmas the tension that they capture is essential to who we are as pluralistic beings constituted by many, sometimes conflicting, roles.

Theoretical Dilemmas

What of theoretical dilemmas? These dilemmas never arise in their purest form, but are used as devices to test and refute ethical theories. The conflict can seem so apparent and explicit that no solution can be found. The thought experiment involving the strongman and the various trolley cases are standard examples. In these cases we must choose between letting more people die and actively involving ourselves so that fewer people die. They can be adjusted in various ways to bring out the needed conflict for an individual. They are not addressed as clearly by the identity based approach as the pedestrian dilemmas. Yet this should not dishearten us—they are highly artificial and so it is bound to be the case that theories do not have immediate application. The question to ask is whether or not we can better understand these cases on the approach adopted here. I believe we can.

The key to such an improved understanding of these examples is to focus on what it is that makes these cases so extraordinary. It is tempting to simply dismiss them as unreal. But this isn't a productive strategy—they are meant to test theories, not correspond to reality, and hence it is a clear misunderstanding, much like inadvertently changing the subject, to make this move. The fact that they are extraordinary is important not as a route to dismissing them, but as a route to understanding what is so troubling about them. Ordinarily we take it to be our role not to kill people, even if we can concoct some larger benefit. This is a good rule of thumb for several reasons. First, killing is wrong and compromises legal/political, social, and natural roles. Second, our epistemic situation is rarely if ever such that we have enough of a handle on the future to make the necessary determinations with confidence, even if we have suspicions of our own. Third and most importantly here, making judgments for the common good and acting with such authority far exceeds our place. We have no role that confers such responsibility and legitimate power. We are human beings, not gods.

In theoretical dilemmas each of these ordinary facts is changed. Killing is still wrong but killing is going to happen no matter what we decide. Second, there is no epistemic limitation. The case is theoretical and so by mere stipulation we are placed in an unnatural epistemically perfect position. This is a major change not to be ignored. Our ordinary epistemic position affects the sorts of roles we take on ethically and hence changing our epistemic situation in this important way changes a great deal regarding our ethical judgments. Finally, in constructing the cases we are forced into positions of unnatural power and authority. Roles we do not normally possess and do not consider central to our identities are forced on us by the situation. We are then asked what to do. In these situations the world forces new roles on us. This, in fact, is quite a common occurrence that deserves a great deal of attention. Who we are and who we become is in many ways out of our hands and rather a function of a larger world, social and natural, in which we play a small part. Theoretical dilemmas stretch this phenomenon to the extreme in that they give us a role quite out of the ordinary with massive and pressing duties that conflict with other massive and pressing duties that follow from roles we ordinarily occupy. The extremity is rare, but the thought that the world foists roles upon us captures something quite ordinary and worth paying attention to.

These changes are crucial. As individuals our roles lead to judgments that we should not actively kill or cause harm, even if we think benefit may come from it. But in the theoretical cases this general disposition is challenged. In the case involving the strongman one natural result is to try to find a way out of the dilemma by negotiation or by pointing out that one doesn't know that the strongman will really have all of the prisoners killed. But since this is a theoretical dilemma it is easy to close the door on these considerations. Any epistemic limitation can be eliminated and we find ourselves forced into an unnatural situation. We are also placed in an awkward position of power and authority in making a judgment regarding the fate of the prisoners. We are mere tourists, not governmental officials or the like. We are not acting on behalf of any corporate individual as would usually be the case when making such decisions.

The role of "decider" in this case is entirely foreign and compromises some individual roles that we have going into the situation. We are still individuals with various roles and a propensity not to do harm but pushed into a role in which we have power and responsibility over life and death. It is the profound tension between the ordinary individual roles that favor keeping our hands clean and the new and pressing role of an individual with more than an individual's power and authority that generates the dilemma. By adjusting the numbers accordingly we can favor one side over the other and create problems for various ethical theories.

The trolley cases function in the same way. In the original case we stand at a switch and know exactly what the future contingencies are. By standing at the switch we have unwittingly been placed in a position of extraordinary power and responsibility. Even if we are not in charge of the tracks ordinarily, by being in the position we find ourselves in this role becomes one we occupy and it brings various normative constraints. By resolving any epistemic issues and introducing a new and unnatural role with a powerful normative import a dilemma can be constructed.

There is one additional point of interest. Most people are more willing to actively sacrifice a few to save many in the trolley case when at the switch than when able to push the fat man in front of the train. One reason for this is likely the physical proximity—the physical distance of the switch from the situation distances us psychologically from the horror of the act in a way that pushing, and touching, the man in front of the train. Yet we are still left with what seems to be a definite contradiction in ethical intuitions, mitigated only by the squeamishness associated with direct physical contact in the situation. But there is also another clear difference between the cases. When at the switch, one is put in a situation where one clearly occupies the role of someone with control over the track and the situation. When standing next to the fat man this is not the case, if only because the "role" one finds oneself in is entirely local to the situation at hand and can only be understood in reference to it. Switches are normal ways of controlling trolleys, pushing a fat man or any large object onto the tracks are not. So in the former case we find ourselves in a normal role while in the latter case there is no such normal role to fill. To push the fat man onto the tracks would mean taking a rather robust role onto oneself that the situation has not forced one into. It makes sense, then, that more people are reluctant to intervene in such cases—the role that would force intervention is more distant from us.

But wait—what is the solution to these dilemmas? I have none to offer. In such cases the roles we find ourselves in bring different ways of making normative judgments into conflict with one another. Again, we must take a pragmatic approach to these dilemmas. The proper response will likely be a function of how deeply one is pulled into the situation since this will change one's perspective on how various roles are in play in the situation as described. In these dilemmas there is a strong argument to be made that one ought to rescues oneself from the situation as much as possible. Once one is involved then the new role of power and authority can take over. Just how we see ourselves and how much we become involved mentally will likely determine the correct course of action. The way out of the dilemma, then, is to analyze what set of roles one occupies in the case and consider whether or not certain roles can be and should be avoided. Such analysis may not yield clear answers, but at least given this approach we can understand the situation in a way that countenances the genuine dilemma in the situation and get a grasp on how the moral dilemma functions. This is certainly a vast improvement over many approaches.

It may seem that at this point I have retreated to an "anything goes" moral stance by cowardly failing to come down on either side. In a sense I am allowing that both decisions could be proper, but two caveats need to be attached. First, to say that either choice would be morally acceptable is manifestly not to say that anything goes. Far from it. It is not morally acceptable to decide to kill all three individuals yourself or to somehow manipulate the situation so that all involved die. These are unacceptable actions. It would also be unacceptable to simply freeze up or run off crying in either case. This would display an unwillingness to deal with the world as it manifests itself.[1] There remain many ethical constraints, despite the dilemma.

Allowing the propriety of both actions in a theoretical dilemma, then, does not mean giving up on ethics altogether. Rather it means rejecting the idea that we can sit in the study and come up with absolute rules for such cases. This leads to the second caveat. In order to determine the correct action on my view we must immerse ourselves into the particular situation, determine how involved we are, and take stock of the roles involved. Since this cannot be done from the comfortable distance of a philosophy seminar we should not expect a principled solution to theoretical dilemmas. Philosophy will only bring us to understand why the dilemmas emerge and help us think about them. This in and of itself is surely a laudable accomplishment. Moreover once we adopt a roles based analysis we don't have to pretend we have or need a solution to them to avoid embarrassment. They are constructed to create deep tensions between roles and so of course they present dilemmas. This is really only a problem if one has a totalizing theory to defend. I do not.

Furthermore the result that we cannot legislate correct action at a distance is a natural result of a claim made above: facticity—the particular factual context we are thrown into—plays an enormous role in our moral obligations. Some roles are natural, some roles are chosen consciously, some roles are chosen unconsciously (one takes an action that results, unintentionally, in a role; think unexpected pregnancies here), and some roles are accidents. What one's duties are in the situation will depend on antecedent facts that got one in the situation and thereby the roles one occupies. There is no clear distant answer because duties flow from roles, roles often are determined about details in context, and by stating the

---

1 This is not the same as someone who would simply reject the role explicitly and thereby attempt to remove himself from that situation. I am imagining someone who cannot handle the situation, not someone who reflects on the situation and attempts to reject it. This is an interesting response and I am not sure that if one can truly reject the situation as given in the example. It is worth noting, however, that in similar real life examples this may be a way to deal with the problem. One of the features of theoretical dilemmas is that they posit (because they can) the unavailability of any escape hatches.

dilemma abstractly we have a radically incomplete context.

My treatment makes even more sense once we begin to think of actual cases that are like these dilemmas. Decisions of state involving war or other means of destructive policy are the clearest examples because in such cases we place ourselves in a political role in which it is proper to cause direct harm to maximize the good. One common justification for a war or for the use of a weapon during a war (e.g., the atomic bomb) is that the alternative would bring more death and destruction and thus one has a duty to take action that though regrettable is the best course. Similar considerations apply to the currently popular thought experiment of the ticking time bomb. If one has reason to believe a terrorist has knowledge of an imminent attack that would allow us to prevent it is it morally acceptable to torture the terrorist? Would it be morally acceptable to torture his children in front of him?

These decisions are difficult and epistemically cloudy. Leaders must often make decisions having little grasp of the contingencies. This is as close as we get to the situations created in theoretical dilemmas. But in these cases the person with the decision has taken on a role of power and responsibility as integral to his or her identity. By being a leader there are normative constraints that apply. Often leaders must take actions as representatives of corporate individuals that as mere individuals they would and should reject as abhorrent. Leaders, then, must live with increased tension as the price for increased power. These dilemmas arise because of duties generated by different roles that in this particular case conflict with one another.

Leaders or others with some responsibilities that puts them in such situations may be forced to act in a morally deplorable manner because of the particular political role or other sort of role they play. Their role mitigates the sin, but it does not erase it. The price of responsibility is living with the acts that are required of one. Leaders hence often ought to have troubled consciences even if they believe they acted rightly. Fulfilling their political role requires them to act against other roles, social, familial, and natural. The key lesson to draw is that the role based approach clearly applies to such cases and hence is a promising way to explain theoretical dilemmas as well.

By analogy with the dilemmas political leaders face, we can see cases like these in our lives, though they rarely if ever present stark dilemmas. Sometimes we find ourselves in a role of public responsibility and must act in accordance with it. Sometimes this may require actions that we as individuals are uncomfortable with. Rarely would we think of such cases as instances of moral dilemmas since there does not seem to be a clear contradiction. But on my analysis we can see that they are instances of moral tension arising out of variant roles. Theoretical dilemmas work by playing on this tension in such a way to create an outright contradiction. To exacerbate the tension inherent between public and private roles cases must be invented that pit principles we appropriately associate with different roles against each other.

We must note this but also realize that the tension is quite real because we adhere to both consequentialist and deontological principles in virtue of the different roles we inhabit. As individuals in a community we often find ourselves with roles of different scope. Political leaders are clear manifestations of this common phenomenon. Dealing with the tension bound to arise from such variant roles can be quite difficult. But such tension is a natural consequence of the sorts of beings that we are.

One final note on theoretical dilemmas. In current thought often they work by placing consequentialist and deontological principles against each other (as these are two predominant theories). We oscillate—a very bad intuitive result for both theories since both claim absolute precedence. I am urging that different sorts of roles are responsible for the contrary intuitions. Some roles we occupy favor consequentialist ways of judging right action while others favor the deontological approach. This is only a problem if one demands one absolute ethic, exactly what I am rejecting. On an identity approach we can be both deontologists and consequentialists by understanding how the two principled approaches fit into various roles that constitute our identities. Both capture proper ways of moral thinking relative to various roles and hence each will hold sway in particular cases or when thinking about moral problems in a particular way (indeed the impossible complexity that is introduced into theories of either type in order to account for intuitions that favor an opposing theory is further evidence that a pluralistic roles approach is a better way to understand what is going on).

I am skeptical that one or the other can be shown to be superior; rather, a correct treatment of the conflict would be to trace how the various roles we undertake and find ourselves in function in either deontological or consequentialist ways (and other ways as well) and then how these roles can be harmonized to create a coherent moral agent. Again, this wouldn't bring us a theoretical solution to a merely theoretical problem, but it would lead us to understand why both are appealing and in conflict with one another. By thus finding our way about perhaps we can better understand our moral condition as captured by both theories and the conflict between them. While such an understanding would no doubt displease partisans of either stripe, it would be quite helpful in assuaging the false anxiety that accompanies conflicts between seemingly plausible moral theories through the rejection of the conceit that there is such an abstract, totalizing theory to be had in the first place. An identity approach to ethical understanding offers a dissolution of just this sort, permitting us to accept the dilemma as real without being pushed into an ethical crisis or a threat to ethics generally because of the dilemma.

Critical Dilemmas

Critical dilemmas are rare but tend to strike at our moral core. They involve irreconcilable conflicts in which we are forced to choose between two seemingly essential alternatives. The standard example is the forced choice between becoming a freedom fighter and caring for an aging parent. Both are absolute duties yet are mutually exclusive. Failing to become a freedom fighter against unspeakably evil tyranny would be an unforgivable moral failing. But so would failure to care for an aging parent. The key feature of critical dilemmas is that whatever choice is made requires one to abrogate a seemingly essential role—by so acting one utterly fails to fulfill the dictates of a role that is important to who one is.

The thought of some is that this horrid conflict produces a situation that transcends any moral code and leads to a situation of absolute freedom. Here we have free choice as to our own essence and there is no right or wrong until we make the choice. Above I expressed a good deal of skepticism regarding these conclusions. No doubt there are these sorts of dilemmas in life. They often involve basic choices as to what we will do in life: which career to pursue, whether to sacrifice career for family or vice-versa, how to behave politically, etc. They are, however, rare compared to pedestrian dilemmas and so it is a stretch to think they undermine any possible moral system. To think otherwise would mean to hold that a failure of a system in a rare case showed that system to fail in all cases. Such a principle needs substantial motivation as it appears initially quite absurd. Even so, critical dilemmas do pose a difficult challenge to moral systems because they present choices that are so important and yet cannot be handled. If we adopt the identity based approach favored above, however, we can make sense out of these dilemmas. Critical dilemmas involve direct and stark conflict between two or more roles that are essential parts of one's identity.

Pedestrian dilemmas are similar but differ in at least one of two ways. First, they generally involve roles that are more peripheral to one's identity and so sacrificing one role does not undermine one's very sense of self. Second, though pedestrian dilemmas involve sacrifice in a particular case this sacrifice is not so stark that one must forfeit the role entirely—e.g., one can still be a good friend even if one fails on a single occasion. In pedestrian dilemmas one is forced to fail to uphold the norms associated with one role or another but is not forced to choose which role is to be compromised and forfeited by one's action. Critical dilemmas must involve essential roles and pose a choice that requires the abandonment of one or the other. If one of the roles involved is one we can part with without a loss of our sense of self and what we truly value then this can be done relatively easily, though with some regret. If the choice involved does not require us to entirely forfeit our role but only engage in a singular failure then our sense of self is not challenged in a deep way. Critical dilemmas must require us to sacrifice something about ourselves that we are not prepared to sacrifice. In acting in the face of such a dilemma an essential role must be entirely forfeited, not just acted against. This is why these dilemmas are so critical.

The examples fit this analysis well. In Sartre's example one is torn between a political role and a familial role. The stakes are high and both are essential to who one is: one is both a dutiful child and a patriotic supporter of freedom. Yet given the situation—the invasion and occupation—one is in a situation in which one role must be abandoned in favor of the other. Because both are, prior to the situation, essential, a crisis ensues. What does one do? There are no clear answers. But on this analysis it is clear that the radical conclusions do not follow. The moral universe does not collapse. We do not get to choose our essence. Right and wrong do not disappear. Our lives do not become completely unhinged.

Rather we are in a situation that makes us pay a large price for the plurality of roles we inhabit. Even so, there are many decisions in such cases that are clearly wrong. Running off to the circus senselessly compromises both roles. Moral systems hence do not collapse when critical dilemmas emerge; norms are merely in conflict, yet all the same remain in force and rule out a great deal. Various norms speak for particular courses of action in a substantial way, though in dilemmas there are multiple and conflicting motivated actions. We must come to a solution wherein we can fulfill both roles as best as possible. In the rare case an absolutely stark choice must be made we must decide what role is most important. This can be done through deep reflection and by reference to other roles. As a human being which is more important? Where does our duty really stand? Are there other roles that will be compromised by one choice or the other? There is no calculus here, but that does not mean that we are in normative anarchy.

Actually, on my analysis the situation is almost the opposite of what the existentialist takes to be the case. For her the lesson to draw is that there is a contradiction such that ethical norms collapse and we have absolute freedom. On my view we should conclude rather that there is a tension because there are too many ethical systems functioning in reference to different essential roles in play. Neither ethical system collapses—rather two draw us into a dilemma and we must determine which is more important. Ethics is not underdetermining our action and hence inadequate but rather over-determining it because our identities involve a plurality of roles, some of which we take to be absolutely essential to our sense of self. Such situations do undermine old theories that claimed to have a right answer but they do not create a normative anarchy once we realize this. We do have absolute freedom in some sense in that we have to make a dire choice that will bind us in the future, but this is not creating our own moral space but having to change moral space, unfortunately, that was already there because the geography cannot be maintained because of the situation we have found ourselves in.

My reading is much more intuitive and tracks how we feel in these situations. We feel trapped, not free. Both ethical freedom and confinement bring anxiety, but of a different sort. The existentialist would have us believe that the anxiety is one of absolute power to shape who we are, a condition of such freedom that there is no basis of choice whatsoever. No doubt we do have the power to alter ourselves in deep ways in response to critical dilemmas. But I am arguing that the anxiety is one of feeling overburdened by ourselves and thus trapped in a situation we cannot live with as we are. To get out we must alter our identities by casting off a role we desire and wish to retain. We do have the power to change ourselves, but this power is unwanted and severely limited by the norms that follow from who we are. In critical dilemmas our identities are in crisis because an important part of who we are cannot be sustained. To deal with them we must discern who we ought to become, and while there is a great deal of freedom here, it is freedom conditioned by an overabundance of grounds out of which we must do our best to shape who we are and who we will be.

The Antigone case can be easily explained as well. Antigone is trapped between a political and a religious/familial duty. The tragedy is that she has done nothing wrong to find herself in this situation. But in it, she must act wrongly. She must discern who and what sort of person to be and forsake either her political or religious and familial duty. In acting as she does she violates her role as citizen and is liable to face consequences for doing so. It matters not whether or not the law was just. In this case we think it isn't for the most part and so take Antigone to be our protagonist. But the question would not have been as clear to the Greeks and we should imagine a case where we thought the law just. It still might be right for Antigone to act as she does because she cannot act against her religious and familial identity. But then she must face the consequences of her actions and reconcile herself to a situation wherein she can no longer occupy the political role that before was integral to her identity.

This isn't really a solution, but in large part that is the point. Antigone is a *tragedy*—we can see the disaster on the horizon but also see that Antigone must steer towards it. Cruel fate overcomes the protagonist. Such is life. If

Antigone had but one simple role as her identity then there would be no play to speak of, or at least there would be less dramatic value in the play that remained. Action would be obvious and though bad things may happen to her, we would not identify with her predicament. We identify with her because we see her dilemma as the tragedy that it is. Rather than needing an absolute resolution to this dilemma, the identity approach to the grounding of norms allows us to understand the tragedy as a tragedy. To my mind this is a far superior result than an imposed resolution of the tragic situation that would lead us to believe there is no tragedy here but only injustice.

I do not wish to deny the feeling labeled absolute freedom as unreal in some way. I do countenance such situations. Where I blanche, however, is an analysis of the situation wherein it is thought that we have come unhinged from all norms altogether. This cannot make sense on my approach, not just because I do not think we could ever get true norms out of it, but because this analysis would entail that in such a situation one abandons *all* roles and since I think we should view ourselves as constituted by a system of roles the imagined situation could not exist as there would be nothing left to experience a state of absolute freedom. Simply put, if it does exist, who exactly is enjoying or suffering from this freedom? We would be back to the ethereal self all over again.

None of this means the phenomenon is impossible. Rather I believe that we analyze it incorrectly and over-dramatize the collapse of norms.[1] The situations that lead to them are critical dilemmas wherein norms we can countenance are no help whatsoever and lead to nothing. We must simply choose and accept our fate. My point throughout has been that it may be the case that no norm provides a definitive answer (indeed I think that failure is quite common and unremarkable) but that does not entail that no norms are in play and everything is thrown into question. Rather much stays stable and we can argue on both sides. We are torn because two or more fundamental roles are in deep conflict and cannot be retained.

What changes in such situations is that so much is thrown into question that we are forced to take a very deep look at who we are and who we will become. This is where the stress comes from. One is torn between two important aspects of identity and so one comes to question much, much more than usual and in a sense re-conceptualize who one is based on what roles one occupies and the situation we face.

In my view, Antigone is a better example of this process. It is a tragedy, but we don't see it as the collapse of morality and all norms. Rather she must struggle and question herself, and, yes, live with the fate of who she decides

---

1 Indeed this conclusion is drawn from the dilemmas by those who already accept the conclusion for other reasons—the dilemma isn't so much the argument for the conclusion as a dramatic display of it.

to become. In doing so she must embrace her death. The modern examples are much more artificial and used to claim a specific conclusion and hence are not as true to the phenomenon of such cases in life.

Indeed to reach a state like this we need not confront a strict dilemma. Often we rethink the course of our lives. Midlife crises might be of this sort for many people. Young people often throw much about their lives up in the air and try to decide who they fundamentally ought to be. But this is a matter of degree, not type. More is in question but not everything is in question. The phenomenon, then, is not one in which one is absolutely free but when because of reflection or a situation in the world many of one's roles, including ones that are not well defined and/or have been essential, do come into question in a way that they often do not.

My analysis is even better when we turn to the way critical dilemmas emerge in most peoples' lives. The explicit cases cited by the existentialist are rather rare. They require a singular choice that clearly requires one to choose between two roles one already holds dear. More often we face a series of choices regarding who and what sort of person to be—whether to have a family, what career to pursue, where to live, what religion to adopt. These choices are absolutely essential to our being and can rise to the level of a critical dilemma. Yet it is rare that the dilemma presents itself in such a stark and explicit way. Rather these dilemmas are implicit in our lives. Often it is only in retrospect that we can see the dilemma since a multitude of stressful, but smaller, decisions reveal a profound development in who we are.

Moreover, when we are faced with this critical tension in our lives it is not always the case that one or the other role is rejected or abandoned. Take the commonly discussed tension between familial and professional roles. Can one have a family and be a good parent but also be very ambitious and have a successful, profound career? The question is most often discussed in terms of young professional women, but it need not be gender-based. It is most pressing for women because of the different contours we have attached to the roles of motherhood and fatherhood.

In response to the tension one could, of course, forgo a career or forgo a family. But one could also try to do both. In so doing one might fail in one role or the other, or indeed both. Or one might strike a balance. This is obviously what is desired. What is required is reforming our commitment to and understanding of the roles in question. So, if I am to be a good father and have a successful career I might need to keep my career ambitions in perspective and make sacrifices in how I am going to be a good father. Perhaps I will put my children in daycare but make a commitment to be home every evening to spend time with them. There is nothing wrong with this, but it may require tempering some of my desires as to how to be a good father and accepting some detriment in my career for not being able to work late. The process here is one of reforming our roles so that the tension is eased, which will sometimes require substantial changes in our commitment to and understanding of the roles involved.

The central feature of critical dilemmas and tensions is that they force us to confront who we are and to change that in an important way. We must abandon deep commitments about who we are or change various commitments so as to hold onto to others. They are the often drawn out processes of the reformation of one's identity in the course of one's life whereby one must make difficult choices, adjustments, and sacrifices.

On the identity approach to ethics this phenomenon is altogether sensible. We have many roles and must in our lives make choices as to precedence. We can only do so much. Yet, being the pluralistic beings that we are, we seek to do more. In shaping one's life various roles will come to the fore, others will be downplayed, and still others will be rejected. This process will mean confronting implicit critical dilemmas and resolving them through a series of difficult choices. That this process is implicit is no surprise on an identity based approach—rarely will a situation emerge that brings the critical choice out in such an absolute and explicit way. In reality such large and important facets of our identity are formed and shed over long periods of time as we work to redefine ourselves, become who we are, and work to find an inner harmony in our identity.

While actual critical dilemmas are quite rare, the tension they capture is an important part of being human. We must work to become who we are and through a series of often implicit choices determine who and what sort of person we are. The highest aim of an applied and useful ethics would be to provide some understanding and guidance in this process. Life is short and only so much can be done. We must decide what to become and which roles are the most important. This is the process of shaping one's identity. It is difficult and, given our pluralistic identities, fraught with tension. Critical dilemmas work by distilling this tension into one clear and explicit decision that must be made. Though such cases are rare, the tension they exploit is commonplace. Hopefully understanding how critical dilemmas work can aid us in understanding the essential tension we face of discerning who and what sort of person to be.

A similar sort of phenomena occurs in pedestrian dilemmas—we must alter who we are in some way to deal with an unfortunate situation. Pedestrian dilemmas differ as stated above: they don't require the wholesale sacrifice of a role and the roles in conflict are not as central to our identities. These are major difference but the underlying analysis is really the same. The analysis works for theoretical dilemmas as well. Often these dilemmas cast our consequentialist intuitions against our deontological intuitions. The conflict is so stark that we have a real dilemma. The way out is to somehow motivate one type of theory over the other in a way robust enough to resist the opposing intuitions. The dilemmas are supposedly so crippling because neither theory type can gain absolute supremacy. But on the analysis I have been offering it is a mistake to ask for any one theory to reign. We have roles as part of our identities that operate in both types of systems. Hence when we think of the sorts of situations described in theoretical dilemma it should be no surprise that we have a problem—they are manufactured so as to put us in roles that bring different sorts of normative demands upon us at the same time.

Again I have offered no definite solutions. One approach to dilemmas, critical dilemmas included, would ask that given the dilemma the ethicist be able to respond with a clear final answer. I have not done so. Indeed on reflection the thought that one could do this is rather absurd. Should one join the resistance or stay with one's aging parent? I don't know. That is why it is a dilemma. Do we really think that we could pitch this situation to an ethicist and be given a ready answer? I can't think of any ethical system that would do so—such an ability seems entirely foreign to human ethics.

As humans we are complex pluralistic beings with various obligations, desires, needs, etc. We do not control the world and so it should be no surprise that sometimes, indeed oftentimes, the world pitches us a situation that leads to dilemmas. Indeed it would be astonishing if we could sit in the study and would work clearly and perfectly in all situations. The study of ethics is abstract while dilemmas are highly particular. In resolving them, hence, we must deal with the objective particularities of the situation and proceed on that basis. This is the ethical challenge of being human we all face. The study of ethics should seek to help us understand our ethical condition and provide rules of thumb that can be used in particular situation, not purport to offer abstract and absolute rules that must be followed in all cases. Such a response in the production of ethical theory is based on a misunderstanding of the human ethical condition. I hope here to reveal that misunderstanding for what it is using moral dilemmas. If we grasp the lesson moral dilemmas teach us we can begin to look at our moral condition from a different angle and realize that totalizing theories are something we can do without.

I have offered no solutions or theories. But I hope to have offered some understanding. In critical dilemmas, like the others, we should be able to see why we find ourselves in dilemma and how to think about what to do next. Abstractly there is no one final answer, but again clearly this doesn't imply that anything goes. Rather it means that the individual must approach the situation with an appreciation of the dilemma and make a choice based on his identity and the particularities of his situation. On an individual level there may very well be right and wrong answers. And further, no matter what one decides it is necessary that one live with the results. This holds for all dilemmas. While an identity ethics can't tell us generally how to resolve them it does imply that once we do resolve them one way or another or choice has repercussions for us. So in Sartre's case if one chooses to fight in the resistance that role must be embraced but one must also the failure one has become as a child. This failure is mitigated by the choice, but not erased. Our actions have repercussions for our characters and identities. The approach favored here helps us understand both how to think about moral dilemmas and also the sort of repercussions they have for our lives.

The Treatment Reviewed

In this chapter I have tried to show that an identity based approach to ethics and the grounding of ethical norms can account for each variety of moral dilemma. My approach hence fulfills the third criterion of adequacy given in chapter four. It is not important that clear solutions be offered—after all, these are dilemmas—but it must be the case that a proper ethical approach explains the moral dilemmas we encounter. The identity approach does this. Moral dilemmas arise when two or more roles compel incompatible actions in such a way that duties, principles, are aspects of character are in conflict. Since ethics is grounded in who we are and we are constitute by a web of many roles we are prone to moral dilemmas. We can see, then, how and why moral dilemmas arise. Though this understanding does not solve every moral dilemma immediately, it does teach us how to go about dealing with moral dilemmas when we encounter them. This is surely a great virtue of the identity based approach.

It should be clear that I have not offered something resembling an ethical theory. Indeed, I do not think that an ethical theory in the traditional sense is really possible or practically helpful. As we've seen above, there are real problems with ethical theories and they seem to be able to account for moral dilemmas only by an epistemic approach. Because they claim some general understanding of ethics there can be no dilemmas—rather there are only misunderstandings. This strikes me as incredibly implausible and a mockery of actual ethical experience. Indeed the singularity and generality of ethical theories that leads to this deficient approach to moral dilemma also makes ethical theory rather irrelevant to life.

This is an unhappy state of affairs we should seek to change. Human life is too complex for one general ethical theory to account for it. Moral dilemmas show this and the identity approach to ethics helps us understand why. We occupy a plurality of roles and hence depending on how we see ourselves we subscribe to different ethical theories to varying degrees. Theoretical dilemmas make this most clear—we are both consequentialists and deontologists depending on which role we focus on. By adjusting the case we can highlight various roles and hence motivate various actions. On the approach motivated here there is no possibility of a generalized theory. Rather the identity approach is just that: an approach. It helps us understand ethical experience and think about the relevant questions and problems. It shows us how to find our way about difficult ethical issues. Rather than abstract universal rules characteristic of theories it offers rules of thumb: general pointers for deciding particular cases. Anything as definite as an ethical theory would be must be pursued pragmatically as applied to particular cases. My aim here is to motivate a way of thinking about moral dilemmas and ethics in general that helps us in this important task by producing a better ethical self-understanding.

An identity based ethics helps us understand our moral condition since it explains the tensions we find therein, made explicit in moral dilemmas, in terms of the complex beings we are. We must come to understand how norms are grounded in a nature that is partly out of our control and how our particularities shape the objective moral terrain. This understanding available, moral dilemmas fall into place as extreme examples of common moral tension essential to human identity. This understanding doesn't offer a theory that resolves any dilemmas, but it does explain where they come from and helps us thereby deal with them in more productive ways.

The most identity-based ethical theory can offer us in terms of resolution of moral dilemmas is generalized rules of thumb to apply to specific cases. These might identify what sorts of roles tend to be more important and counsel us to consider the damage done to different roles by different examples. The most constructive rule is simply this: avoid moral dilemmas.[1] This doesn't help those who find themselves confronted with one but it is quite helpful. We should seek to conduct our lives and harmonize our roles such that these conflicts do not emerge. Sometimes it may beyond our control, but often we can do things to avoid tragic situations captured in moral dilemmas. In any case, in the conduct of actual lives aimed at virtue a better understanding of our ethical condition and the way moral dilemmas arise and function is much more important than a theory that claims to solve them all or show that they do not exist. Without understanding such theories will not be useful, and they come in such variety that it is hard to

---

1 This is much like Robert Fogelin's "solution" to the liar paradox (e.g., "This sentence is not true"): a stern injunction not to utter instances of the liar. Fogelin, Robert, *Walking the Tightrope of Reason*, ch. 2.

rationally believe one or the other. The necessary move is to step back and try to understand what is going on. The identity approach has been offered as a beginning of just such a process of understanding.

CHAPTER ELEVEN: BETWEEN INSULATION AND IMPERIALISM

Introduction

The first worry that emerged after pointing to identity as the grounding of moral norms was that I have merely moved the question around rather than answered it, like a child who cleans his room by putting the mess under the bed. The previous three chapters aimed to provide a deeper explication of what exactly identity is such that we can understand how it can ground ethics and how we can understand moral dilemmas on this basis. Doing this, however, is likely to have deepened a more principled worry about the identity approach. There is a tendency in ethics to swing wildly between insulation and imperialism, slipping into a formless relativism or an untenable absolutism. We either seem to proclaim that there is only one good way to be or that no form of life is any better than others. Both are unacceptable, yet hard to avoid.

The immediate worry for this project is that by pointing to identity as the grounding of ethics I am joining the relativists despite my protestations to the contrary. This is so because contemporary discussions of identity focus on what makes us different. Popular culture and modes of thought focus on finding yourself as the key to being happy and achieving success. The idea here is that we have some unique authentic self that we find or create and that this ineffable, paradoxical search provides meaning to life. So my identity is what sets me apart and gives me meaning as against others. I want to avoid this for a rather simple reason. I am not engaged in a moralistic or motivational project. I come to identity as the grounding for moral norms as a whole, not within a particular project of achieving a sort of moral perfection or self-actualization. So if I look to identity and see only what is different, there is no way for me to rescue any sort of normativity because anything goes—if any identity is morally permissible then there is no real force to the project of *grounding* moral norms in identity.

Projects that focus on identity in the sense that stresses finding or creating your own true and unique self generally have, at least implicitly, objective constraints from elsewhere that prevents the decent into nihilism. The upside of having those constraints is that they can trumpet identity and authenticity in an uplifting way. The downside is that they need an account of these objective constraints if they want to provide a complete picture. But if they generally lack such developed accounts, they open themselves up to attack from opponents who charge that they have licensed an anything goes morality, which would be no morality at all. The upside for my approach, which says that all that grounds ethics (again in the sense of what one ought to do and who one ought to be) is identity, is that I don't need some other implicit account to solve my problems with objectivity and normativity. And I don't need to hold a robust ontology. The downside, of course, is that I need to show that grounding ethics with identity does have objective constraints and in so showing must not totally abandon the import of what makes us unique, autonomous individuals. This chapter is an effort to address this downside and in the process provide a deeper understanding of our moral condition.

The Challenge

We seek norms of conduct and constitution—norms that establish what one ought to do and who one ought to be. In order to validate them against criticism it is tempting to adopt a formless relativism and thereby insulate them from criticism by making them independent of any sort of rational justification external to the mere choice to adopt them on no objective basis at all. Our norms are valid for us, but not in any general way. We can hence hold our norms to be valid without needing to provide *any* defense of them since there is no such thing to be had—norms on this understanding are simply not the sort of things that are subject to justification or *rational* criticism. They can only be criticized as matters of mere taste. I don't much like your actions, but there isn't anything wrong with those actions—I dislike them in the same way that I dislike mayonnaise on sandwiches or pink dress shirts.

Such a position creates polar opposite reactions. Some find it comforting, liberating, and simply fact about modern enlightened life. It is comforting because one's personal norms cannot be questioned by anyone and one can also avoid disagreeing with others or having to argue. But such a situation is only acceptable if we are happy not to do ethical investigation and critical inquiry. If we want more than a shrug of the shoulders when querying what makes life have purpose and what our life ought to be, then this formless relativism is a nightmare because exactly what we seek and need is put out of reach.

This is obviously unacceptable. Indeed such "norms" wouldn't be norms at all because they would not truly constrain us—we can change such things at will without any impropriety since the normative aspect of norms has disappeared because there is no real right or wrong. We have kept the word by abandoning the content. And we can do this only by turning away from the desire for the search for good life, wherein "good" means more than absolutely anything at all. The nightmare of moral nihilism is only avoided by forcibly shutting one's eyes and hoping—usually in vain—for better dreams.

Upon inquiry we hence flee from the pole of absolute insulation because anything "grounded" in this sense is beyond reason and so not grounded for the purposes of inquiry at all. No doubt one could live like this by avoiding searching inquiry. Yet in a project of inquiry we must avoid formless relativism since it fundamentally undermines ethical inquiry. In doing so, however, we often swing to a sort of imperialism wherein we are forced to assert that our way of life and norms are universally valid for all peoples in all places at all times. We have a theory of the good life and anyone who has deviated has gone wrong. In claiming this, however, we lose sight of any sort of tolerance and must impose our values universally. Actual variance in ethical forms of life suggests this is unacceptable. Not only is it a fact that conceptions of the good life differ markedly but we also have the intuition that there is some legitimate variance. It would be best to be able to assert a grounding for morality that left us with truly normative norms that could also make room for tolerance. Yet in avoiding one extreme we slip into the other.

An acceptable ethical theory must steer between the poles of an insulation achieved by a formless relativism and an imperialism implied by an ethical absolutism and dogmatism. This is no easy task. We tend to oscillate between such that when one appears untenable we quickly swing to the other, only to be forced back and forth again and again. Somehow we must find a way of thinking about ethics that allows us to ground norms as absolutely valid but does not force us to the implausible and unattractive view that there is but one set of norms that are valid and all others fail.

The challenge is clear in pointing to identity as the grounding of ethical norms. If one stresses what varies in identity from human to human then the threat of a formless relativism looms in that by stressing a difference in identity anything goes and norms are easily insulated—to "ground" a norm we only need change our identity appropriately and on this understanding there is no anchor as to what our identity ought to be, it is rather merely stipulated and manipulated. But if one stresses what we all share when talking of identity, then an untenable absolutism threatens in that we have little room left for legitimate variance. It becomes impossible to countenance any variance since ethics must be grounded and fixed by some facet of identity that we all share and hence constrains us in the same way.

Usually when we talk about identity we think of features quite local to us and our backgrounds and hence will slip into an isolated, insulated ethics. But we could also mean by identity what it means to be human. This is a less common use, but there is nothing absurd about it—what separates a human being from most everything else that exists is that he or she is a human being. But if ethics is simply what follows from being human then the move to identity is indecisive and we will further have no room for legitimate variance in ethically proper forms of life.

The Fluidity of Identity

This issue can be cast in the present context by asking: how fluid is identity? How easily can roles be taken on and rejected? In order to avoid the oscillation between insulation and imperialism we must find sensible answers to these questions. Initially, in pointing to identity as the foundation of ethics, it seems I have swung wildly to a baseless relativism familiar in modern society.[1] Roles are seemingly arbitrary and more importantly can be changed at will. To take an extreme example, it seems that a murderer could rightly commit murder if he takes on the role consonant with being a murder and hence acts out of his identity. How could I condemn him? My identity is no more privileged than his and his actions are grounded in who he is, not who I am. If this is where we end up I have clearly failed to offer any grounding for ethics. There is, indeed, no real field of ethics to develop on such an account but only a descriptive study of how any given individual can in fact "justify" various actions by adopting certain roles.

The example is extreme but the worry quite real. In response we should reject the view of identity and the roles that constitute it as self-chosen and

---

1 Indeed in my experience it is quite common among young college students when they are confronted with moral conflicts. This generally takes the form of a soft relativism that avoids the blanket pronouncements of the hard relativist about the contingency of all "norms," but the radical conclusion is a natural implication of the soft relativist position—the soft relativist just prefers not to say this and not make the commitment explicit. The position feels quite comforting. One can have ethical views of a sort and also tolerate all others. Awkward conversations are avoided and there is no need to rationally defend personal ethical commitments. Such views break down, however, when pressed to explain how the ethical commitments are genuinely ethical and can provide real constraint and meaning.

extremely fluid. Some roles are like this but others are not. Some roles simply cannot be truly disavowed or abandoned—this much clearly follows from the point that the self doing the choosing is composed of a web of roles already. Foremost here is one's role as a human being, an autonomous self-conscious rational being. If we can trace some moral norms to our identities as human beings, then these norms cannot be escaped on a whim. One may act against them, but then one is in fact creating a tension within or even a contradiction with oneself. One can act against and even disavow such norms, but one cannot escape them in life. As such they can anchor a genuine and genuinely objective ethics. Other roles are similar. For example, familial roles can be avoided—e.g., by not having children—but once occupied cannot really be abrogated. One's existence and actions automatically commit one to roles that form an essential part of one's identity. These roles provide the truly grounded basis for ethics.

Ethics is grounded in identity and is not arbitrary because some of the roles that constitute identity are essential. Norms have power over us because of who and what we are. Why ought we be this way? In some cases we have choice and in others we point to other ways we are that make the ought to be norm in question valid for us. A regress threatens, in this instance of ought to *be* norms: one ought to be one way because one is another way, but then it is an open question as to why one ought to be that way, and so on. The way out is to point out that at bottom we reach normative categories of roles that cannot be abandoned because the sort of beings we are are by nature constrained in identity as a condition of existence. Why ought we be this way? Because we would not be if we were not this way. This is like asking why we should be human beings. Various relationships engender similar situations—one simply is something and would not be who one is without it. There is no further grounding for such norms because they constitute our essential identity. Certain roles form such critical parts of who we are that it makes no sense to ask why we ought to inhabit that normative category since it is who we are. Hence we can end the regress in a normative category of being that is the sort of normative fact necessary to both be both grounded and grounding.

The Essential Self-Conscious Self

This inevitably will seem questionable because it appears we can always make sense of the question of why we ought to be a certain way. This is simply an exercise in self-conscious reflection. I am claiming that the regress must stop with some feature about ourselves but in fact we do tend to keep the regress going when conducting ethical reflection. The opposing thought, however, is this: self-conscious reflection permits me to reflect on myself as a whole. Hence when doing ethics I have the ability to ask why I should be a certain way. I can even ask why I should be human and reflect upon it. The self-conscious "I" floats free of embeddedness in the world and in who I currently am. If this is so then any grounding in identity is subverted. Perhaps as a matter of fact we cannot bracket all roles, but this is immaterial—we can make sense of queries about why I ought to be any role and so any "grounding" is arbitrary and hence no real grounding at all.

To reveal the mistake of this view we must push and ask the following: what is this self-conscious "I" you speak of? Tell me about it. As soon as one begins roles are used to describe the being that is supposed to be beyond all roles in order to show the normative inertness of roles as a whole. Remember, a human being in moral space simply is an autonomous self-conscious rational being. It makes no sense to ask why I should be an autonomous self-conscious rational being because if I were not I would not be—there is nothing left there that I can understand as myself that could serve as a being from which I could question and thereby undermine the normativity of this role. We aren't doing ontology and so the point isn't about whether or not it has a body or soul or whatnot.[1] To make a jump to that nest of vipers is to make a category mistake.[2] Or rather, it is to assume that to develop an understanding of ourselves as moral agents we should and must engage in ontology. If you assert that the self-conscious reflective "I" is not this autonomous self-conscious rational being in moral space you should at least be able to tell me what it is. But this can't be done with any specificity. It is some ethereal self mistakenly created by a misunderstanding of self-consciousness. It has no form, no characteristics, and no features. When I am conscious of something, say the pen on the table, I, one thing, am entertaining another thing, the pen. We are not one in the same. Note again that this isn't to posit any physics of the external or internal world, etc., just a basic note that the I that is conscious of the pen is not the same thing as the pen.[3]

Extending this basic point when we engage in self-conscious reflection the object of the pen is replaced by the self and becomes the object of consciousness. But what is the subject here that is conscious of the object self? We quickly jump to some other mystical, ethereal self that is formless and can make an object of the self that exists within a world and context.[4]

1 As far as I'm concerned here, any ontology is compatible because I'm trying to understand the moral self as it is, not through reduction.
2 Gilbert Ryle coined the term in *The Concept of Mind*.
3 Even if one has some abstract metaphysics in which some larger self makes them one and the same—this is a point about the self as engaged in inquiry.
4 Wittgenstein's comments on the "visual room" in *Philosophical Investigations* are worth comparing on this point. When thinking of perception we tend to think of some homunculus in our heads that views the perceptions of the self in the world and that I am really this homunculus. But put this way we aren't helping the situation: now we shall want an analysis of the perception

This self can question why one ought to be a certain way to no end because it is not defined to be a certain way. If we hold that the ability to reflect on something means that the subject reflecting is separate from the object reflected upon self-consciousness entails that there must be some ethereal self and questioning in ethics can never come to an end.

The misunderstanding here is the failure to realize that consciousness and self-consciousness are quite different animals. Self-conscious reflection takes the subject as object and does not create or imply a separate subject doing the reflection. I can reflect on my conscious states but that does not mean I am not constituted by those conscious states, looking on from nowhere. In the same way I can reflect on rationality and what it means to be a human being but am still doing so using the faculty of reason and as a human being. So I can question whether or not a particular form of argument is good, but it makes no sense to argue as to whether or not to be reasonable as a whole because in doing so I am engaging in reasoning. Self-conscious reflection allows us to inspect and question much of what and how we are and think but it doesn't permit us to question that as a whole simply because much must be held in place to engage in self-conscious reflection. Self-consciousness is fundamentally different from consciousness because it does not follow the subject-object split of consciousness.

A related point has been made throughout this essay: we must start where we are and work from there, not imagine some god's eye view or view from nowhere from which we can construct the world through inquiry. We are located in the world as beings and so when engaging in inquiry must work from the inside. We have an amazing capacity to query roles, call them into question, and change the roles that constitute who we are. But this is always done as a being constituted by a system of roles, holding some roles in place in order to challenge others, and in the case of what we can call essential roles like being an autonomous self-conscious rational being, always relying in part on the role in order to engage in the questioning and challenging part of our identity. So in ethics when we seek to ground ought to do and ought to be norms we end up digging back into the sort of beings we are by essence, by accident, and by fact. This not only ends the regress but by pointing to aspects of our identity that are based on being in moral space, being an autonomous self-conscious rational being, we can avoid a formless relativism that insulates any and all moral choices. Identity properly understood as a grounding isn't about finding a true authentic self

---

of the homunculus. As soon as this is offered we will need to go further back. The point I want to take from this is that it is a mistake to too easily equate the process of consciousness with reflective processes of self-consciousness. Doing so quickly hides the important identity of subject and object in self-conscious reflection.

but a rich combination of what we share by nature and who we have become in the world—understanding the moral self in inquiry requires looking to what we share.

The Amoral

The argument so far has been that identity is grounded in aspects that cannot be changed. This must be the case based on who we are. Thus regresses must end because at some point what is being asked about disappears when something is questioned. This, then, provides a response to the worry of insulation or relativism: we share basic aspects of identity that serve, in part, to ground norms and thus we are all anchored in the same way. As beings in moral space this is objective in that it is the basic foundation of moral space as such. Departures from this, for example failing to become an autonomous self-conscious rational being, leaves something outside the scope of inquiry and hence the relativistic worry does not emerge. Variance in identity is curtailed but be what we all are and must be in order to be included in the scope of the "we" inquired into.

What, however, of those who do not seem bound by morality at all? This is a threat because it seems to suggest that even the most morally basic categories are a matter of choice, not essence. We must initially distinguish between the unmoral and amoral man. The unmoral or vicious man occupies moral space but acts contrary to essential ethical norms. He does wrong and though he may enjoy it and make it a habit, in doing so he acts contrary to an essential role he in fact occupies. An amoral man is quite different: he does not occupy moral space at all because for some reason he does not occupy the roles that would give rise to the norms of ethics. He does not act viciously though he may do vicious things (or for that matter may do extraordinarily virtuous things though he cannot act virtuously). He is not subject to the moral condemnation of the unmoral man because he is beyond norms of condemnation.

The amoral man is the anomaly and is treated as incapacitated in some deep way. He simply cannot take on the basic roles that form morality, often because of a severe mental defect of sorts. This sort of person simply cannot tell the difference between right or wrong and is not socialized or socializable. Such people are rare. They are not condemned to punishment but treated as sick in some way. Those we punish rightly are those who occupy moral space but act against the good. Hence though there may seem to be those who are not bound by any norms either they are sick or deficient in some deep way or they are bound by norms by being who they are but chronically act against them.

The truly amoral man is unrecognizable as a moral being because he does not inhabit moral space. There may be some reasoning and norms going on in there, but it is so only by analogy because we cannot recognize him as a human agent because of the radically deformed way in which he engages in practical "reason," which is to say that we have trouble understanding what he is doing as practical reason at all. Rather, we see him as consumed by, or better, defined by, a compulsion. A clearer comparison is to someone who has been in an accident and has suffered severe mental injuries. Obviously the person has moral value, but we do not see her as responding to moral norms like she did before because she has lost that mental capacity. A genuine amoral man, should he exist, might appear more normal on the surface but simply does not have what we would term the faculty of practical reason. We could not truly understand such a man, though of course we would work by analogy to attempt to explain his behavior. But this would be imperfect, his behavior would not really be actions in the strong sense of the term. We would treat him as deeply sick, in need of care and control.

This seems implausible only because we speak in absolutes about a phenomenon that occurs in gradations. People who we think of as amoral are not fully amoral. They still respond to many norms and we can recognize their exercise of practical reason. But they have been severely damaged in a way so that parts of moral space are not available to them. In dealing with them we try to open that space up to them and treat them as diseased. That we do so means that they are not just different, but deficient as moral beings. They are what we can call morally disabled—missing some capacities to engage in moral reasoning and life that handicaps them.

Avoiding Ethical Imperialism

Now, however, the opposite worry emerges: in sticking to roles that are not fluid I have offered an untenable moral absolutism and imperialism not consonant with reality. Indeed we each have individual identities, not one overriding singular identity that is the same for all. Have I now failed to allow for some sensible ethical and role variance?

No, for two reasons. First some aspects of identity are quite fluid. For example, many friendships, political affiliations, and views of all sorts are quite easy to shed. Their grip on an individual is not very deep and so an individual has a good deal of choice in which roles he or she occupies. This allows for some variance. Indeed the fluidity of roles isn't binary but lies on a spectrum. Some roles can be appropriated/inhabited or disavowed implicitly in action or explicitly in speech while others—like being a human being—cannot be disavowed in any way at all. To act against such a role leads to a deep and profound tension in the individual's identity.

Most roles fall in between. They cannot be simply disavowed but with work and time can effectively be vacated. Some friendships are like this: though when we were children simply saying that one is no longer friends with another sufficed to end a friendship, adult friendships are made of sterner stuff. They must decay and only over time and neglect or a grand gesture can they be ended. In the same way taking on the role associated with friendship takes time and work as well. It cannot be faked and cannot be simply declared.

Citizenship is also much like this. One is born with a certain citizenship and though it is possible to take on another citizenship or disavow one's own this process is quite difficult and complex. One cannot simply declare that one no longer considers oneself a citizen of the United States because one disagrees with the President and hence divest oneself of various norms of conduct. Rather formal procedures must be followed and one must disavow all benefits such citizenship affords one.[1] Community membership functions in this way as well, as do many intellectual and religious roles that have a grip on us. For these sorts of roles a simple disavowal is mere show. It is rather in a profound change in the way one thinks and acts and aspects of one's character that manifests the change in role. Such a change takes work.

The second way to allow for ethical variance is to point out that even though the same roles that ground ethics in identity function for all the way they function differs by culture and even individual. In large part this is accomplished by the confluence of the various roles that constitute one's identity. Though all share some roles they do not share others. Hence how the common roles function and manifest themselves will vary based on the individual. Further, the roles we share ground rather basic maxims. In many cases they can be followed in various ways to various ends. Helping others is a good example. As human beings we have an implicit duty to aid others when we can. But there are many ways this can be done depending on the individual and the situation. The other roles occupied by the person will shape this as will other factors and mere whim. The norm is universal but the expression of it is particular.

For example, the duties of a paramedic, lifeguard, and passerby all vary when a man is drowning in a lake. They all have a duty to help but because they occupy different roles they ought to help in different ways.[2] To take

---

1 It seems in each election there are those who declare that if one candidate wins they will leave the country and disavow it. Rarely, if ever, do they follow through. Citizenship is much deeper than political agreement with those in power and abandoning the role requires a great deal of sacrifice and work.

2 I speak generally here, but this is also an example wherein legal and other norms differ—as a member of the community and a human being I have a duty to help if I can though as a matter of law there is no duty on a mere passerby. The law does, however, recognize legal duties for other roles, such as lifeguard, paramedic, or parent.

another example, a very rich woman may have a duty to donate a great deal of money to a charity of her choosing in order to help others while a poor man may have a parallel duty simply to do what he can. These examples are rather obvious, but the differences can also be quite subtle.

We all harmonize our roles in various ways and occupy different roles. Laying down rules of conduct for all will often proceed on a very general level that lacks the specificity to prescribe definite actions. Which actions these general rules prescribe will depend on the person, but this is not a sort of relativism because virtue is not relative to framework or whatnot—rather virtue is shaped by the circumstances of the world and the individual such that it comes to be expressed in varying ways. Because we are all the same sort of beings there is one virtue of humanity. But because we are different individuals with different identities human virtue expresses itself in a plurality of ways.

The way out of the untenable oscillation between ethical absolutism or imperialism and a formless relativism that isn't ethical at all because it can countenance no genuine norms is to adopt a sensible pluralism. Pluralism is often thought of as the claim that there are many different and perhaps even incommensurable goods. This is not the view I hold as it quickly degenerates into a formless relativism. Rather I hold that there is but one good (simply the good) that can take on a plurality of individual *shapes* as it is actualized in a life. Who we are and ought to be is anchored in our natures but in our lives takes on an individual form that makes us who we are and ought to be. We avoid the oscillation between insulation and imperialism by adopting an objective pluralism that holds onto a basis we all share but allows for differences based on the individual's roles within the larger, more basic, elements we share.

There are many sorts of norms and roles that are proper for us to include as part of our identities. They will vary from person to person and culture to culture. But the fact that they are many does not mean that they are merely relative and not objective. They are objectively valid as expressions of one's humanity and can be rationally criticized. Because we find room for a pluralism of roles occupies, relations to other roles, and way the roles are occupied we can make sense of a middle road that avoids absolutism and relativism. The good is singular and objective but manifests itself in many ways.

Threading the Needle

Norms are grounded in identity and identity is constituted by the plurality of roles one occupies. Many of these roles are given and some are essential. Others we can take on and shed on the basis of other roles we occupy. Norms are objective and subject to rational criticism because they are anchored in roles we all share. But because of the plurality of roles in identity there is legitimate variance. We end up with an objective pluralism: ethics is objective because as autonomous self-conscious rational beings we share moral space and thus by nature can be right or wrong in how we live and who we are but it is pluralistic because of particular facts and roles that can and do vary between groups and individuals such that the particular contours of moral space can in fact vary without undermining that form of life. This is the way between insulation and imperialism.

This idea is incredibly simple but also difficult to grasp because it is contrary to the predominant ways of thinking. When thinking of identity as the basis for morality we can move to both extremes. Most often discussions of identity are associated with senseless relativists because identity is usually used to refer to what separates us from each other. So if identity grounds norms then we find the basis of morality in culture, race, religion, etc., and no real foundation at all because each of these is equally arbitrary. This is the route of insulation. Against this I have urged that we must focus on those aspects of identity that are universal and that thus tie us to one another. There are some roles that are not fluid at all and it is these roles that prevent us from descending into a formless relativism. One may explicitly reject various facets of one's identity but fail to do so because by being one implicitly takes on that role. By being one takes on a normative role.

The opposite temptation now presses and indeed historically the focus when talking about identity is to stress only what makes us the same—if it is these roles that rescue us from relativism then we are led to believe that they *alone* constitute the ground of ethics in our identity. Hence we quickly find ourselves grounding morality in what it means to be a human and then lording our conclusions over everyone, or at least feeling as if we ought to be doing so (but perhaps refrain because such behavior is socially impolitic or dangerous). This, however, fails on two counts. First, this singular role cannot possibly account for all of the norms we would take to be part of ethics unless it is unhelpfully expanded so that so much is built into human nature that it is no longer natural.

This is a common problem in ethics. We seek to ground norms in nature, but in order to get the robust norms we want out of nature a great deal that is implausible gets built into nature such that it is no longer natural. Second, it is in principle opposed to any tolerance and cannot make sense of any variance. It views the good life wholly in terms of what we share and so must posit one correct way of being. Any variance means one has failed to live the good life. We cannot tolerate any ethical diversity. At present this is not an attractive position and in any case presupposes a privileged epistemic and ethical position from which to declare what it means to be a human being that is not available. Quite simply it seems that we should be able to allow for some variance in the good without losing all sense of objectivity. To do so we must accept all of the roles that make up one's identity, not just what we share. It is imperative to allow what differs and what we share to work together to help us understand the human ethical condition.

The way out is to countenance both aspects of identity—both the fluid and the fixed. There is but one good, but it is manifested, or can be exemplified, in various ways. This is the key to objective pluralism—we accept variance in good forms of life but only insofar as it is constrained by objectivity to which all forms of life respond. In pursuing the good life we must find a way to harmonize our various roles so that our identities reach a balanced way of being. Some roles will vary from person to person and hence the way the roles are harmonized will vary as well, meaning there will be many forms of the good life. Yet because we share many roles and must come to terms with them the particular harmonized identities will all be similar and come to take a sort of family resemblance to one another.

There are some roles that we all share, paradigmatically being an autonomous self-conscious rational being, and these form the basis for the most objective normative appraisal and grounding we have. Others are shared by large groups of people, for instance citizenship or familial roles. Some roles are not shared but are objective in the sense that the individual who occupies that role cannot abandon it. Some familial roles are like this, as are roles whose existence is secured by some past action or event. But there is still much room for variance. Different individuals have different given roles depending on circumstances out of their control, past choices and events, and the like. And different individuals choose different roles and thereby become bound by different norms or by similar norms in different ways. And different individuals have different interrelations of roles which will affect both how they play particular roles and how they handle conflicts and tensions in roles. But such variance is anchored in shared aspects of identity. So we retain an objectivity to normativity and genuine grounding rather than slipping into a formless relativism.

Acknowledging an objective pluralism therefore permits a way between insulation and imperialism. We do not insulate the good life because we allow that all forms of it respond to the same good. But we avoid imperialism we allowing that the way the good manifests itself in a harmonized identity will vary depending on individual particularities. Because identities are made up of a conglomeration of roles we can acknowledge a principled pluralism without descending into relativism. We ought to be individuals with harmonized identities and we ought to act from such. Since there are inescapable roles we must countenance these in shaping who we are by taking, abandoning, recalibrating, and recasting roles. But there are many ways to harmonize our roles depending on what we do, what we think, how we relate to others, etc. Hence when I say that we ought to be harmonized individuals there is universal constraint as to how this can be done because we start with roles that are the same and cannot be abandoned. But by becoming who we are there is a great deal of room for legitimate variance in how exactly we become harmonized. The good is one but can be expressed in many different ways in each life because of the differences in who we are by nature, accident, or choice.

Ultimately the problem of being forced to choose between insulation and imperialism in ethics can be traced to a misunderstanding of identity and the self. We seek ethical grounding, some way to end the ethical regress. Why ought I do x? Because of principle y. Why ought I follow principle y? Because you are z. But why ought I be z? To this question there may be further answers concerning the sort of being that one is or there may not. If there is not then it seems like we have reached bottom and it is unclear we have grounded anything at all. The ethical imperialist will urge that there is one moral way of being that grounds all others, some abstract, ethereal human role that rules over us all. The ethical insulator will reject this thought and hold rather that one ought to be z only because one chooses z. The imperialist will rightly object that this makes ethics entirely arbitrary while the insulator will rightly find the former view too intolerant and absolutist.

Understanding identity in the way I have above, we see that the mistake of both is to offer answers to the question. In our regress we feel tempted to ask why we ought to be z. Correctly understanding identity, in many instances this question is simply asking the following: why ought I be me? The predominant urge is to answer this in some way but the correct response is to point out that the question is a piece of patent nonsense. It relies on assuming that there is some separate self asking about the self, that when I reflect upon who I am I thereby cease to be that person and become some abstract formless self that does the reflecting and inquiring. This is what I am rejecting. There is no reason I ought to be me simply because if I were not me then I would not be. Both the imperialist and the insulator assume a concept of self that stands beyond worldly existence, inhabiting a view from nowhere. For the imperialist this is constituted by one immutable identity that constitutes the whole of the ethically relevant self while for the insulator this is some abstract chooser that can adopt various roles at will and therein arbitrarily ground ethics. We must end the regress with the moral self as absent this there is no domain for the question while also realizing that part of my normative nature is objective and universal.

Once we reject the idea of the ethereal self and instead focus on the phenomenon of identity in this world we see that we reach grounding in who we are and that who we are is both anchored in an objectively valid good and shaped by our particularities. Put another way, in becoming an autonomous self-conscious rational being in a community one is initiated into moral space but the particular contours of this moral space will vary depending on one's particular identity and circumstances and can change over time. By locating moral grounding in our identities and understanding identity in terms of a plurality of roles we can find a way out of the oscillation between insulation and imperialism common in ethics.

A Note on Ethical Thought and Reflection

Some comment is now in order regarding what it means to engage in ethical thought when deciding what to do and who to be. A feature that is commonly identified to distinguish ethical thought from other forms of practical reasoning is that it abstracts from the particularity of the individual and takes account of others. All within the ethical community (whether it be a family, tribe, political unit, or humanity, etc.) have inherent value. Unethical thought discards the value of a person (or thing) that should be considered, usually in favor of the agent engaging in the thinking. We generally term this selfishness, self-centeredness, and self-will. It is a lack of respect for the ethical dignity of others. The scope of the ethical community is important—in past times it did not encompass humanity in any strong way whereas in the modern west we take it as a given that the ethical "we" includes at least all human beings[1] and that each, from the ethical perspective, has equal inherent value.[2]

It may appear that an identity based approach as developed here loses this basic intuition about ethical thought—roles, after all, are localized in a way and allow us to refuse abstraction to a sideways on point of view or God's eye point of view or view from nowhere. I've resisted the possibility of such a perspective on the grounds that it is defined as having no perspective

---

1 Historically this is not the case. For example, when Diogenes the cynic termed himself a cosmopolitan he was making a radical statement, refusing to identify primarily with a particular city and community. For us things have swung the other way such that we can find it hard to square ethical thought with particularized attachments, instead deeming such localized roles as parochial and archaic.

2 This is not to suggest that we do not or cannot ethically value some individuals more than others. We obviously do. We can, even while holding onto the equal inherent value of all humans, by holding that a particular individual by her life work or action or whatever provides more benefit to humanity as a whole than another. The *inherent* value is equal for all, but the practical value differs because of what different individuals can offer humanity as a whole.

---

and hence can't be a view. We must start where we are as human beings thrown in the world. But the doubts continue: am I not just saying that there is no such thing as what we hold to be ethical thought?

This is a parallel worry to the threat of insulation that has been the focus of this chapter. The above response in hand, I can now address the present worry as well. To think ethically is to ask, "what ought I be and do?" As an exercise in reflection this manifests itself as "what ought one be and do?" Circumstances matter and to some degree need to be built in. But even so the "one" in the question needs to be defined. Here is where roles come into play. I am a complex, fluid system of roles. When I ask what I ought to be or do I am asking, in part, what I ought to be and do as *a particular role*. What we find central to ethical thought generally is our role as human beings, as moral agents. So I ask, "what ought I be or do as an autonomous self-conscious rational being?" This is the way to cash out the general ethical insight that values all moral agents and pursues ethics abstractly, asking "what ought one do?"

It is tempting to stop here and hold that such a question and perspective is all there is to ethical thought. I do not do so. First, it radically underdetermines what a particular person ought to do and be and in so doing restricts the scope of the ethical greatly. Second, insofar as it makes assertions they are totalizing absolutes, hard-pressed to account for legitimate variance. Moreover, when we state such duties they are so general that it is unclear how they are to be filled.[1]

Identity as grounding gives us a richer approach. When I ask what I ought to be and do in a particular domain, I engage in a form of thought that asks what ought I do as a [role] across a whole series of roles that are relevant to the discussion. And I must balance them in terms of each other based on how central they are to who I am. There may be tensions and even contradictions. I may be obligated to abandon various roles as inconsistent with my identity either by being less important than other roles or by failing to accord with roles I cannot abandon and are central to my being. In the clear example, if I have adopted the role of a thief or murderer I do not act rightly when I rob or kill. I cannot justify myself on the grounds that I happen to be defined in terms of the role of their or murderer. The correct analysis is that I may have adopted such a role but I shouldn't be that way because as an autonomous

---

1 In practice we tend to deal with these issues by building roles into the circumstances we construct around the question of what one ought to do. So instead of just acting what the duty of an autonomous self-conscious rational being is generally we ask what the duty of an autonomous self-conscious rational being *that is a father of a child and an American citizen and a devoted Catholic etc.* is. There is nothing wrong with this—what I am doing in this section is making the roles we often build into circumstances explicit as what is considered when engaging in ethical thinking rather than hiding the roles in the circumstances.

self-conscious rational being (as well as a host of other roles), I shouldn't be a thief or murderer.

This can get quite complicated because ethical thought and reflection is the continuous process of coming to understand who one is and making judgments as to who one should become by resolving tensions, abandoning roles, downplaying roles in favor of others, and recognizing and acting in accordance with roles one is necessarily constituted by (by nature or by circumstance). Ethical thought is characterized by abstraction in the sense that it leaves whims and mere preferences aside in abstracting to what ought to be done from the perspective of a role and in the sense that it asks this across sets of relevant roles including natural roles in which the perspective adopted is quite broad, e.g., as an autonomous self-conscious rational being and further in the sense that ethical thought is the process of questioning roles from the perspective of others, throwing part of who we are into doubt, and being open to change to become more coherent and flourishing human beings. It is this generalized unity that ensures objectivity in ethical thought while it is the relevance of more particular roles that provides for legitimate variance within the ethical. Ethical thought display a structure that is objectively pluralistic. It is the process of engaging in abstracted reflection objectively bound by the basic contours of moral space but taking on legitimate variance based on features of the identity engaging in such thought.

Conclusion

Norms are grounded in identity. We ought to be or act a certain way because we are such and such a way, or we are such and such a person. Identity allows for normative facts such that norms can be grounded without committing the naturalistic fallacy, or perhaps we should say it allows us to overcome the naturalistic fallacy by articulating normative nature in the moral self without engaging in ontology. Identity should be thought of as a complex system of roles of the types enumerated above. Together these work to produce who we are and hence how we ought to be and act. Some are quite fluid while others cannot be abandoned. We may deny them in behavior or comportment but in such cases we develop a false consciousness or false being wherein we have become a contradiction or harbor a deep tension within our identity. Identity is not insulated because of objective components of moral space based on roles that we share and cannot escape, but allows for legitimate variance because many roles are fluid. The way between ethical insulation and imperialism is to recognize both the bounded and complex and fluid nature of identity, revealing the possibility of an objective pluralism in who one ought to be and in the structure of ethical thought.

CHAPTER TWELVE: CONCLUDING REFLECTIONS

Summary

Moral dilemmas have been the focus of this essay. But I hope to have motivated some quite general points about the foundation of ethics, the nature of identity, and the way to a sensible objective pluralism in ethics. Though moral dilemmas are often discussed they are rarely taken seriously. It is more likely one will confront them as an amusing intellectual puzzle than as a topic in need of serious inquiry. When there is serious inquiry into moral dilemmas, it is almost always limited to a very specific dilemma and used to a very specific purpose. The neglect of a general intellectual inquiry into moral dilemmas is an unfortunate mistake.

Here I have attempted to begin the process of remedying this mistake by trying to come to understand moral dilemmas generally. After dealing with preliminaries in chapter two I sketched three types of moral dilemmas we encounter: pedestrian, theoretical, and critical. Though each type is different from the others all present legitimate dilemmas and hence it is reasonable to think that we ought to be able to deal with all at once. Chapter four examined the use to which each sort of dilemma is put. Though this varies a great deal I argued that what we really seek in responding to each type is the same: a sort of grounding of ethics would allow us to solve or understand the dilemmas.

Chapter five turned to ways that this is done. After critiquing theological, consequentialist, deontological, and virtue-based approaches to ethics as insufficient to ground ethics in such a way that we could come to terms with moral dilemmas I sketched an identity-based approach that in my view can do so. Moral dilemmas are helpful because they put stress on our ethical systems and hence lead us to seek more grounding for them. What is needed, I concluded, is a sort of normative fact. Identity is the answer. We ought to act such and such a way because we are such and such a way.

It is easy to say this, but difficult to make good on the promise of an identity approach. Chapters seven and eight attempted to explain identity in such a way that we could see how it grounds ethical norms. I argued that identity is a complex system of interrelated roles. Identity is thus pluralistic and complex. These roles come in different types, some of which I described, that stand in various relations to each other. Chapter nine provided several examples of how to think about ordinary moral issues—from understanding legal ethics to the relationship between solidarity and cosmopolitanism to how we can view the moral situation of a recovering addict—with reference to the identity approach. Chapter ten returned to moral dilemmas and offered an understanding of each variety that explains why we encounter them and how we might deal with them.

Chapter eleven turned to the familiar oscillation between insulation and imperialism. Identity approaches to ethics will be liable to fall into either unpalatable extreme. To avoid this we must stress that some roles are unavoidable—predominately natural roles—and that identity is made up of a plurality of roles. Noting both facts allows us to ground ethics in such a way that norms legitimately constrain but there is room for legitimate variance in proper norms based on who a given person is. To be good is to become harmonious in one's identity, balancing the various roles that make up who one is.

The Lessons of Moral Dilemmas

The usual approaches to moral dilemmas are misguided. Most ethical theories perceive them as challenges to overcome, simply ignore them, or draw dramatic, radical conclusions from them. I have argued that we ought to adopt an identity based approach to ethics and view our identities as complex conglomerations of roles that each brings normative demands upon us. We have a plurality of roles and there is no guarantee that they will always lead toward the same end in a particular situation. Moral dilemmas of any sort are the result of finding ourselves in a situation where roles are in some stark tension with one another, that is, tension that is quite beyond ordinary moral tension because, in a sense, we cannot act rightly. This is to be expected as a result of being the sort of beings that we are. So rather than offering a theory that solves all sorts of moral dilemmas I am offering an approach to ethics in which we can understand moral dilemmas. In fact, rather than serving as a challenge to an ethical theory, moral dilemmas are great evidence for the approach I am advocating. If morality is grounded in identity understood as a pluralistic system of roles, then it is to be expected that moral dilemmas will emerge.

Moral dilemmas are facts of our lives that arise from our complex identities and our lack of control over the world we live in. I take it as a criterion of adequacy of any approach to ethics that we be able to make good sense out of each of the varieties of moral dilemmas. Most fail to do this on two counts. First they often ignore all or most types of dilemmas. Second the understandings offered are questionable. My response has been to reorient our approach, developing a view of how we are to approach ethics that begins with the fact of moral dilemma. Each type leads us to query how ethical norms are grounded. The most plausible way to do so is to focus on our identities because this can provide a normative fact. Norms can thus be grounded without committing the naturalistic fallacy. Identity is to be understood as a complex system of roles. These roles in turn lead to various norms in different situations. Each of the moral dilemmas arises when various roles lead to starkly different actions and we must discern what we ought to really do. Hence dilemmas are quite stressful and can be de-habilitating.

Rather than viewing moral dilemmas as embarrassments, we ought to take them as a basic ethical datum. On the approach offered here, this can be done and though we may not be able to avoid dilemmas or solve them we can understand why they arise. Doing so opens the way for an identity based approach to the grounding of norms as a fruitful research project. In relation to moral dilemmas, this approach offers understanding and rules of thumb for dealing with dilemmas and tensions as they arise. Though moral dilemmas as stark as those discussed here may be rare, the tension that these dilemmas thrive on are commonplace in daily life and in the ethical challenge we all face of determining who and what sort of persons we ought to be. Hopefully adopting this identity approach can lead to a better and more enlightening understanding of the human ethical condition.

The Larger Project and Approach to Ethics

Through examining moral dilemmas in this essay, I have argued for some rather general lessons about ethics. I am skeptical of the ability of any ethical theory to give an account of moral dilemmas and believe that we should rather move away from the idea that our job is to provide robust ethical theories. Rather than looking for a set of abstract principles that hold universally, we ought to transition to a sense of ethics wherein we attempt to suggest ways to think about who and how we ought to be and provide rules of thumb for dealing with the ethical situations we encounter. This reorientation may be of little interest to professional ethicists, but in my view it provides a realistic way to think about and do ethics that is actually relevant to life.

Essentially I have been seeking a way to think productively and seriously about ethical problems we face in life—centrally who and how we ought to be in order to live a meaningful, flourishing life and understand and be at peace with our moral condition—without claiming to know the answers and without importing an extrinsic theory of the nature of things. We begin with ethical confusion. And no matter how much we are convinced of our own theory of how things are by nature, it would be helpful to not need all those other theories to be correct and understood in order to engage in productive ethical thought. Hence my questions have been directed at discerning how we should think about ethics. I assert no ontology and have no grand story of the nature of the world. Neither do I hold an ethical theory of the sort that is usually presented, detailing what exactly one ought and ought not to do.

Rather, I have presented an approach to ethical problems that can be used to deal with them. This approach is to look for moral grounding through identity and an analysis of the various roles that constitute who we are, coupled with our freedom to structure our life and our selves so as to become who we ought to be. The result is small in the sense that no final answers or ultimate norms have been presented. But it is large in that it gives us a way to think about ethics sensibly without ontology and without theory. This is important: if provides a way for us to engage in critical and productive thought and conversation about important ethical questions without having to either assume or defend robust commitments that are quite disputable.[1] To borrow from Wittgenstein again, the aim here has been to develop a way of thinking such that we know our way about natural ethical problems that confront us as autonomous self-conscious rational beings.

The identity approach to ethics developed here has yielded a number of very interesting points worthy of further consideration. The aim of this essay has been to reorient our approach to ethical inquiry so that identity is the locus of our investigation. This begins with stressing the importance of the question of who and how one ought to be and became even more important in the argument that when we attempt to ground ethical norms we should

---

1 When we hinge ethical discourse and thought on such commitments instead of arguing about and understanding ethics we end up arguing about and defending other topics, predominately ontology and theology and the like. The ethical discourse is put on hold but since we can't make headway on grand theories of the nature of things we tend to forget about the ethical discourse altogether, removing it from the realm of critical thought and argument. Here I am providing a way to engage in such thought and argument, which I find important, without having to get bogged down in tangential and supposedly foundational issues.

look to identity. We then look to an analysis of identity and from this can return to ethical problems. Above I've argued that doing so sheds new light on moral dilemmas, provides a better understanding of ourselves, and opens the way to embrace a sensible ethical pluralism. Many related points have been made throughout or are implicit in the analysis. To conclude, six general issues deserve comment: tolerance and respect, moral imperfection, authenticity, moral angst, the moral self, and the contours of moral space.

Tolerance and Respect

Most of us believe in tolerance of moral systems and conceptions of the good that differ from our own. We wince at the thought that we should force people to be moral or to live what we believe to be the good life. We also stress the importance of respecting other moral systems—not just letting them exist unmolested, but acknowledging their worth. The trouble with this is that it is hard to tolerate and respect other moral systems without undermining the force of our own because as soon as we acknowledge another it is unclear why ours is one that one ought to adhere to. And once we acknowledge one other valid moral system it seems we have to acknowledge them all. We end up the soft relativist retreating to a common refrain of "right for you" and "true for you," even when we are living and embracing our own moral system.

Chapter eleven explained how to avoid the theoretical aspect of this problem. Given the middle ground that an identity-based approach offers between insulation and imperialism, formless relativism and strict moral absolutism, we can now make better sense out of how we can tolerate and respect others and also how the two stances are not the same. This may all seem minor in that tolerance has been a central tenet of a liberalism that we now almost all endorse.[1] But that is actually the problem: our conception of the good slips into treating tolerance for conceptions of the good *as* our conception of the good (and raising the thorny issue of whether or not to tolerate the intolerant). The result is that any substantive conception of the good gets hallowed out, including the one that consists of tolerance for others. I do not think this is necessary, but if this is so some account must be given about how we can tolerate and respect other's conceptions of the good.

Tolerance contrasts with intolerance and repression. To tolerate someone is not to approve of them in any way but simply to refrain from using coercive force to make them be and do what you think they ought to be and do. To us this is anathema, but in many ways repression has been the norm.

---

1 At least on its face—we often differ as to what tolerance means and some will countenance tolerance in word though fail to practice it in any meaningful sense in their other claims and their actions.

For most of history it has been commonly accepted that a well-functioning community needs to share a robust moral conception, e.g., a religious creed. This may appear heresy of a sort to us, but it should be noted that organized police are quite new as well.

Further, if I believe that I know the good, that is, I have a moral theory that I believe tells me what everyone ought to do and how everyone ought to be, then it is perfectly natural to force it on others. I know better, and so I am doing them a favor by repressing them. Put another way, I am forcing them to behave a certain way in order to save their souls. Outside of the religious context, to us Plato seems much too repressive in the *Republic*, but in his view he has discovered justice for the city and soul and hence it is entirely proper to create that justice above all else.

Obviously this is all problematic for us. The first issue is simply how to justify political tolerance of others. This was the heart of the wars of religion, which were incredibly awful. The solution in, for example, the Treaty of Westphalia was a political solution: the prince decided the religion and we weren't going to fight about it anymore. This is not liberal society wherein multiple points of view are tolerated because within each principality intolerance was still accepted. But it does point the way: the settlement was based on the recognition that it was better for everyone not to fight because no one was powerful enough to prevail once and for all.

Transposed into liberal society the same point carries: we do not engage in repression of those who have different conceptions of the good because then they would do try to do the same for us and we would be in danger of being repressed. We thus all make an instrumental decision to mutually disarm, so to speak, and live together in a less perfect situation rather than face extinction. We now have political tolerance, but it is unstable and shallow. It is unstable because as soon as one group thinks it has enough power to enforce its conception of the good then the compromises of the past will likely be abrogated. It is shallow because no one really values tolerance in such a society: they value self-preservation and have decided that tolerance is the best means to that end in the current situation. This does not mesh well with the great value we do afford tolerance in contemporary liberal society.

In *Political Liberalism* John Rawls attempts to provide more.[1] His key idea is an overlapping consensus that embraces the core political values of a liberal state. We can imagine a diverse society with competing and antagonistic conceptions of the good. Eventually they make the move sketched above: tolerance and other liberal values are adopted as a modus vivendi. Over time, however, the democratic institutions develop and liberal values take on a

---

1 Rawls, John. *Political Liberalism* esp. Lecture IV.

robust form and become part, in their own way, of each group's substantive conception of the good. Put another way, they are integrated and made to fit within most of the conceptions of the good in play in that society. We are thus left with an overlapping consensus among most of society (the reasonable) about the democratic and liberal values on a substantive level even though other parts of the conceptions of the good (or, for that matter, how those values are endorsed) differ greatly.

Rawls' argument is somewhat compelling, though I will not explore it in detail here. I do not want to reject the view, but at the same time I want more than what it can offer. First, even though tolerance and the like happen to have become part of the substantive conceptions of the good for society it seems that they have done so only because they perpetuate the survival and freedom to pursue the favored conception of the good. The real justification of tolerant liberalism is still merely instrumental; it is a compromise to survive. We only can really value it for itself because we have been trained to because it proves to be instrumentally helpful. I would like more: an account of why we *ought* to value tolerance on its own terms but also one that does not hallow out our own conceptions of the good. Second, Rawls can only get us (and is only trying to get us) tolerance for others. I want to get respect: belief that while affirming my conception of the good wholeheartedly I see the virtue in other, different conceptions of the good (though of course not *all* other conceptions of the good). The identity approach to understanding our moral condition can answer both worries.

First, why should we value tolerance? Two responses, both good, can be made. First, we should be humble about our grasp of the good. We are not gods and we could be wrong. All we can do is live how we see best. Our intellectual limitations do not permit us to force this on others. Personally, I think this is right. But it will not work for someone who has certainty, and most people are quite certain about their conceptions of the good. For religious people it may (though does not need to) be the case that their faith gives them certainty and they really ought to force others to live properly. Legal restrictions may limit them, but within the legal structure they ought to work to force others to be good.

The second response is deeper and it is here that an identity approach is helpful. We can derive it from a point of Kant's: the only good thing is a good will, meaning that it is the motive that causes an act that is important normatively, not just the act itself.[1] So if I have a conception of the good I believe with certainty and I believe others ought to follow it I can still come to tolerate them because I recognize that I cannot change their motive, or

---

1 Though of course an act may still be good even if we enjoy it, so long as it derives from the good will.

who they are. Through repression I can force them to appear externally to be the sort of person I think they should be, but I cannot change their identity. I may attempt to destroy their identity to build it anew, but it would be better if I could convince them without force or repression to adopt my conception of the good. Hence I will tolerate them.

This gets us some tolerance, but it doesn't get us very much. Our modern liberalism wants more than toleration—it wants to see a way to respect some (though, again, certainly not all) differing conceptions of the good. This is difficult. To respect other conceptions we end up undermining our own and descend into a formless relativism that ends the conversation and stifles reflections, even for an individual, of who and what *one* ought to be.

The identity approach can get us to respect. I am a system of roles, many of which I cannot escape and many of which I share with others in my community and in the human community as a whole. But because I am a pluralistic being who occupies many different roles in various ways I can see how my conception of the good will differ from others based on their prior choices, natural circumstances, events in life, particular talents and interests, etc. That is, I can acknowledge that my conception of the good is what one ought to be but also that there may be other ways one ought to be as well. I need not say all are equal. I can sensibly hold that some (whether mine or not) are better than others in that they creates a more harmonious life or better captures parts of roles that we share. I can engage in conversation and reflection about how one ought to be and make normative claims while at the same time asserting my own and allowing for others to be right as well.

Intolerance is believing I am right alone and trying to force it on others. Formless relativism is believing that we are all right and so none of us is really right at all because anything goes. Mere tolerance is believing that I alone am right but refraining from forcing it on others. Respect can be found when I believe I am right but I also acknowledge that others may be right as well even though they are different. A roles-based account of identity as the foundation of moral norms permits just this.

Note that respect and tolerance can be extended in different measures. For example, I do not tolerate someone's form of life because of the odious consequences it imposes on society at large. I believe that he ought to be repressed because of these harms. An example here would be someone who engages in terrorism. He may claim that his conception of the good and moral identity require him to engage in terrorist acts in the name of his ideology, but I do not tolerate him and believe he should be imprisoned and resisted. I think his identity and conception of the good deeply wrong and confused and because it is so harmful for the world as a whole, I repress him.

I tolerate another form of life though I find it misguided. Take a man who has chosen to spend his life at leisure, wasting talents and simply waiting to die. I will try to reason with him, I will seek help for him, but I will not condemn him to prison or repress him. I tolerate his conception of the good though I think he is confused and misguided. I do not respect his form of life and think it wrong, not just wrong for me but wrong for him and for everyone. There are other forms of life that differ from mine though I acknowledge that they are good forms of life with their own conceptions of how one ought to be. I recognize my conception of the good in them in various ways and see that a different sort of life has been built in different circumstances. I need not think that they are perfect, but I respect them because I see how they have a worthy conception of the good from my point of view even though we differ.

Moral Imperfection

It is often taken as an obvious truth that "ought" implies "can." Simply put, ethics does not require the impossible of us. If it did, it would be quite unfair. If we are unable to be a certain way or do a certain thing then we are not to be morally blamed and are not morally sullied for failing to be that way or do that thing. This principle is related to our notions of responsibility and freedom—to be morally blameworthy or praiseworthy an individual must have had some choice in the matter. If a particular act or role is beyond the realm of possibility then it is beyond moral judgment. Conversely, if one must be a certain way or do a certain thing then it too is beyond moral judgment.

I have rejected the idea that there is one totalizing moral code or theory that can tell us what we ought to do and who we ought to be in all cases. And I have argued that there are situations, like moral dilemmas, in which we must act against a role or abandon a role that we wish to and perhaps ought to retain. In doing so, however, I run afoul of the principle that "ought" implies "can" because in a moral dilemma one ought to do (or not to do) both things and be both ways but one cannot do or be both (or not do and be both). Is this not, then, a clear refutation of my approach?

I think not. We must be careful with how we understand "ought" and "can" in this regard. In most cases in which two duties conflict there is one sense in which one ought to fulfill both duties but cannot but another sense in which one really ought to fulfill one over the other. For example, I am a member of the PTA and also a good friend of Joe. There is a PTA meeting this evening and as a member I ought to go, as I've said I would. But Joe has recently been divorced and lost his job and is very depressed and has phoned saying he needs to talk. As a good friend of Joe I ought to go and talk with him. Consequences for the friendship and for Joe could be dire if I don't fulfill this duty and leave Joe to his own devices. So I ought to do two things but cannot do both (suppose there is no way to re-arrange life so as to do both). In such cases most find it obvious that what we really ought to do is go talk to Joe, shirking our duty as a member of the PTA. The idea here is that we have two prima facie duties in conflict, but when compared we really only have one duty, an all things considered duty to go talk to and help Joe in his time of need. It is more important and so it trumps and thereby eliminates my duty to go to the PTA meeting.

My approach need not disagree with any of this. I just want to be careful about how we think about the "trumped" duty. Rather than asserting that it becomes no duty at all when Joe needs to talk, I wish to say that it remains a duty that I justifiably fail to meet. This does not, however, magically erase the duty from existence. I am not morally blameworthy even though I have failed to do my duty. Life intervened and another more important duty arose. But I will still likely apologize for my absence and explain it in order to make amends and retain my moral standing as a member of the PTA.[1] We should not become too obsessed with exact words. The point is only that "ought" (and here I'm concerned only with the moral ought, bracketing other senses of the term) can be used in varying ways, roughly corresponding to prima facie and all things considered duties, and we should be careful in how we are using it.

But this is not all. There are other situations in which the conflict is deeper. Moral dilemmas are such cases. Here the temptation is to retain the above analysis and insist that because "ought" implies "can" there must be one all things considered duty that trumps the other one and resolves the dilemma. But this is just the move I have been rejecting, arguing instead that moral dilemmas are a sort of moral tragedy that must be resolved in tragic ways by choosing who and what sort of person to be when doing so means taking an action one ought not to take or violating or abandoning a role one ought to uphold or retain.

In these situations, I suppose we can talk about an all things considered duty that is the right answer, but I do not think this is particularly helpful. Different people will choose differently depending on their roles and how those roles fit into their identity. And they ought to choose differently in

---

1 We can continue the example: suppose that I constantly miss PTA meetings because of other more important duties to friends and family. Even though I haven't acted wrongly I am a bad member of the PTA. I never show up. Where I am wrong in such a case is in retaining the role of a member of the PTA. I should apologize and quit if I am rarely able to fulfill my duty to go—even if I have justifiable reasons not to go on each occasion. My moral fault is not my moral judgment in the moment but poor handling of my life and identity such that I attempt to take on a role that it turns out I cannot act in accordance with.

some cases. Chapter eleven showed how we can make sense of this without sliding into an untenable relativism. Instead we are left with an objective pluralism.

More importantly, using the principle that "ought" implies "can" here to argue that there *must* be some all things considered duty that trumps and eliminates the other duty, even if that all things considered duty varies from person to person, unacceptably downplays a key feature of our moral condition. Quite simply, autonomous self-conscious rational beings thrown into the world and composed of a system of roles are prone to moral tragedy and are defined by moral imperfection. We cannot be perfect and by nature will morally fail in some ways. We do not control the world and we cannot prevent conflicts in roles, even deep identity altering conflicts in roles. Sometimes we cannot do what we ought to do and instead of pretending that there is some mysterious perfect moral state for us in this world we must learn to accept our moral imperfection and work within our failings and our capacities to retain and build a coherent, sound moral identity as best we can in the circumstances.

The point I am urging is not akin to the doctrine of original sin in its various guises. Doctrines of original sin hold that humanity is infused with sin by nature, that humans are all immoral beings to some degree. Sometimes it is claimed that this is a sort of passed on marker originating in Adam's sin. More secularly, it is the view that humans are by nature driven by some immoral instincts and are disposed to do wrong. Our task is to overcome this sin, perhaps with the aid of the divine, and clear our accounts with the universe or God or whatnot.

There is a great deal of truth in this—we are beings driven by ambition, self-will, and fear who act selfishly and wrongly toward others. We are tempted to behave immorally for personal gain, or at least what appears to be personal gain. But out moral imperfection takes on another form on my approach. It is not just base temptation that makes us imperfect but simply the fact of being a moral being thrown into the world, pulled by a variety of roles and having to make moral sacrifices in who one is because of one's limitations and complex identity. We are doubly broken as moral beings, driven by immoral impulses to act and be as we ought not to act and be and also constituted as moral beings by a plethora of roles in tension with one another. In the course of human events we are required to make choices amongst conflicting roles and both do what we ought to do, and what we ought not to do.

How do we respond to this sort of moral imperfection? We might embrace it. Accept it just as we accept the past and all that we cannot change. In accepting it, we make the best we can out of what we have, trying to live a flourishing life and have a flourishing identity and knowing that there is something lost in the process, and that one is in many ways in tension with oneself. But we can make progress, building coherent, rich identities that allow us to minimize the tension while also embracing life in the world.

We might also retreat from the world and seek to minimize our roles. There is a great historical tradition of such approaches throughout the world. We become like the hermits in the desert, abandoning everything but the communion alone with god, or the monks who seek to rid themselves of all attachments.[1] We may be the philosopher, abstracting himself from all particular circumstances in the world to engage in deep thought. In a way, we can seek to find a way not to truly live by not engaging with the world (another sense in which to philosophize is to learn how to die). We attempt to rid ourselves of attachments, of ambition, of fear, of will in general and by so doing become morally and spiritually whole; distancing oneself from the roles one has been thrown into, and seeking instead to be only an autonomous self-conscious rational being.

Is there a correct response, a correct way to deal with this moral or perhaps spiritual imperfection? It strikes me that there is not, and that no response can be pursued in purity. We can accept our imperfect moral state, but we still must live it and be torn by what we have lost, and what we will lose. We can attempt to leave this world, yet cannot totally do so, for however much we abstract from it in thought, we still live. We can minimize many roles, but we cannot eliminate them all. We are torn in a sense, anchored to a world that gives content to our lives because of the roles we have been placed in, but able to abstract from it in reflective thought and seek an otherworldly moral purity outside of those roles and our perspective.

But this is all just another layer of moral imperfection and part of the moral angst discussed more below. Indeed one can pursue both avenues in life, seeking through thought and mediation to abstract from the world and the roles in life that constitute the violent waves crashing at cross-purposes in our identities while also recognizing that we must continue to live and doing so as best we are able.

As human beings and moral beings we are essentially autonomous self-conscious rational beings engaging in reflective abstraction from the world *and* beings thrown into and embedded in a world not of our making in which much is out of our control. There is a tension here—between the reflective agent engaging in abstract thought away from the vicissitudes of ordinary life and the actual living being who must engage with the world. One may reject the life of wholly abstract thought, ethical or otherwise, and embrace one's roles in the world, seeking to live a vibrant, flourishing life and accepting the

---

1 Compare Schopenhauer on this point.

inherent tensions and contradictions in doing so. Or one may seek freedom from the world, from will, ambition, attachment, and fear and seek a life of thought, eschewing the actual process of living as much as possible. Neither extreme can be pursued in purity because the tension between our reflective meditation on our lives and our world and active engagement in our lives and our world is part of what is essential about being a human being. We are neither wholly because we are essentially both. We have great capacity to engage in reflection and change our roles and our world, but at the same time we are fundamentally limited by our thrownness into the world, our belonging to a time and place and context, and our finitude. In coming to understand our moral condition we must come to see both our capacity and limitations, accepting that we are essentially morally imperfect and defined by tension.

Ethics and Authenticity

Authenticity is a state of being in which one is one's true, unique self, not acquiescing in what outside forces attempt to make one. We are obsessed with it. This was not always so. Most times and places have not made an issue out of authenticity. Most had or do have clear ideas as to what constitutes the good life and the proper roles individuals ought to play. So there is no need to make a big deal about ensuring that one is authentic. Rather one easily fits into a larger society playing a particular set of roles that society reinforces and teaches. There is a sort of implicit faith in the larger societal scheme that we have come to lack. We struggle with authenticity and worry that the sort of life we have been led to within society is a matter of mere inertia and not a true valid life. When young, and likely beyond, many worry that they are somehow inauthentic, that they have weakly acquiesced into a life that they did not choose.[1]

The stress on authenticity is interesting because authenticity as a value determines nothing about the content of a form of life. Rather, it focuses on how we arrive at that form of life. An inauthentic form of life is just one that was not personally chosen. Our conception of autonomy requires that we personally choose our form of life for ourselves, not have it imposed upon us. Note that this concept of autonomy is quite different that that we find in earlier periods (and as I want to understand it). Autonomy was thought to be a constraint on the form of life that was good because we had to determine what it meant to be a free being and what that meant for our lives. But as our conception of a moral foundation crumbled and nature lost its purpose and was unmasked as brute events, autonomy transformed and lost

---

1 See Charles Taylor, *The Ethics of Authenticity*, for a nice discussion of the concept.

any constraint: what was important was the fact of being free and exercising choice alone. There could be no wrong choice. The only wrong would be in failing to rise to one's freedom and hence not choosing at all. So continually we rebel against the past, even if that means rebelling against rebelling. We are self-defined and that makes us good. The self is not so much discovered as created in an act of pure will absent any constraints. This is a sort of absolute freedom that has haunted modern ethics: we see there is no basis for choice and hence are free to create value in pure choice.

I reject this simply because I see no normativity involved in a choice that cannot be right or wrong and all that matters is the choice. Taken to the logical extreme this is simply anything goes. The position is absurd if only because it is unclear why choice has any value once value is shown to be empty. Accepting that life is meaningless does not magically falsify that conclusion. Moreover, I don't think that we truly ever are in this sort of position: rather there are tensions and conflicts, we are overly bound and thus free to change, not totally unbound and thus free to burn our past and rise anew from the ashes of our identity. It sounds pretty but it is unclear what it means in reality. There is no abstracted state in which we can totally choose from nothing our form of life. We exist in a context.

Observation of my fellows suggests that being authentic means just doing something different to show others, and perhaps yourself, that you are authentic. This is just as shallow as the supposed sheep who accept traditional conceptions of the good life. Authenticity as a value does not specify a different form of life at all. It simply specifies a "free" sort of life that was chosen. So why do people who seek authenticity seek to be different? The answer I think is that by being different they go against the flow and somehow prove their authenticity to themselves. Deviance is a way to demonstrate, or prove to others or oneself, one's freedom. This strikes me as confused because the search for authenticity has gone to such an extreme that there is nothing discovered and no basis for choice of a form of life. By valuing it alone nothing else has value.

Nonetheless it is important to give some account of authenticity since there is something important about the concept, both for us and for a good life in general. Authenticity is not to be found in just being different to demonstrate one's freedom but in engaging in serious self-conscious rational moral reflection on one's life. We are bounded in who we are and can only work with who we are and our particular situation. Attempting to reject this somehow isn't authenticity—accepting, reflecting, and realistically reconstructing who we are in the world is. The colloquial sense of authenticity is right in seeing the value of being true to oneself and not having one's form of life forced upon one but quite wrong in the next step that holds that to do this we must paradoxically create ourselves anew. Authenticity is accepting where we are and engaging in the sort of personal inquiry in which we harmonize and reform our roles rather than merely acquiescing in the given and avoiding moral reflection.

Our roles are often in tension with one another because we cannot be everything. They help define one another and we are able to discard some roles and take on new roles. Authenticity is found in the task of investigating who one is and discerning who one ought to be and building an identity as much as possible that is coherent and captures that. We are free and we have choice, but that freedom is valuable because it is bounded. To get both authenticity and value we must work at becoming who we ought to be based and bounded on who we essentially are by nature and circumstance. There are good and bad ways to be, but many of each. That is the point of a pluralistic and objective ethics that is based on identity understood as a web of roles. Authenticity is not found in the vain quest to step beyond one's moral self in the world to create it anew but in accepting it and working within it through moral inquiry and reflection.

Moral Angst

The search for and struggle with authenticity is an expression of a moral angst that is part of our moral condition. In moments of reflection we worry that somehow we are not getting it right, that we do not even know how we ought to be and yet the clock is always ticking. There are no timeouts in life and eventually we all will die. Whether or not one thinks there is something after this, it matters that we get life right, that we find some meaning and purpose within our lives. Reflection, however, can lead us to find this impossible and life absurd.

Some proclaim, and claim to embrace, the emptiness of life. Yet they tend to find some meaning in their brave and noble acceptance of the absence of meaning. If *everyone* held their view there would be no bravery in the truth. It would just be dismal. Indeed these claims often target not meaning generally, but a particular traditional (and usually theological) sense of what meaning is. They often then find or really posit meaning elsewhere. Reflection, however, can lead us to sense that there is no *possible* meaning or purpose, no roles that we ought to be.

I seek to do ethics without theory, without ontology by understanding our condition and the question of who and what sort of person one ought to be. This question is essential even if we don't have a full understanding of the nature of things. I want to know how to think about how to live without having to accept some religion or ideology that is in deep dispute. Looking to understand, rather than give a reductive account of, identity has been my path. Within this approach to ethics we can better understand moral angst and the feelings of meaninglessness that can torment us. For most people at most times what constitutes a meaningful life has been clear because the proper roles for a person have been clear. One had a place in society and in the world that was not disputable. One simply lived it without reflection.

Most of the time our *acquiescence* in roles that gives life structure and meaning. But being human means being able to engage in critical inquiry about what roles one ought to occupy. And though the questioning must stop, our sense of what it means to live an essential role can become confused. This inquiry is liberating: we can move in new directions and restructure parts of our lives. But it can also lead to crisis: we lose a sense of purpose because too much has been cast into doubt. The ability to choose undermines real value. Engaging in reflection about our identities can alienate us from them—we find it hard to embrace the questioned roles, yet unable to find roles that banish the insecurity. We must be ourselves, but cannot find peace in this.

Moral angst is not a bad thing. The alternative is lacking the ability to engage in critical reflection. Losing this means losing freedom to shape the course of our lives through rational reflection. The cost is moral angst. But this is not the sort of all encompassing moral angst we can feel when it seems like there could not possibly be a right way to be and that the question that seems so important—who and how I ought to be—is utter nonsense because there is no possibility of living life well or finding meaning. Abandoning the sideways on view from nowhere, from an impossible vantage beyond the world, and accepting that we are constituted by roles, some of which are essential and many of which are given, we can avoid the abyss-like sense of moral angst. Properly conceived moral angst is the worry that we have gotten it wrong, that our lives are poorly constructed and have been poorly managed and we do not fully know how to go about making things right. This sort of moral angst is quite troubling, but at least it is a sort of angst we can understand and deal with in our lives. Rather than attempting to rid ourselves of it, we should understand its source and learn to live with it. Looking to identity as a system of roles can help. It does not answer the problem of meaning, but rather productively frames the question.

Because I am an autonomous self-conscious rational being, I can restructure and change my roles. Meaning and purpose is to be found in exploring the roles that by nature or circumstance I cannot give up or devalue. Moral reflection should seek to identify roles, and hence norms, that fix my existence as a moral being. Purpose should be sought in understanding these roles and in structuring my life to exemplify them and others I have attached importance to. Thinking about ethics as grounded in identity and seeing the possibility of an objective pluralism allows us to accept that we can find meaning that is real though not universal. The way to live with moral angst is to grasp our limitations as beings in the world, embrace the freedom we do enjoy in structuring out lives, and reshape and organize a life with purpose guided by our essential and deeply held roles. We should embrace ethical doubt and seek peace and meaning by living our limitations rather than bemoaning the loss of something we never had.

The Moral Self: Beyond the Ghost and the Machine

A recurrent theme here has been the rejection of the ethereal, formless self. I have argued instead that the self, our identity, is *constituted* by a system of roles. This understanding of identity has then grounded moral norms in that at some point one cannot sensibly ask why one ought to be *y* because to call that into question would be to undermine the agent we are looking into. This point has been echoed in the methodological maxim that we should start, as we must, where we are. Hence, there have been no ontological or metaphysical commitments about the nature of the self and whatnot. Rather I have attempted to begin only with the autonomous self-conscious rational being because that is the description of a moral agent, that is, an agent in moral space.

No doubt many will be skeptical about this shift in perspective. We are quite used to beginning with what there is and then trying to make sense of the object of inquiry, here ethics, in terms of that extrinsic, prior ontology and theory. I see this as problematic because modernity is characterized by the removal of telos or final cause from nature. The result is that it is hard to understand how norms could apply to human beings conceived of as a natural thing. Rather a descriptive, or demystifying, account of moral phenomena is offered. At present, evolutionary approaches are popular. Now that alone is fine and an interesting inquiry. But it goes part and parcel with a background view that there is *nothing* substantive to say about the human being as a moral agent because that sort of an agent is an illusion. The theory provided tries to explain, naturalistically, why we fallaciously think we are moral agents. This I have rejected.

Another reaction to modern naturalism is to argue that we are in fact bound by norms and thus conclude that there is something beyond the natural, something supernatural, that defines us. Here we get conceptions of souls and the inquiry allows natural science to do its thing with the constant proviso that it must miss something very basic and important. We need not be theological to make this move. We might rather say that normative phenomena take priority and thus are the basis for ontology more basic than the naturalistic picture of the world. Here we seek to unmask modern naturalism as insufficient, replacing it with some sort of phenomenalistic metaphysics, whatever that turns out to be.

Both miss the moral agent as a self to be understood instead of reduced to ontologically basic categories (whatever we decide those are in our favored theory). They do so because they are mired in difficult ontological debates that can be avoided if we seek first an understanding of the human being as a normative agent. Why start with the human being as a normative agent? Because we are conducting inquiry, proposing and evaluating theories and beliefs, engaging in the task of justifying and explaining. *This* is where we must begin as inquirers (because it is what it means to be an inquirer) and *this* is a normative activity. If you undermine all normativity you've undermined all epistemic norms as well and thus your own theory—there is no reason to believe it because *reasons* have been unmasked as unreal. Inquiry cannot validly produce a theory that undermines normativity because doing so undermines inquiry as well.

This basic point is important to realize, but does not show very much. It only gets the idea that I must begin where I am as an inquirer and as a moral agent and come to understand what it means to be that sort of thing— that is develop an intrinsic account of normative phenomena attached to identity. That is the project I have begun here. It licenses no inferences to conclusions extrinsic to the project of coming to a self-understanding of being an autonomous self-conscious rational being. It says nothing about what exists in nature, as we now understand "nature" or further how we ought to think of "nature."

Modernity has profited by taking the human being as a natural thing and investigated it absent telos. As we do this the human being becomes a machine following causal laws extrinsic to that human being. We become gears in a massive machine, not agents. Those who recoil—and certainly historically the originators did reject this understanding of the human being—argue that there is some ghost in the machine. Descartes' thinking thing is a nice example of this ghost. The body is the machine and the ghost somehow controls it.[1] One camp scoffs at the idea that we need a ghost in the machine and dismisses it as dangerous superstition. The other recoils at the thought of reducing man to machine and argues that there simply must be more.

The moral being, for me, is the autonomous self-conscious rational being

---

1 The historical development is very interesting here. Malbranche is bothered by the interaction problem between mental and physical substance that Descartes papered over with the pineal gland and adopts occasionalism: mental and physical events correlate with each other but the link is not causal. Rather *God* makes it be so. Idealists like Berkeley (though coming at the issue from a different direction) end up not needing the physical substance anymore at all, rather reducing the physical back to the mental as ideas.

and this is neither ghost nor machine. Those conceptions have their place in the inquiries they belong to. But they should not be blithely imported to this sort of inquiry. By focusing on understanding ourselves as moral beings who are pressed by the question of who and what sort of person we ought to be we can get back to an understanding of ourselves as normative beings as a matter of fact. The moral being must be understood as part of a world in terms of an identity related to the world, not some ethereal formless self. But it also is not a machine because the moral being cannot conceive of itself that way and still be a moral being. By eschewing ontology and beginning with the moral being as we find it, we can better understand ourselves and moral inquiry. That has been my task, and we are led astray if we confuse ontological issues with the separate quest for moral self-understanding.

Understanding Our Moral Condition: The Contours of Moral Space

Our moral condition is the moral space we find ourselves in as moral agents. Throughout I have spoken using the metaphor of moral space. In doing so I am not referring to some realm like the physical realm that we inhabit like that realm. Rather it is a rough analogy to our standing in moral inquiry and life, the various rights and duties and possibilities that are open to us as moral beings who engage in moral reasoning. The project of coming to understand our moral condition is one of trying to sketch the outlines of moral space, to make sense of our position within it reflectively. We begin by looking for norms or action and being. This leads to a quest for grounding, in the space analogy an attempt to understand the basic contours or geography of moral space. We could, of course, simply trace how we in fact do tend to reason and act when we ask what we ought to do but the quest for grounding wants more: it worries that we are floating in nothingness and the solidity and security we seek and often feel is an illusion because on reflection everything is simply arbitrary and our pretences for a good life with purpose is, in the end, just brute feeling and altogether irrational.

Theoretical ethics attempts to provide some grounding, but I have argued that each predominant approach fails precisely because it points to something that in principle we cannot understand or really tries to ground the normative with the non-normative, a fallacy hidden only by using the same word in multiple sense: one which points to some fact that we understand and another which captures the target normative content. But a gulf has been opened up between the two for us. We cannot return to antiquity's conception of teleological nature without resorting to the supernatural and thereby abandoning the quest for ethical self-understanding.

My argument has been that we must start where we are and ask, within moral space as we find it, what could ground norms. The answer was identity.

We ought to act a certain way because we are a certain way and that is what someone who is like that does. Why ought we be that way? Well usually we have an answer based on other facts about ourselves, other ways we are. But eventually we hit bottom and the question does not make sense. Not only does removing the aspect of identity strip us of something essential but we cannot imagine what remains as human in anything more than the brute biological sense. Since we are in moral space we cannot and need not dig deeper. Rather than looking outside of moral space for a grounding we must take our identity as a normative fact and it can ground moral space.

A great deal of time has been spent tracing various roles that constitute identity, how they work together and are in tension with each other, and how we can understand moral dilemmas and other ethical problems within this framework. I have further argued that this approach leads to a sensible objective pluralism. We begin with identity and realize that it includes things which we share, some of which we must share, and things we do not. Hence we can allow for legitimate variance while still being anchored by who we essentially are. There are right and wrong ways of being, but one may construct a virtuous identity in different ways. This makes sense because different people are defined by different roles in different ways and to different degrees. But much of our identity is shared with others and forms a common basis upon which we can both understand and evaluate others and ourselves. Moreover, even contingent parts of our identity are, as a matter of a fact, outside of our control: we have no choice regarding many of the roles that define us. They are necessary for us as part of who we are, even though others do not share them. They fix who we are and shape who we can become.

Translating this approach to ethics into the spatial metaphor makes the point in terms of our moral condition quite nicely. In order to be in moral space, in the sense of being able to respond to norms, one must be an autonomous self-conscious rational being. We are free to make some choices as to what we do and who we are. We are able to reflect upon ourselves and conduct inquiry. And we give and ask for reasons and engage in the process of justifying claims and actions. This also gives us moral value, but (quite importantly) it is not the sole source of moral value for humans or other things. What we all share in being such beings is the basic structure of moral space. It creates a sort of dignity of reason and freedom. It is the basis for the quest for purpose. It makes reflective peace and understanding valuable.

Entering such a space means acculturation and learning a language in a society so that we can realize our human potential to engage in self-conscious rational reflection. The way this is done also shapes moral space—it forms various features of geography within it. Various contingencies of our lives also create part of the geography of our moral space. In both of these ways my moral space may differ from others but we still share basic features because we have the same basic structure and our roles are very similar. When we make choices as to who we ought to be we further alter moral space, we stress or take on various roles that create duties we need to balance with others. In life we share an essence, but part of a good life is constructing, or rather crafting from within, an identity from who we find ourselves being that is coherent and meaningful. Moral dilemmas show us that as moral beings we are fraught with tension, bound in various ways and needing to figure out who and what sort of being we are and ought to become.

There is such a thing as the objective good life that we all should live. But the geography of moral space is malleable within each life and hence the shape the good life takes can vary. One can go astray and end up in bad faith or so deform one's identity that we cannot understand the moral space within which the person lives. And because we are autonomous, we can act against our identity and compromise roles that we implicitly hold onto.

There is a potential worry that has been lingering for quite awhile and has emerged in various guises throughout. I've agreed with Cicero's claim that the most important question of all is who and what sort of person one ought to be. In figuring out how to answer that question I pointed to identity as the grounding of moral norms, the basic structure of moral space. I've also maintained that we are free. But if the question is who I ought to be, and the way to answer that question is to examine who I am such that my norms are grounded, isn't the answer to the question automatically that I should be who I am, that is, exactly what I am right now? And if so aren't we in a rather tight circle in that we are tasked with constructing who we are but do so out of who we are. The structure is finished before self-construction began and there are no materials with which to modify it.

In response to this recurring worry we must point to the open-endedness of identity, the inherent tension that we ought to work out within it, the possibility of bad faith, autonomy, and above all self-conscious rational reflection that we conduct in ethical inquiry. Ethics is grounded in identity, but identity is complex and open-ended. There are roles that cannot be changed and there are roles that can be altered in various ways. Moreover, because we are complex, there is tension in our roles. I cannot do and be everything and must make choices. The choices I make as to what I become depend on my valuation of roles and the way I come to understand myself. I can reflect on my life and see how I am failing to live up to roles I must hang onto by necessity or because of the choices I have made. So I can reflect and say that I ought to be *x* instead of *y* and base that judgment on parts of my identity that are not up for grabs at the moment or, in some cases, ever. I can reflect upon tensions in my identity and work to resolve them. Our moral condition is one of complex confusion in who we are coupled with the ability to shape who we become on that basis.

To return to the metaphor, ethical inquiry is the task of tracing our moral space and remodeling it from within. The foundation is in essential roles that are the basis of some norms and importantly the basis for ethical reflection cannot be changed. When I engage in such reflection, much is simply not up for grabs, even if later I might contest it. Other things are not up for grabs because of particular facts of my life and context based on accident or prior choice. But at the same time I can note, like a city designer, what is unsatisfactory about the landscape and city as it currently exists and work to improve it. Our moral condition is one of chaos and sparks of freedom. We are thrown into a world and become who we are in that world. We are able to build and structure our lives within our situation and it is our difficult task to come to terms with who we are and ought to be and construct a rich, coherent, and meaningful life. This means coming to terms with and being true to who we are, and developing our identities in the world as we find it.

Ethical inquiry, at its best, leads us to accept where we are and helps us figure out where we can and ought to go. It is an exercise of both self-discovery and self-creation. This project has been predominately concerned with providing a way to understand how we can productively and critically go about ethical inquiry. Moral dilemmas lead us to look for grounding, that leads us to identity, and understanding identity leads us to the plurality of roles that constitutes who we are. Based on this self-understanding I have argued that we can deal with and grasp moral dilemmas and other problems in ethics. Our moral condition is one in which we are thrown into the world. We are autonomous self-conscious rational beings who are constituted by a variety of roles, some of which are by nature essential and some of which have become essential because of our past and place in the world. Our task in inquiry is to determine who and what sort of person we ought to be based on where we are. Reflecting on the various roles we play is a fruitful way to pursue this project both in terms of coming to understand and accept the tensions inherent in our moral condition—our moral imperfection and angst—and the magnificent possibilities for forging and living a good and meaningful life, and in doing so finding understanding and some measure of peace.

BIBLIOGRAPHY

Alcoholics Anonymous. 4th Ed. New York: Alcoholics Anonymous World Services, Inc., 2001.

Alibrandi, Tom and Frank H. Armani. *Privileged Information*. New York: Dodd, Mead, 1984.

American Bar Association. *2009 American Bar Associate Model Rules of Professional Conduct*. In *Professional Responsibility Standards, Rules & Statutes*. 2009-2010 Edition. Ed. Dzienkowski. West Publishing, 2009.

Appiah, Kwame Anthony. *Cosmopolitanism: Ethics in a World of Strangers*. New York: W.W. Norton & Company, 2006.

Aristophanes. *Clouds*. In *Four Plays by Aristophanes*. Trans. Arrowsmith et. al. New York: Penguin Books USA Inc., 1962.

Aristotle. *Nicomachean Ethics*. 2nd ed. Trans. Inwin. Indianapolis: Hackett Publishing Co., 1999.

Aristotle. *Politics*. Trans. Barker. New York: Oxford University Press, 1995.

Ayer, A.J. *Language, Truth, and Logic*. Mineola, NY: Dover Publications, Inc., 1952.

Bell, Derrick A. *Ethical Ambition: Living a Life of Meaning and Worth*. London: Bloomsbury, 2002.

Bentham, Jeremy. *An Introduction to the Principles of Morals and Legislation*. Mineola, NY: Dover Publications, Inc., 2007.

Bentham, Jeremy. *Rights, Representation, and Reform: Nonsense upon Stilts and Other Writings on the French Revolution*. Ed. Pease-Watkin et. al. Oxford: Oxford University Press, 2002.

Blackburn, Simon. *Being Good: A Short Introduction to Ethics.* New York: Oxford University Press, 2001.

Carroll, Lewis. *Through the Looking-Glass: and What Alice Found There.* Mineola, NY: Dover Publications, Inc., 1999.

Cicero, Marcus Tullius. *On Duties.* Ed. Griffin. Trans. Atkins. New York: Cambridge University Press, 1991.

Dennett, Daniel Clement. *Consciousness Explained.* Boston: Little, Brown and Co., 1991.

Descartes, Rene. *Discourse on Method and Meditations on First Philosophy.* 4th ed. Trans. Cress. Indianapolis: Hackett Publishing Company, 1998.

Dostoyevsky, Fyodor. *Crime and Punishment.* Trans. Garnett. New York: Modern Library, 1994.

Fogelin, Robert. *Walking the Tightrope of Reason: The Precarious Life of a Rational Animal.* New York: Oxford University Press, 2003.

Foot, Philippa. "The Problem of Abortion and the Doctrine of Double Effect." *Oxford Review* 5 (1967): 5-15.

Grayling, A.C. *The God Argument: The Case Against Religion and for Humanism.* New York, Bloomsbury USA, 2013.

Greene, Josh. *Moral Tribes: Emotion, Reason, and the Gap Between Us and Them.* New York: Penguin Press, 2013.

Hare, R.M. *Moral Thinking: Its Levels, Method and Point.* New York: Oxford University Press, 1981.

Harris, Sam. *The Moral Landscape.* New York: Free Press, 2010.

Heidegger, Martin. *Being and Time.* Trans. Macquarrie & Robinson. New York: Harper & Row, 1962.

Kant, Immanuel. *Groundwork of the Metaphysics of Morals.* Trans. Paton. New York: Harper & Row, 1964.

Long, A.A. and D.N. Sedley. *The Hellenistic Philosophers* Vol. 1. New York, Cambridge University Press, 1987.

Maxwell, John C. *There's No Such Thing as Business Ethics: There's Only One Rule for Making Decisions.* New York: Warner Business Books, 2003.

Mill, John Stuart. *Utilitarianism.* In *Utilitarianism, On Liberty, Considerations on Representative Government.* Ed. Williams. London: J.M. Dent, 1993.

Montaigne, Michel de. *The Essays.* Trans. Cotton. Ed. Hazlitt. *Great Books of the Western World* 25. Ed. Hutchins. Chicago: Encyclopedia Britannica, Inc., 1952.

Moore, G.E. *Principia Ethica.* Mineola, NY: Dover Publications, Inc., 2004.

Nietzsche, Friedrich. *Beyond Good & Evil.* Trans. Kaufmann. New York: Random House: 1966.

Nietzsche, Friedrich. *Thus Spoke Zarathustra.* Ed. Pippin. Trans. Del Caro. New York: Cambridge University Press, 2006.

Nozick, Robert. *Anarchy, State, and Utopia.* New York: Basic Books, 1974.

Plato. *Euthyphro.* Trans Grube. In *Plato: Complete Works.* Ed. Cooper. Indianapolis: Hackett Publishing Co., 1997. 1-16.

Plato. *Phaedo.* Trans. Grube. In *Plato: Complete Works.* Ed. Cooper. Indianapolis: Hackett Publishing Co., 1997. 49-100.

Plato. *Republic.* Trans. Grube, rev. Reeve. In *Plato: Complete Works.* Ed. Cooper. Indianapolis: Hackett Publishing Co., 1997. 971-1223.

Quine, Willard Van Orman. *Word and Object.* Cambridge, MA: The MIT Press, 1964.

Rawls, John. *Political Liberalism.* New York: Columbia University Press, 1996.

Readings in Ancient Greek Philosophy: From Thales to Aristotle. Ed. Cohen et. al. Indianapolis: Hackett Publishing Co., 1995.

Russell, Bertrand. "The Elements of Ethics." In *Philosophical Essays.* New York: Simon and Schuster, 1966. 13-59.

Ryle, Gilbert. *The Concept of Mind.* 60th Anniversary Edition. New York: Routledge, 2009.

Sandel, Michael. *Justice: What's the Right Thing To Do?* New York: Farrar, Straus and Giroux, 2009.

Sartre, John-Paul. *Being and Nothingness.* Reprint Edition. New York: Washington Square Press, 1993.

Sartre, John-Paul. *Existentialism and Human Emotions.* New York: Citadel Press, 1985.

Sellars, Wilfrid. *Science and Metaphysics: Variations on Kantian Themes.* Atascadero, CA: Ridgeview Publishing Co., 1992.

Schopenhauer, Arthur. *The World as Will and Representation.* Vol. 1. Trans Payne. Mineola, NY: Dover Publications, Inc., 1969.

Sextus Empiricus. *Outlines of Scepticism.* Trans. Annas and Barnes. New York: Cambridge University Press, 2000.

Singer, Peter. *How Are We to Live?: Ethics in an Age of Self-Interest.* Amherst, NY: Prometheus Books, 1995.

Sophocles. *Antigone.* In *The Three Theban Plays: Antigone Oedipus the King, Oedipus at Colonus.* Trans. Fagles. New York: Penguin Books, 1982. 55-128.

Spinoza, Benedict de. *Ethics.* Trans. Curley. New York: Penguin Books, 1994.

Styron, William. *Sophie's Choice*. New York: Random House, Inc., 1979.

Taylor, Charles. *The Ethics of Authenticity*. Cambridge, MA: Harvard University Press, 1991.

Taylor, Charles. *Sources of the Self: The Making of Modern Identity*. Cambridge, MA: Harvard University Press, 1989.

Tolstoy, Leo. *Confession*. Trans. Patterson. New York: W.W. Norton & Company, 1983.

Tolstoy, Leo. *The Death of Ivan Ilyich and Other Stories*. Trans. Wilks et. al. New York: Penguin, 2008.

Tolstoy, Leo. *The Kingdom of God is Within You: Christianity Not as a Mystic Religion but as a New Theory of Life*. Trans. Garnett. Lincoln, NE: University of Nebraska Press, 1984.

Wittgenstein, Ludwig. *On Certainty*. Ed. Anscombe and Wright. Trans. Paul and Anscombe. New York: Harper & Row Publishers, 1969.

Wittgenstein, Ludwig. *Philosophical Investigations*. 2nd ed. Trans. G.E.M. Anscombe. Malden, MA: Blackwell Publishers Ltd., 1997.

INDEX